Making Home Work

Making Home Work

Domesticity and Native American Assimilation in the American West, 1860–1919

Jane E. Simonsen

The University of North Carolina Press

Chapel Hill

Designed by April Leidig-Higgins
Set in Adobe Garamond by Copperline Book Services, Inc.
Manufactured in the United States of America

This volume was published with the generous assistance of the Greensboro
Women's Fund of the University of North Carolina Press.

Founding Contributors: Linda Arnold Carlisle, Sally Schindel Cone,
Anne Faircloth, Bonnie McElveen Hunter, Linda Bullard Jennings, Janice
J. Kerley (in honor of Margaret Supplee Smith), Nancy Rouzer May, and
Betty Hughes Nichols.

The paper in this book meets the guidelines for permanence and durability
of the Committee on Production Guidelines for Book Longevity of the
Council on Library Resources.

Library of Congress Cataloging-in-Publication Data
Simonsen, Jane E.
Making home work: domesticity and Native American assimilation
in the American West, 1860–1919 / by Jane E. Simonsen.
p. cm. — (Gender and American culture)
Includes bibliographical references and index.
ISBN-13: 978-0-8078-3032-1 (cloth: alk. paper)
ISBN-10: 0-8078-3032-1 (cloth: alk. paper)
ISBN-13: 978-0-8078-5695-6 (pbk.: alk. paper)
ISBN-10: 0-8078-5695-9 (pbk.: alk. paper)
1. Arts and society — West (U.S.) — History — 19th century.   2. Arts and
society — West (U.S.) — History — 20th century.   3. Home economics
— Cross-cultural studies.   4. Social values — West (U.S.)   5. Women —
West (U.S.) — Social conditions.   6. Indian women — West (U.S.) —
Cultural assimilation.   I. Title.   II. Gender & American culture.
NX180.S6S572 2006
305.48'89707809034 — dc22   2005034946

Parts of Chapters 3 and 5 were previously published as " 'Object Lessons':
Domesticity and Display in Native American Assimilation," in *American
Studies* 43, no. 1 (Spring 2002). They are reprinted here by permission.
Copyright © Mid-America American Studies Association, 2002.

Chapter 4 was previously published as "The Cook, the Photographer, and
Her Majesty, the Allotting Agent: Unsettling Domestic Spaces in E. Jane
Gay's *With the Nez Perces*," in *Arizona Quarterly* 58, no. 2 (2002). It is
reprinted here by permission of the Regents of The University of Arizona.

cloth   10 09 08 07 06   5 4 3 2 1
paper   10 09 08 07 06   5 4 3 2 1

To my parents,
Pat and Jim Simonsen

CONTENTS

ILLUSTRATIONS

ACKNOWLEDGMENTS

I tell my students that writing a research paper is like building a house; the work and design are your own, but you cannot do it without relying on the efforts and wisdom of others. Because I have written a book, my debt goes even further.

A number of groups provided generous financial support for my research during graduate school. I am grateful to the University of Iowa Graduate College; to the P.E.O., particularly the members of Chapter AF in Eau Claire, Wisconsin, for a P.E.O. Scholars Award; to the Charles Redd Center for Western Studies; and to the University of Iowa Department of American Studies.

I appreciate the generosity and expertise of archivists for their help in locating materials for this book. The staffs of the University of Iowa's Special Collections, the Cumberland County Historical Society, the Iowa State Historical Society, and the National Anthropological Archives; Carolyn Bowler at the Idaho State Historical Society; Jacalyn Blume at the Schlesinger Library; Patricia Kervick at the Peabody Museum; and Barbara Landis have all answered questions, provided leads, and helped open western women's lives to me.

My interest in the lives and writings of western women began during my undergraduate years at Gustavus Adolphus College. Gretchen Flesher Moon introduced me to the powerful ways women revealed their perceptions and ambitions through personal writings and gave me the freedom to make my own discoveries. At the University of Iowa, Laura Rigal, Linda Kerber, Kathleen Diffley, Joni Kinsey, and Malcolm Rohrbough encouraged me to think of my research not as a dissertation but as a potential book. Other readers along the way have helped me to see my chapters as more than a collection of interesting stories. Members of the history and American studies dissertation writing groups at the University of Iowa opened new disciplinary perspectives and asked far better questions than I could have asked myself. Thanks especially to Mike Augspurger, Bill Bryant, Mike Lewis, Sean Meehan, Kevin Quirk, and Jennifer Rasin for taking my work as seriously as they took their own. Jacki Rand, Linda Kerber, Eileen Boris, Megan Kate Nelson, and anonymous readers at the University of North Carolina Press provided crucial comments on various portions of this manuscript. I am grateful to Charles Grench and

Amanda McMillan at the University of North Carolina Press for their dedication to this book and their encouragement through the process of revision.

I was lucky enough to have an extraordinary group of colleagues in the University of Iowa American Studies Department. In so many ways, they helped to make home and work compatible. From painting the lounge to serving themed snacks at guest lectures, from vigorous discussions over lunch to Thursday nights at the Mill, they made the months of research and writing not only bearable but fulfilling in more ways than I could have anticipated. The Honors College at the University of Central Arkansas has also stretched my mind in new directions; not every scholar is fortunate enough to have colleagues so dedicated to interdisciplinarity. Conversations with them and with my students have enriched my thinking.

I am grateful to my family for always encouraging me in my work, from my first forays into storytelling to sharing professional struggles and successes. My mother read my manuscript as voraciously as she reads everything else, and my father helped me, from the beginning, to notice connections between seemingly disparate ways of seeing the world. I thank my sisters, Ann Oswood and Julie Dennert, whose stories about home and children have reminded me every week that making home takes work. Finally, there are not enough thanks in the world for Mike Augspurger — colleague, reader, best friend, husband. He accompanied me through research and writing, marriage, building a career, making a home, and starting a family. His unflagging confidence in my writing reminds me of what I love most about my work. And my daughter Solon, who developed and came into being in perfect tandem with this book, I thank you for teaching me that there are many ways to labor, and many ways to love.

Making Home Work

Squaring the Circle

In 1889, ethnologist Alice Cunningham Fletcher arrived at the Idaho Nez Perce reservation along with her companion and fellow reformer E. Jane Gay. Fletcher and Gay, both well into middle age, had left the home they shared in Washington, D.C., for the more rugged climes of the West bent on convincing the Nez Perces that home ownership was the quickest route to civilization. As a government agent empowered to allot homestead plots to Native Americans under the auspices of the 1887 Dawes Severalty Act, Fletcher was to untangle the threads of tradition that bound the Nez Perces to each other and to their land and to bring them into the ranks of individual property owners. With land surveyor, marking chains, and plat book in tow, the reformer the Nez Perces called "Measuring Woman" was determined to persuade the people to embrace Euro-American lifeways in exchange for plots of land and eventual citizenship.

Yet Fletcher found the reservation in turmoil. The Nez Perces were writing petitions to reject their government-appointed Indian agent, three of the agency officials were on trial for infighting, and settlers were grumbling that the government had sent a woman — an easterner, no less — to perform the allotment. "The introduction of the square idea has a depressing effect," Jane Gay wrote of white cattlemen's response to the enterprise, "for hitherto they have worked only in rings, but I dare say they really have no faith in anybody being able to square their circle." Likewise, many Nez Perces rejected Fletcher's carefully marked corners and the patrilineal family lines she recorded in her plat book. "The Indians often destroy the Surveyor's corners as soon as his back is turned and make corners of their own," Gay lamented, and she noted that Fletcher was plagued by "a sort of kaleidoscopic shifting of the wives and husbands and children, to the detriment of the family group system of allotment."[1]

Gay's letters home to relatives and reformers as well as the photographs she made while in Idaho portray Fletcher's work as a constant struggle to make straight the crooked ways of the agency and to rectify the needs of the Nez Perces with the official property descriptions the government demanded. Fletcher's tasks included convincing Nez Perces of the value of home ownership; encouraging legal, monogamous marriages; and stressing the necessity of adopting Euro-American gender roles. Amazed at — and often exasperated by — Fletcher's unflagging commitment to the assimilation plan that Gay called the "square idea," Gay looked with irony at most efforts to achieve any kind of order on the reservation. Her letters contain a mixture of admiration for Fletcher's persistent idealism and an equally persistent suspicion that deliberate attempts to force Indians to accept Euro-American domesticity would be futile. In spite of the government's fantasies of orderly incorporation, neither Nez Perces, white cattlemen, nor even Jane Gay were willing to "do everything on the square."[2]

Gay had resisted some aspects of the square idea by remaining unmarried and spending her life with female companions. A woman with a keen understanding of the power of social institutions, Gay nonetheless recognized that "home" had definitions beyond what could be photographed or recorded in a plat book. It also consisted of community bonds, tribal histories, and personal intimacies that ran counter to tidy notions of patriarchal family homesteads. Gay's narrative discloses the conflicts that arose out of the clash between the ideal of a civilized home and the reality of home as improvised, shaped by intimacies, and sustained by women's unpaid labor. Perhaps most important, her letters and photos insinuate that the square idea undergirding white, middle-class domesticity was not natural but had to be made — through imposing legal order, through taking photographs of domesticated homes and bodies, and through the household labor that sustains the economic providers of families.

The deliberate, arduous, and often self-conscious production of domesticity that is at the heart of Gay's narrative is also the subject of this book. Underlying Fletcher's square idea were arguments that promoted the Euro-American, patriarchal, middle-class home as the pinnacle of civilization. Reformers, politicians, and domestic scientists staunchly believed that assigning homestead plots to Native Americans could force them to drop their tribal ways in order to cultivate farms, build homes, attend school, and participate in local economies and national government. But in the American West, contact between whites and Native Americans made for, as Gay notes, more "kaleidoscopic" conditions that challenged government order and demanded the constant remarking of the ideological as well as the geographic corners that delineated home. Reformers like Fletcher drew on antebellum beliefs in the morality of the family home and on more recent theories about the home's role in evolutionary progress. But, I argue, even assumptions about the value of home that drew authority from science could not simply be exported to western spaces in the post – Civil War era. Instead, domestic ideals had to be painstakingly produced and reproduced in response to the changing conditions and new cultural systems that women like Fletcher and Gay encountered.

Making home, in other words, took work. In the American West, sustaining home as a cultural ideal entailed the public work of writers, artists, anthropologists, bureaucrats, and reformers. At the same time, making home demanded the domestic labor of cooks, housekeepers, and caretakers whose daily rounds and duties did not always square with prevailing aesthetic, legal, and scientific definitions of home. Knowing the home through work not only means seeing that Euro-American and indigenous domestic workers took part in complex conversations about class, racial progress, and the nature of civilization; it also means seeing, perhaps for the first time, the literary, legal, and aesthetic manufacture of domesticated spaces and bodies — the production of white, middle-class identity — as a laborious process in itself.

Women's Work in the Contact Zone

Scholars have argued convincingly that domesticity was an imperial construct used by the white middle class to uphold its power in a diversifying and expansionist nation. Creating the illusion of a coherent national identity in this era was a crucial aspect of the cultural work that domestic writers did. The efforts of these writers and reformers to define domesticity as a white, middle-class trait were attempts to assert power over the lives and bodies of those whom they deemed foreign; bad housekeeping became a marker of racial inferiority. Critics have also recognized that women excluded from this version of domesticity due to the color of their skin made radical political claims by asserting the virtues associated with their own housekeeping.[3] Scholarship in American studies has turned up rich new ground in this attempt to explore the dimensions of "home" and "away," and "domestic" and "foreign," by looking to photography, iconography, film, and women's writing, but researchers have not explored these texts as products of work.[4] More than just a metaphor, domestic imperialism was mediated not only by gender and race hierarchies but by economics, material conditions, and class divisions. While studies of international imperialism have demonstrated that conquest plays a role in creating and cohering domestic national identities against foreign dependents, the domestic as a category of inclusion and exclusion in the incorporation of the American West has been less thoroughly explored.[5] I borrow from these new methods by looking at the diverse ways that home was imagined during expansion to the trans-Mississippi West, but I also look at such texts for ways they represent ideas about and expressions of women's work.

Looking at imperial domesticity in terms of women's work necessitates seeing domesticity as a pattern of working relationships rather than as a finished product, as a messy process rather than a polished ideal. Postcolonial theorists have adopted the term "contact zone" to designate any site where cultures meet, clash, and create new meanings.[6] The idea of the contact zone foregrounds the struggle between diverse groups for control not only of the physical territory but of the ideas that would define identity: labor relationships, gender roles, and racial hierarchies. New western historians emphasize that the American West is best understood not by tracing an idea's slow and steady progress across the continent but by recognizing how confrontation between groups alters, undermines, and reveals faults in those ideas.[7] White women who went west, and native women who encountered Euro-Americans there, were forced to rethink what it meant to do women's work in the face of alternatives. Each chapter in this book brings to light a different western contact zone, from eastern Iowa to northern Idaho, in which women struggled to reimagine what domestic work could mean, attempted to reposition themselves within class hierarchies, or labored to shore up domestic ideals that were challenged by cultural others just outside their doors.

The centrality of work to the process of cohering American identity in the contact zones of the West required domesticity to be more than a symbolic ideal embedded in texts. As scholars of Native American history have shown, images of assimilated Indians also record histories of labor relations. Americanization involved training native boys to work in skilled trades and girls to work in homes.[8] Likewise, even those middle-class white women who popularized the cult of domesticity recognized their authorship as a form of work.[9] A photograph or literary text, then, not only documents the ideals of its maker but, like the faded image of a double exposure, can document the more complicated history of its production. To explore this hidden history is to trace the kaleidoscopic shifts and zealous remarking of domestic spaces that Gay acknowledged as the daily work of assimilation.

Scholars of material culture have long recognized the dual function of artifacts as records of labor relations as well as shared cultural ideals. Material artifacts reveal information about a culture's loftiest goals as well as the conditions of their creation. Woven into a Native American blanket sold in Santa Fe, for example, are the economic relationships and aesthetic expectations that structured exchanges between artist, seller, and collector. Feminist geographers and historians of women's work have looked at homes as similarly complex creations, recovering the economic, material, and physical dimensions of women's labor in the nineteenth and early twentieth centuries. They have investigated domestic chapbooks, diaries, and home design in order to reveal the contributions that women have made to family and national economies through their paid and unpaid work. These scholars have shown that when a culture assigns economic values to different kinds of work, it creates hierarchies based on material power — hierarchies that often create divisions between male and female, white and nonwhite workers.[10] A keen awareness of work and labor relationships is also necessary to an analysis of imperial domesticity. By looking to literature, photographs, and homes for signs of the work relationships that produced them, I show that women undermined domesticity's benign parallels between homemaking and nation building as often as they upheld them.

Each of these kinds of texts thus explores different ideals and realities associated with different types of women's work. The aim of this book is not to trace the history of women's domestic labor in the American West but to argue that the forms through which domesticity was produced there — forms that ranged from Alice Fletcher's maps to Jane Gay's photographs, from Caroline Soule's western fiction to Arikara Anna Dawson's field matron reports — came into being through vastly different kinds of "women's work." As Nicholas Bromell has argued, we can never assume that the definitions of either "work" or "labor" are static or commonly held across gender, class, or ethnic lines.[11] For Gay, Fletcher, and a host of other women who encountered the American West during the late nineteenth and early twentieth centuries, "women's work" could refer to a multitude of different activities necessary to settlement, creation of culture, and assimilation. Housework, child care, artisanal production, artistic display, charitable efforts, political activism, scientific inquiry, and domestic science all fit into the capacious category of women's work. Although each of these pursuits could be and was referred to as women's work by women who undertook them, they offered widely varying amounts of power and authority. They posited diverse relationships between women and men, between white women and indigenous people, and between women of different social classes. Moreover, women often defined the value of one kind of women's work by contrasting it with another. The divisions within what counted as women's work during this era show that women recognized that domestic work was as varied as the women who performed it; they knew that the different forms of women's work indexed differences between women.

Thus domesticity was yet another field of contest in western contact zones between 1860 and 1919, as women attempted to claim the authority to define the values and identities associated with various kinds of domestic work. Situating an investigation of imperial domesticity within sites in the American West brings into sharper focus contrasts between ideology and actual conditions and reveals a more diverse range of participants. We risk reproducing the hierarchies that structured women's work in this era if we retain strict divisions between cultural and material work. In recovering the history of assimilation, we tend to draw lines between white women as culture workers who created imperial domesticity and Native American women as domestic laborers. Certainly middle-class white women were largely responsible for the writing, image making, and scientific study that justified their authority over Native Americans; they helped turn domesticity from a sign of gender subordination to a pillar of race and class privilege. Because indigenous women produced fewer of these texts, we understand their participation in tribal cultures and in the allotment era largely through the study of their labor.[12] Hannah Arendt's distinction between work and labor suggests that middle-class women's activities, because they generated lasting products such as books and images, were work, while native women's subsistence activities should be defined as process without product — as labor.[13] This distinction is useful for understanding how market value affects social value, but it hides the effort involved in cultural work and effaces the cultural meanings of domestic labor. Certainly white women's "unproductive" housework shaped middle-class women's attempts to change the meaning of home and to wield this knowledge as authority over Native Americans. The work of native women as writers, artists, and domestic laborers also made them participants in creating their own homes and identities.[14] How did indigenous women attempt to shape or alter ideas about the relationship between women and domestic labor? In what ways did they publicly and privately offer up their own cultures as alternatives to Euro-American domestic ideals? *Making Home Work* attempts to recover some of the indigenous voices that can be lost even as scholars have discovered how images of Native Americans have reflected back the ideals of whites who produced them.[15]

Native American assimilation provided opportunities for middle-class white women to assert the civilizing function of domestic work, to suggest that the cultural and economic value of their work separated their domesticity from the drudgery of working-class and native women, and to claim professional expertise in domestic work as teachers and fieldworkers. What middle-class white women defined as "women's work for women" (a phrase reformers often used to describe efforts to assimilate their native sisters) in the West differed in value from the "women's work" both white and native women performed as laborers in their own households. Because the domesticity so crucial to assimilation involved distinctly different kinds of work — and such different conceptions of home — the economic devaluation and social power assigned to women's work affected women differently. Home, domesticity, and women's work took on a range of meanings contingent on the status and aims of the various women who produced them. Rather than investigating historical changes in a single genre's representation of domesticity, each of my chapters explores a different form through which women produced domesticity. Because various kinds of texts necessarily represent different kinds of creative and physical work, exploring a single genre fails to account for diversity and conflict within the capacious concept of domesticity. My sources reveal the relationship between domestic work and Native American assimilation that women constructed, both imaginatively and materially, through literature, household labor, evolutionary science, and visual displays. By looking at domestic object lessons across genres, we see the dangers women faced in placing the weight of civilization on a concept made fragile by internal fault lines. While domesticity appeared to have the solidity of the square idea, in fact it is, as Gay suggests, more like a kaleidoscope, in which new patterns constantly shift into view.

Rewriting Women's Work

Midcentury domestic writers helped to establish literary metaphors of women's work as "labors of love" that mystified the economic value of women's work.[16] The popular notion that women's work was moral rather than economic participated, historian Jeanne Boydston has argued, in making "the non-economic character of housework a simple 'fact of nature'" rather than a "question of exploitation."[17] Boydston's careful analysis of white women's records during the heyday of domestic writing shows that the very writers who promoted the home as a refuge from financial concerns were preoccupied with their own domestic production, which did not fit neatly into moral definitions of home. Some of the most prolific domestic writers were prolific precisely because they were supporting themselves and their families when their husbands failed to earn a living wage. A gap existed between men's wages and families' needs, and women recognized that their unpaid household labor filled that gap. In fact, Boydston shows that the value produced by women's unpaid domestic labor allowed business owners to pay their male employees less than a family wage. The excess value needed to support the family was made up through women's work at home, while employers used the money they saved in wages to support the further growth of industry.[18]

Boydston's study reveals the rift that existed in the antebellum era between the cultural work of domesticity and domestic labor. By describing domestic chores as labors of love rather than work with economic value, writers helped to produce a "pastoralization of housework" that disguised women's domestic labor in rhetoric that labeled it as an intrinsic, natural, and spiritual outgrowth of womanhood.[19] Midcentury novels and manuals reinforced distinctions between the domestic economy and the market economy, domestic women and foreign workers, and the moral and economic work of sustaining the family, even as private diaries recorded the volume and value of women's domestic labor. Domestic writers recognized the toil involved in domestic work — toil often associated with the working class and foreigners — yet regarded such work as an expression of higher moral values that allied it, instead, with artistic invention.[20] Like writing itself, domesticity established its value to the world by erasing signs of its creation; in order for both the home and the novel to exert influence, they needed to appear without effort on the part of their creators.

The conditions of the American West, however, complicated attempts to present domestic labor as effortless. Western contact zones, where the ordering structures of American "civilization" seemed most threatened by the wilderness and by native others, intensified the need to define domesticity as a sign of middle-class status and values. Yet domestic ordering ideologies carried west by government agents, novelists, and even rank-and-file women ran head-on into physical environments and alternative practices that defied such order and threatened to reveal home as the fragile structure it was. White women's cultural work and domestic labor acquired new urgency in the West as ways to maintain both the idea and reality of home in an environment that threatened socially constructed distinctions between home and market, and savagery and civilization.[21] Those categories, white women believed, were sustained through women's work. Middle-class women did not necessarily regard their housework only in terms of economic value or strictly as a labor of love, but mingled those definitions as they struggled to articulate differences between themselves and the laboring classes, and between middle-class moral housekeeping and native women's drudgery.

The conditions of western contact zones also gave new meaning to home and domestic work as frameworks for comparing cultures, as science articulated the differences between what it defined as "savage" and "civilized" lifeways. By the time Alice Fletcher arrived in Idaho, ethnologists had spent decades looking at family life in order to understand the progress of civilization. Beginning in the 1850s, scientists on both sides of the Atlantic saw the key to social evolution in changing gender roles and household forms. This theory, turned into popular knowledge, helped to put domestic values into a new scientific context.[22] Europeans such as Jacob Bachhofen, Sir Henry Maine, and Herbert Spencer and American Lewis Henry Morgan explained evolutionary progress in terms of three stages: savagery, barbarism, and civilization. Each stage carried with it more highly developed political and economic organizations, systems that were rooted in family structure. In savage society, these scientists believed, families were extended, matriarchal, and matrilocal. As groups developed, increasing political sophistication was accompanied by increasing patriarchal control — and sexual differentiation. Drawing on evolutionary biology, these early ethnologists regarded the signs of women's submission — frailty, economic dependency, and confinement to the home — as necessary to advancement. Sexual differentiation and separation of tasks within the household were the engines behind progress toward civilization.

Popular scientific definitions of civilization in the later decades of the nineteenth century increasingly affected the ways Euro-American women understood domestic life and the gendered work roles that structured it. Science made it clear that woman's role as household worker was a product of evolution and that her disempowerment was part of progress. But a number of women used the new science of evolutionary theory to suggest new ways of looking at household labor. They suggested that women's confinement to home was, in fact, a remnant of barbarism, and in order for a race to reach its fullest potential, women needed to be liberated from housework to share in the same liberties and opportunities that men enjoyed. Foremost among these theorists were the women Dolores Hayden has called the material feminists: those who argued, as early as the 1840s, that the physical structure of American homes contributed to the economic erasure of household labor and thus to women's political, economic, and social exploitation.[23] Material feminists often departed from moral arguments about women's worth to society in favor of claims that rooted the power and influence of women in their material conditions, such as their control over household space, their access to wages and property, and their physical and economic integration into public life. Like early ethnologists, they saw family organization and home architecture as maps on which to read the progress of civilization. They believed that by reorganizing the home and educating women, they could advance civilization itself by releasing women from the kinds of work that kept them from intellectual and economic advancement.

The rise of popular evolutionary discourse in the latter half of the century shaped the ways that material feminists understood their work. Catharine Beecher and Harriet Beecher Stowe, though firm believers in women's inherent morality, incorporated the material and scientific aspects of housework into their domestic manuals in the 1840s and 1850s. By better understanding the science behind domestic work, Beecher and Stowe argued, women could improve their health, their families' welfare, and eventually, civilization itself.[24] Later feminists were more overt in their focus on evolution, suggesting more radical changes to homes and women's household labor. Charlotte Perkins Gilman, writing in the 1890s, believed that both the human race and the physical forms of houses should evolve toward cooperative models in an effort to free women from the submission made material in the family home. A staunch evolutionist, Gilman argued in *Women and Economics* (1898) that women were, in fact, physically and intellectually inferior to men but that changes in home architecture would force progress through the professionalization of domestic work.[25]

But as the trend toward professionalization legitimated some forms of domestic work, it also suggested that most women's housework was not specialized at all and that a categorical divide existed between domestic science and daily domestic labors. Francesca Sawaya argues that some middle-class women who participated in discussions about domesticity in the early twentieth century relied on images of the "premodern" to fashion professional identities.[26] Particularly for Gilman, ethnicity was a great barrier dividing women able to educate and professionalize themselves from those who were not. Emerging theories of scientific home management and rising immigration near the end of the nineteenth century helped middle-class white women to claim specialized understanding of systems of orderly home administration and to justify their work based on the very real need to improve the health and condition of working-class and immigrant families. Home economists such as Ellen Swallow Richards and Sophonisba Breckinridge helped, by the turn of the century, to define the home more clearly as a woman's workplace and to acquire legitimacy for domestic work by elevating it to professional status. Schools and settlement houses offered courses in home economics, chemistry, and domestic design that produced a generation of women whose knowledge of home work was based not on female instinct and influence, as earlier writers had suggested, but on specialized knowledge firmly rooted in the sciences.[27] Women's assimilation work among Native Americans shows that the professional legitimacy of some kinds of domestic work was tenuously premised, in part, on the illegitimacy of other forms.

Nineteenth-century observers looked at women's work in other cultures through the lens that ethnology provided — a lens that, Native American historians have pointed out, was often distorted by Euro-American ideas about gender differentiation. Most Native American societies did divide work roles along gender lines; in many cases, women were the primary agriculturalists, while men provided meat and hides. Though these divisions were not necessarily hierarchical, Euro-Americans who encountered native societies in the latter half of the century thought in terms of the value systems that divided men's and women's labor in their own societies and thus judged Indian women's work as lower in status than that of men. Indian women tanned hides, erected homes, carried wood and water, and maintained gardens—signs of their disempowerment and drudgery. If this work was devalued in Euro-American society, observers reasoned, how much more must it be in native societies? In fact, these very tasks accorded many indigenous women esteem and even rewards and status within their tribes. In evolutionary terms, whites saw women's performance of what seemed to them to be male tasks—farming, home building, and supply gathering—as a corruption of gender roles and an impediment to progress.

Evolutionary beliefs about home and gender roles were thus a crucial component of the General Allotment Act of 1887, backed by Senator Henry L. Dawes. The Dawes Act drew on theories, common to both ethnologists and material feminists, that saw environmental change as a way to effect social change. The act was meant to destroy both native cultural patterns and the government-implemented reservation system by allotting 160 acres to each head of family, 80 to each single person over eighteen and each orphan under eighteen, and 40 to each child under eighteen. Heads of families would select allotments after reservations had been surveyed; land and individuals would be duly registered and, after a period of twenty-five years' severalty, Native Americans would own their lands outright, with freedom to sell or lease the property. Native Americans would become citizens at the time of allotment but would remain government dependents during the period of severalty. Property ownership was the cornerstone of the Dawes Act; however, reformers drawing on social evolution believed that civilization could only be effected by concomitant changes in social life. To that end, they promoted Christian marriages among indigenous people, forced families to regroup under male heads (a tactic often enforced by renaming), and trained men in wage-earning occupations while encouraging women to support them at home through their domestic activities. Both the Hampton Institute in Virginia, founded in 1868 as an industrial school for freedmen and -women that also began admitting native students in 1877, and the Carlisle School in Pennsylvania, established in 1880, developed systems whereby Indian children would learn industry and housekeeping—and the value of money—through exposure to Euro-American homes and habits. Educators hoped that the children would return home to spread the new ways among those still living traditional lifestyles.

Making Home Work shows that the redefinition of women's work and Native American assimilation were part of the same phenomenon, in which women used science to reimagine domestic space and the role their work would play in building a nation. White and native women's responses to and criticisms of domestic work undermine the message of popular texts that naturalized imperialism as benignly domestic. By making home and domestic work as central to understanding relationships between natives and whites in the West as they have been to studies of Americanization attempts in the East, I hope to open new spaces and new kinds of work to scrutiny. Assimilation ideals took shape not only in the halls of Congress, Indian school classrooms, and portfolios of professional photographers but in women's writing and the daily processes of housework. Forced assimilation also was carried out in Native American homes across the West, often using tools associated with domestic work — scrub brushes, sewing needles, and buckets of water. Far from centers of Euro-American institutional power, these homes were fragile representations of white, middle-class norms and offered spaces where Native American women could create their own understandings of home, domestic work, and progress.

Domesticity on Display

Domestic literature, evolutionary theory, and the science of housework all helped to make the gendered and racial order of the world visible by locating it in the home. The home stood for the achievements and imperatives of civilization as well as for the work that women did; home was a way to initiate others into the order that it represented. Cultural theorist Tony Bennett argues that evolutionary science was, like other late nineteenth-century theories and institutions, a "response to the problem of order, but one that worked differently in seeking to transform that problem into one of culture — a question of winning hearts and minds as well as the disciplining and training of bodies." This winning of hearts and minds was achieved by way of popular and material culture that helped to make the anthropological world order visible. Stories, paintings, photographs, commodities, and even home architecture embedded the ideal of racial progress in the culture. Bennett calls this "extension of anthropology's disciplinary ambit" into sites outside the museum the "exhibitionary complex."[28] Object lessons with popular appeal empowered spectators outside the museum by allowing them to participate in creating civilized order in their lives and to be seen as models of correct behavior — behavior shaped by the narratives of race and nation governing the displays.[29]

The exhibitionary complex was an important component of museum displays, but it also organized late nineteenth- and early twentieth-century American home spaces and women's domestic work. Popular writing that concealed women's physical labors nonetheless stressed women's crucial role in turning a mere structure into a home. Domestic literature lingers over descriptions of homes, for a nineteenth-century home's tasteful interior could reveal the class status, moral sensibilities, and Anglo-Saxon values of its inhabitants. This function made displaying homes crucial for middle-class women interested in revamping the structure of the home and improving the status of working-class, African American, Indian, and immigrant women. Late nineteenth- and early twentieth-century communal apartment buildings and settlement houses were designed to relieve some of the pressures on women to perform all necessary household chores single-handedly and to allow them to venture into new professions. At the same time, other reformers used single-family model homes to enlighten ethnically diverse groups as to the benefits of nuclear family living.[30]

As the Euro-American home moved into western spaces in the second half of the nineteenth century, Native American women and their forms of work were increasingly included in the exhibitionary complex. Certainly the theory behind visual exchange was part of attempts by writers, photographers, scientists, and reformers to convince citizens of the possibility of domesticating indigenous people and to convince Native Americans of the superiority of Euro-American domesticity. Yet Native Americans themselves remained largely outside these exhibitionary exchanges. Native American images and artifacts objectified and commodified Indians without recording either the effort expended by reformers and photographers to achieve this revolutionary effect or the intense labor that indigenous people performed at home and at school en route to their transformations. Those who controlled the spectacle and distribution of native crafts promoted the value of those goods to Euro-American society, suggesting that by purchasing these goods, middle-class homeowners could access a more authentic, pure relationship between self and labor — a relationship that was being lost in turn-of-the-century commodity culture.[31] Yet by celebrating the "pure" and "primitive" life, even those who most heartily appreciated native cultures pushed into the background the economic realities of indigenous life, just as earlier domestic texts had erased white women's economic contributions to the family. They obscured those very power relationships between producers and consumers, and laborers and owners, that they sought to escape by looking west but that were very much alive in those areas as a result of tourism and commodification of native labor.[32] Likewise, in celebrating craft traditions in particular, middle-class enthusiasm for Native American cultures ignored other forms of native women's labor that increasingly shaped indigenous life. Assimilation had stripped away many of the traditional ways women had used to participate in family economies, creating economic conditions that forced them to seek new kinds of work as wage earners.

Seeing various forms of cultural work — writing, home display, photography, and the spectacle of craft — as part of the exhibitionary complex lends new dynamism to our understanding of domesticity as an imperial construct. Indeed, domesticity traveled west through these very forms, as I show in the first half of this book. But Bennett's theory notes that exhibitions are always an exchange in which viewers are invited to see themselves as part of the community whose virtues are on display. Participation in the exhibitionary complex proceeds by way of consumption — reading books, attending museums, and looking at photographs. Indian reformers hoped to use those same strategies in persuading Native Americans to adopt civilized lifeways. I argue that participating in the stories that the displays told was also made manifest in work, as some struggled to construct the display and others selectively adopted its premises by the way they carried out their work. Every display, in other words, stood not just for itself as architecture, novel, or image but for the work relationships it embodied.

The Outer Edges

The chapters in *Making Home Work* range over six decades, from the waning years of domestic fiction to the blossoming of antimodernism, from crusades for women's economic rights in the mid-nineteenth century to women's integration into the professional class in the first decades of the twentieth. The book is not meant to be a monograph on either women's work or assimilation; instead, the chapters are linked by a common focus on the production of domesticity in the contact zones of the West. The first half explores how white, middle-class women exported domesticity to the West through literature, science, and the ideal of the model home. In the first three chapters, I look at how domestic fiction adapted Native American history to define civilization as women's work, at midwestern women's theories of household labor in the civilized home, and at the Women's National Indian Association's home-building campaign of the late nineteenth century. In the second half, I examine more closely the ways individual women responded to the labor relationships embedded in these definitions and displays of domesticity. E. Jane Gay's story reveals her understanding that power came more easily to some women than to others and shows the fragility of the scientific and moral foundations that undergirded assimilation policy. My investigation into the stories of Arikara field matron Anna Dawson Wilde, Mandan reservation resident Ella Ripley, and Winnebago artist Angel DeCora shows that Native American women accepted some forms of work more readily than others. Some native women became domestic professionals, while others adapted traditional forms of housework and accommodated new forms brought by reformers. These women also recognized the power that lay in cultural work, and they struggled to seize that power in order to define domestic work in ways that affirmed indigenous identity. Each of these women used as well as criticized the exhibitionary complex as it was manifested in photography, architecture, professional domesticity, and the arts. In so doing, they revealed the uneven distribution of power in the work required to produce and sustain the displays themselves. Each woman's story suggests that what seem to be conventional expressions of Euro-American domesticity are much more informed by interracial contexts and by changing theories of women's work than they might at first appear.

As a photographer, E. Jane Gay knew that images could be carefully composed and cropped to trim off the "outer edges" in an effort to present a certain picture of life. She compared the process of cropping to Fletcher's allotment work, in which government insistence on well-defined plots necessitated trimming off not only undesirable lands but also untenable lifeways.[33] Her duties as Fletcher's cook, however, taught her that some kinds of work and some domestic relationships, repetitive and unquantifiable as they were, were difficult to adapt to a square mentality. Perhaps this is why Gay's portrait of herself as a photographer (see fig. 4.3) crops the square edges, signifying the difficulty of representing all that her work and identity entailed. In this image, Gay plays with gender identity and work roles, suggesting that undermining these divisions necessitates a new form, circular rather than square.[34]

The camera in this circular self-portrait indicates not only a single photographic moment but the calculated work of photography itself. Putting women's work at the center of a study of domesticity's incarnations in the American West necessitates a search for the outer edges that are lost if we focus only on the cultural work of domesticity or if we regard women's work itself as a stable category. Reading only the "square ideas" embedded in texts and images suggests that the whole process of making identity in the West was much tidier than it really was. Dynamic exchanges between white and native women as they struggled to define home work for themselves and each other show that making culture, like making home, is never a passive process but is the result of conscious intellectual and physical effort on the part of diverse individuals for whom making home has always been intimately connected with the making of a nation and the making of a self.

CHAPTER ONE

Prairie Heirs and Heiresses

Native American History and the
Future of the West in Caroline Soule's
The Pet of the Settlement

n 1830 George Catlin painted a portrait of Tenskwatawa, the "Shawnee Prophet" and brother of Tecumseh. In the years before the War of 1812, Tenskwatawa traveled widely to urge Indians to look to native religion and ritual in order to fight Euro-American encroachment on indigenous lands and minds. He proposed founding new, pan-Indian towns that would meld tribal identities and herald a new era of political and spiritual unity. But economic and material losses, combined with infighting among the tribes, weakened the movement.[1] By 1830, Catlin recalled, the man who was once "quite equal in his medicines or mysteries, to what his brother was in arms" was no longer the powerful force he had been. "Circumstances have destroyed him," Catlin wrote, "and he now lives respected, but silent and melancholy within his tribe." In the portrait, Catlin seems to have attempted to capture what he saw as Tenskwatawa's resignation as well as the ferocity of one who had called thousands to his cause. In *The Open Door, Known as the Prophet, Brother of Tecumseh*, the one-eyed visionary looks west, holding his "medicine fire" in his right hand and in his left his "sacred string of white beans," objects he took with him on his journeys (see fig. 1.1). According to Catlin, his "recruits" would swear to his cause by touching the loop of beans.[2] Yet the Prophet turns away from his portrait painter, his face haggard and lined, his posture soft, as if remembering a vision. The portrait of the aged Prophet records Catlin's belief that the perseverance and faith of men like Tenskwatawa was wasted on attempts to salvage a doomed culture.

Catlin's portraits and writings highlight what he and doubtless many viewers of his Indian Gallery saw as Indian nobility and exoticism. Yet his *Letters and Notes on the Manners, Customs, and Condition of the North American Indians* (1841) show that even as he zealously sought to preserve Indian cultures, he saw them as pertinent to the past, not the future. "I deem it not folly nor idle to claim that these people *can be saved*," Catlin wrote, "nor officious to suggest to some of the very many excellent and pious men, who are almost throwing away the best energies of their lives along the debased frontier, that if they would introduce their prayers and plowshares amongst these people . . . they would see their most ardent desires accomplished and be able to solve to the world the perplexing enigma, by presenting a nation of savages, civilized and Christianized (and consequently *saved*) in the heart of the American wilderness."[3] Catlin exhorts white men to exercise their manhood by laying aside the pursuit of wealth and power and offering Indians paternal supervision. He imagines the civilizing mission, with its twinned components of Christianization and agriculture, as a nobler enterprise for both border men and Indians.

Author Caroline Augusta White Soule, writing some twenty years after Catlin published his notes, looked at the portrait of the Shawnee Prophet and envisioned an enterprise meant for women. In the preface to her 1860 novel *The Pet of the Settlement*, she declares that one of her Indian characters, White Cloud, was inspired by "the 'Shawnee Prophet' of Catlin."[4] Soule, who may have encountered Catlin's writings or his traveling portrait gallery as a young woman growing up in the East, also saw the solution to the "Indian Problem" in saving the Indian soul. Yet where Catlin regarded assimilation as an opportunity to create new work for western men, Soule suggests that the very tendency of men to pursue wealth and make war meant that the task of civilizing Native Americans fell naturally to women. Drawing upon the tradition of sentimental literature that lauded white, middle-class women as the moral center of home and nation, Soule's novel posits that white women who would take on Indians as the objects of their affections could create crucial roles for themselves in colonizing the continent. As teachers and missionaries to the Indians, they could turn moral influence into authority.

Writing in 1860, Soule was informed by decades of domestic writing that cultivated the public image of white, middle-class women as civilizers. Yet in relocating that image to the trans-Mississippi West, Soule's novel represents an important bridge between sentimental rhetoric and civilization policy. Certainly Soule was not the only domestic writer to imagine the American West as the new moral center of the continent or to suggest that white women would civilize the West. Many of these novels, however, take place within an abstract West that functions as a more moral counterpoint to the industrial East or the slaveholding South.[5] In contrast, Soule situates *The Pet of the Settlement* within a specific geographic, temporal, and political terrain: the landscape of central Iowa that between 1842 and 1860, the years in which her novel takes place, witnessed rapid settlement by whites, the piecemeal takeover of native

Figure 1.1. George Catlin, *The Open Door, Known as the Prophet, Brother of Tecumseh*. 1830. Courtesy of Smithsonian American Art Museum, Washington, D.C. / Art Resource, N.Y.

lands, and the gradual resettlement of the Sauk, Fox, and Ioway beyond the Missouri River. The novel is informed by a period of history that witnessed the difficulties of Indian removal policies, as land cessions forced the tribes into closer proximity with whites and with one another. Soule capitalizes on what she regards as the chaos and violence of male-dominated frontier history, repackaging it in domestic scenarios that intertwine the lives of white women and Indians. In Soule's hands, the stock sentimental plot of moral regeneration includes Indians; the self-awareness and independence that the heroines achieve depend on their care and instruction of Indians.

The Pet of the Settlement represents the rewriting of the past that accompanied the attempts of middle-class white women to foresee a new future for themselves and for Native Americans. Yet unlike some earlier writers of historical fiction who appropriated the Indian past, Soule showed an interest less in their wildness or nobility than in their potential for assimilation. She drew on political history, popular representations of Native Americans, and failed Indian policy as well as on the sentimental tradition in creating a western home in which white women preside over their Native American wards. Soule seized on the Prophet Tenskwatawa's fierce commitment to pan-Indian unity and to religion and ritual as a source of identity in order to harness his influence to a different mission, one that involved white women and natives collaborating to spread Christian domesticity "between the Missouri River and the Rocky Mountains."[6] Prescribing education, landownership, marriage, and Christianity as solutions to the Indian Problem, Soule both presaged the Dawes Act of 1887 and posited these as specific forms through which white women could exercise influence in the West. Soule's vision resembled Tenskwatawa's in that it was as forward-looking as it was rooted in tradition and as invested in exerting power through a new political geography as it was in converting souls. She imagined encounters between whites and Indians as opportunities to translate white women's spirituality and domesticity into sites that would offer women new forms of work in the years to come.

In an Indian Land

In order to imagine a home- and woman-centered future, Soule uses the sentimental genre to domesticate a western past dominated in politics and popular culture by white men and "wild" Indians. Soule admits in her preface that while her tale is based on frontier events related to her by an "aged pioneer," it is meant to lead the reader "from the shadows of sin and into the sunshine of virtue."[7] In adapting the male pioneer's story, Soule creates a melodramatic plotline that emphasizes women's experience and regards domestic ideals as prototypes for national values. The novel echoes Soule's willingness to rewrite the old pioneer's story when the heroine, Margaret Belden, appoints a room in her cottage for the crusty old settler Uncle Billy. She decorates it with "pictures of the chase" and fills the bookcase with "tales of hunters, trappers, and Indians, biographies of discoverers and adventures, and volume after volume of natural history." Yet Uncle Billy rejects the space as too civilized for him, and he moves to his own hut, where he can tell tales of the old days. When Margaret subsequently refurbishes the room for their recently widowed neighbor Grandma Symmes, she replaces the bookshelf and its literary legacy of the frontier with "a commodious dressing bureau," and in place of images of the chase she hangs pictures with titles like *The Healing of the Sick* and *The Blessing of the Children*.[8] New inhabitants, Soule suggests, bring new values and necessitate new spaces to house them.

Soule's novel does not completely reject the western past, for though Uncle Billy must tell his stories elsewhere, Soule makes room in her literary home for Indian characters to take up residence there. Exchanges between white women and their Indian "children" are crucial to the sentimental economy of *The Pet of the Settlement*, and the circumstances that bring her Native American characters together with their white "mothers" are made possible by a particular history of dispossession. Soule's domestication of the Iowa prairies depends not only on retelling the old settler's tale but on reframing conflicts and characters drawn from Native American history. In order to project her tale onto a past marked by uneasy and violent relations between whites and indigenous people, Soule first must clear the landscape by converting indigenous history and politics into literary property.

That effort may partly explain the novel's numerous digressions and twists of fate. Perhaps because of its awkward blending of gothic melodrama, prairie pastoralism, and sentimental excesses, *The Pet of the Settlement* has received little critical attention. The plot follows the Belden family—Margaret, her young brother Harrie, and her father—after their arrival in a new Iowa settlement. Early in the novel, the Beldens take in two individuals ripe for the instruction that civilized life has to offer: a Sauk boy named White Cloud and a white baby girl, Allie, the "pet" of the title. As the settlement evolves into a bustling frontier town, Margaret takes on the responsibility of mothering and instructing both Allie and White Cloud. A flashback at midnovel inserts the story of Margaret's lost love back in New York; when her lover is revealed as the settlement's mysterious hunter-priest, a prairie wedding ensues. A party of Sioux disrupt the festivities when they kidnap Allie. After White Cloud returns with the girl and a fresh set of scalps, he embarks on a quest to find the girl's mother. A new subplot reveals that Allie's mother, Mary, is being held captive by a Sioux chief whose daughter, Bright-eyed, becomes her "dusky maid" and pupil. Eventually, the two Indians collaborate to engineer an escape to the settlement. The mystery of Allie's appearance on the prairie is solved in another digression, as Mary tells of her husband's murder and her own kidnapping at the hands of a family friend. Mary's drawn-out sickness and death and the appearance, absolution, and subsequent death of the murderer conclude the historical section of the novel. The ending reveals the prairie settlement and Belden family fifteen years later, rich in happiness and material success.

This greatly abbreviated summary suggests that Soule's novel, in fact, has little to do with daily life in the West. Indeed, those who do discuss the novel have found that it fails to wrestle with the realities of the western condition. Henry Nash Smith, in *Virgin Land*, argues that "the scheme of values in the novel is organized about the superiority of the hero and heroine, whose merits have nothing to do with the West or with agriculture." He laments that "for all her four years on the prairie, Mrs. Soule can not find the literary means to embody the affirmation of the agrarian ideal her theory calls for."[9] Annette Kolodny, in contrast, suggests that the merits of the heroine and the details of her household have much to do with the way white women envisioned the West. Projecting domestic fantasies onto western landscapes, writers like Soule replaced the brutal realities of western speculation, industrialization, and class division with a nostalgic vision of hearth and home in which women still played vital roles.[10] Both Kolodny and Smith emphasize the novel's engagement with eastern class ideals and find that the novel merely projects a model of virtuous, middle-class white womanhood onto a new environment. Rather than engaging with her western subjects, Kolodny argues, Soule is ultimately interested in developing a "human social garden" in the form of a "model town" that assuages fears about the labor exploitation so rampant in the eastern states.[11] Soule exhibits woman's crucial role in bringing civilization to the prairies, where domestic productivity could flourish without the taint of eastern economic corruption.

Smith and Kolodny are correct in noting that Soule does little to illuminate economic realities or interrogate the social changes brought about by industrialization in the West. For novelists like Soule and for her readers, the prairie landscape provided an ideal setting for dramas of progress that cleansed industrialization of its messier inequities by equating community development with nature's growth. It is not surprising that establishing middle-class identity in a western environment should entail erasing signs of labor. Making labor invisible was one of the triumphs of middle-class culture and the literature that sustained it; it was rare for a nineteenth-century writer, male or female, western or not, to represent any kind of physical labor as intrinsically valuable.[12] Certainly *The Pet of the Settlement* indicates that the fates of white women did not depend on the economic value of their labor but on their influential domestic role in the gentle "human appropriation of a landscape."[13] In envisioning ideal households ruled by women whose authority issues not from their labor but from their natural domestic tendencies, writers like Soule were complicit in creating a pastoral ideal that concealed the economic value of women's housework in favor of the more abstract and immaterial concept of women's influence, a process Jeanne Boydston has termed the "pastoralization of housework."[14]

In emphasizing the middle-class, pastoral values that eventually triumph in the novel, however, neither Smith nor Kolodny engages Soule's portrayal of Native Americans or her appropriation of Iowa history as a backdrop to her novel. Refocusing critical attention on the western materials that Soule does rely on — her Iowa setting and the Sauk and Sioux who play crucial roles in her plot — suggests that Indians are integral to her scheme for establishing middle-class status for white women in the West. Though Soule does seem to exalt the "bright, beautiful change" that comes to the settlement as the open prairie is replaced by a bustling town, her elaborate plot investigates the intertwined histories of the landscape, white women settlers, and the Indians who inhabited the land before the change came about.[15] While white women lose some of their more prosaic chores — they can no longer pick wild berries or collect wildflowers when the open prairies have been replaced by private property — the history that left "uncultivated" Indians inhabiting the Iowa landscapes gives white women new forms of work more in keeping with the western narrative of progress.

The Pet of the Settlement is a historical novel set in the decades leading up to the year of the novel's publication, 1860. Like other American novelists before her, Soule was interested in reconstructing the American past to address present concerns. Soule's professional and authorial activities point to her involvement in social reform. She was active in the temperance cause, an editor of several religious and women's periodicals, the first president of the Women's Centenary Aid Association, and a Unitarian Universalist who eventually became a missionary to Scotland and the first woman ordained as a minister there. Her other writings, *Home Life, or, A Peep Across the Threshold* (1855) and the temperance tale *Wine or Water: A Tale of New England* (1862), reflect these interests.[16] Her ties with the Unitarian church suggest that she may have been influenced by reform-minded, Christian writers of the previous generation. Lydia Maria Child and Catherine Maria Sedgwick, both Unitarians who wrote of hearth and home, also wrote historical novels about the relationships between white settlers and Native Americans, and their stories may have shaped Soule's own girlhood. Child's *Hobomok* (1824) and Sedgwick's *Hope Leslie* (1827) are set in Puritan New England and feature the temporary incorporation of Indians into Puritan homes and white women into Indian ones. Mary Conant's marriage to Hobomok, Magawisca's tenure with the Fletcher family in *Hope Leslie*, and the marriage of Hope's sister Faith to an Indian all suggest the possibility of native assimilation but fall short of endorsing it. Child and Sedgwick were sympathetic to the Indians' situation and condemned what they saw as the racism responsible for Indian removal policies, but both were ambivalent about the Indian's position in the nation. While the women in their novels achieve a measure of independence and carve out roles for themselves as agents in their families and communities, even the most sensitively drawn Indians fade back into the forest. The authors' interpretations of Puritan engagements with Indians were filtered through the lenses of abolitionism and the burgeoning women's movements of their own time. While Child and Sedgwick protested racism and insisted on women's sympathy as a potent force in mitigating political conflicts, they failed to enact a literary alternative to removal.[17]

Lucy Maddox speculates that Child and Sedgwick fabricated a Puritan past that would appeal to female readers who responded to Indian assimilation as an endorsement of middle-class family values. She notes that these readers might also celebrate the authors' success in wresting native figures from tales of frontier violence in order to be "offered a home with the domestic novelists."[18] Soule assumed this task of creating a shared literary home for women and Indians, but she took her vision a step farther by writing a western interior that would include and keep Indians within the physical and geographic spaces wrought by domesticity and domestic policy. Though, like Child and Sedgwick, Soule was an easterner by birth, she did live in a western region that more recently had been the province of Native Americans and the scene of skirmishes between settlers and natives as well as intertribal conflicts. Soule married Universalist minister H. B. Soule in 1845, but his death in 1851 left her, at age twenty-seven, with five children and only $300. Her dire financial circumstances led her to move to Boonsboro, Iowa, in 1854 to teach and write, perhaps influenced by Catharine Beecher's program to find teachers for schools in new western territories. After writing *The Pet of the Settlement* and *Wine or Water*, along with numerous other pieces for the *Ladies' Repository* and the *Rose-bud*, she returned to her hometown of Albany in 1864.[19]

While Child, Sedgwick, and other romance writers such as James Fenimore Cooper and Nathaniel Hawthorne set their tales of Indian encounter in a more distant past, Soule relied on recent history. Markers within her text suggest that the bustling town of Belden celebrated at the end of the novel depicts central Iowa in 1859 or 1860. A litany of Belden's features includes a new agricultural college; the State Agricultural College and Model Farm was founded in Ames, Iowa, in 1858.[20] The final scenes of the novel come after a narrative leap of fifteen years; another leap earlier in the novel skips nearly two years. Thus the novel's opening, which shows the newly arrived Belden family accommodating themselves to their shoddy squatter-built home, chronicles events that take place in about 1842. The change from prairie outpost to bustling town reflects the speed of development during that time, when Iowa's Euro-American population grew from 43,112 in 1840 to 674,913 in 1860.[21]

Soule situates her novel geographically, placing her settlers, like herself, in a "valley of the Upper Des Moines" "two hundred miles beyond the Mississippi."[22] She mentions markers such as the Boone Branch of the Des Moines, where Uncle Billy had set up his squatter's home seven years before the novel begins. She notes nearby high bluffs along the Des Moines, the oxbow in the river, and the fort not far from the settlement. The indicators suggest that Soule had no intention of obscuring that the scene of her novel was very similar to her own situation in Boonsboro, in central Iowa between the Des Moines and Boone Branch, about forty miles from Fort Dodge and not far from present-day Ames.

Between about 1835, when Uncle Billy first came to Boone Branch, and 1842, when the Beldens arrived there, central Iowa was home to white squatters and several Indian groups. Uncle Billy, who, like many Iowa settlers, came from Indiana, speaks "Sauks, Fox, Pottowattamie, and Sioux, better than he can English" and has had numerous dealings — both friendly and bloody — with the Indians of Iowa and Indiana.[23] He frequently refers to his wife's capture by Indians in Indiana, noting that he had tracked his "little gal, my purty Sallie," more than 200 miles in order to retrieve her.[24] The native past in which the spirits of "red men" return to "their old hunting grounds" haunts Soule's interior. Margaret contemplates the prairie "where for ages the red man had built his council fires, fought his battles, and hunted his prey," and she shivers at the thought of seeing "dusky warriors with scalp-locks streaming from their belts, dash out from the timber, or rise up, weird-like, in the marsh-grass in which they had lain coiled in ambush." By the end of the novel, the "warwhoop of contending Sioux and Sacs" has been replaced by the whistle of the railway.[25] Like so many of her contemporaries, Soule used Indian history to lend romance to her setting while intimating that war cries echoed only in the past.

The era in which she set her novel, however, was a time of transition between indigenous use of Iowa lands and white ownership of them. In 1804, following the Louisiana Purchase, the U.S. government treated with the allied Sauk and Fox in order to acquire lands along the Mississippi in Wisconsin, Illinois, and Missouri. Yet the Sauk clung resolutely to their agricultural grounds, and many refused to acknowledge the terms of the treaty, which provided that they could occupy the land only until it was sold. Continuing tension between Sauks and white settlers in Illinois resulted in new forts along the Mississippi and, in 1831, settlers' destruction of homes, crops, and graves at the large village of Saukenuk. These conflicts between settlers, the Sauk, and government agents culminated in the ten-week conflict in the summer of 1832 known as Black Hawk's War. Devastated by hunger and disillusioned by lack of support from other tribes and the British, Black Hawk and his band eventually surrendered. The ensuing treaty between the government and the new Sauk leader Keokuk included the cession of 1832, a strip of about 6 million acres along the western side of the Mississippi in Iowa. The terms of the treaty also banished the Sauk and Fox to central and western Iowa, and the government hoped thus to widen the geographical gulf between settlers and natives. But whites — including Soule's fictitious squatter Uncle Billy — poured across the Mississippi in the 1830s, forcing the Sauk and Fox into less profitable hunting grounds and into closer proximity to their Sioux rivals. Weakened by illness, frequent clashes with the Sioux, and internal political divisions over tribal leadership and federal annuity payments, the Sauk were pressed to cede another 1.5 million acres in 1837. In 1842 they signed over the rest of their Iowa holdings. The terms of the 1842 treaty provided that the Sauk and Fox would move beyond the Missouri River by 1846.[26]

The key events of Soule's novel take place between 1842 and 1846, years in which the Sauks in Iowa were pressed between new and old rivals for their hunting grounds and faced enormous pressure not only to give up their lands but to give in to government attempts to civilize and Christianize them. Both the 1837 and 1842 treaties called for part of the tribes' remuneration to be spent on education and missionary activity. Keokuk refused the money earmarked for education in 1837, and in 1842 he resisted the construction of a manual labor school, reportedly declaring, "As to the proposal to build school houses . . . we have always been opposed to them, and will never consent to have them introduced into our nation."[27] Much more so than their neighbors the Ioway, the Sauk remained resolutely opposed to missionary activity, possibly because of their engagement with the nativism and spiritualism of the preceding decades. Indeed, the dissatisfaction of the tribe with the 1804 cession had made it receptive to the Prophet Tenskwatawa's message. According to Black Hawk's 1834 autobiography, in 1808 the Prophet sent messengers to Saukenuk calling for a meeting on the Wabash River. Tenskwatawa returned with the emissaries to tell the Sauks about "the bad treatment the different nations of Indians had received from the Americans, by giving them a few presents, and taking their land from them."[28] Perhaps more important, Black Hawk and the contingent of Sauks who joined him in resisting the turnover of lands in the early 1830s consulted with another leader known as the Winnebago Prophet. Thought to be half Winnebago and half Sauk, the Winnebago Prophet, Wabokieshiek, encouraged Black Hawk "never to give up our village, for the whites to plow up the bones of our people."[29] Black Hawk consulted with the Winnebago Prophet often, responding to what Wabokieshiek reported in his dreams. Subsequent historians (perhaps unfairly) have likened the Winnebago Prophet to a lesser, wilier, and less noble counterpart to the Shawnee Prophet. In spite of his own significant political activities and Black Hawk's commitment to spiritualism, like Tenskwatawa, Wabokieshiek has been characterized as the spiritual counterpart of a political leader.[30] When Catlin painted Wabokieshiek's portrait in 1832, he titled it with the Winnebago Prophet's translated name, White Cloud.

Capturing Indians on canvas and inviting them to participate in public displays were two ways that Euro-Americans expressed their conflicted emotions regarding what they saw as the inevitable loss of Indians and Indian culture. Given Soule's reference to the Shawnee Prophet's portrait, she may have seen Catlin's portrait of Wabokieshiek, titled *White Cloud (Called the Prophet), Adviser to Black Hawk.* The name of the Indian character might also reference an Ioway leader, Mahaska or White Cloud, or his son, also named White Cloud, who traveled with Catlin to Europe in the 1840s and who is the subject of several of Catlin's sketches and drawings. Catlin's Indian displays, like the photographs that proliferated in the coming decades, "represented North American Indians, like mineral deposits, as an inherent part of the landscape to be marveled at, then mapped, contained, possessed, and removed by the expanding nation."[31] Certainly Catlin's paintings, and those native leaders themselves, were drawn into this physical and aesthetic confiscation. After their 1832 capture, Black Hawk and Wabokieshiek were brought to Washington, D.C., and subsequently traveled to Baltimore, Philadelphia, New York, and Albany, where they were exhibited to crowds. Black Hawk's biographer Roger L. Nichols suggests that part of the function of exhibiting the warriors in crowded cities was to impress upon them the sheer numbers of white people — to imply that resistance against such hordes would be fruitless. Black Hawk's 1832 autobiography, probably much influenced by his interpreter, Antoine LeClaire, reports his "surprise at finding this village so much larger than the one we had left. . . . I had no idea that the white people had such large villages, and so many people."[32] It was during this trip, too, that Catlin painted portraits of Black Hawk and Wabokieshiek. In his portrait, White Cloud poses in front of a blank background, which emphasizes that the portrait was made far from his home and disguises the conditions of its creation; the absence of landscape expresses the real removals that attended the leaders' presence in Washington.

Such paintings expressed Euro-Americans' longing for the noble savages of their collective imagination; yet by recording physical removals, the paintings served expansionist goals by recording Indians' incorporation into the "visual territory" of Euro-American art.[33]

Soule's novel participates in this movement. She regards native history and individuals, including Tenskwatawa and Wabokieshiek, as literary property that could be mobilized to promote her hopes for the future of the nation. Her literary portrait of an Indian prophet marks her attempt to move Indian display from the visual territories and political venues of eastern cities, with their male-created treaties, canvases, and exhibitions, to women's purviews — homes and domestic texts. While for Catlin, the prophets were best painted against a blank background, Soule's interest in geography and history helps her claim western history and individuals to create spaces for the work of middle-class women as she asserts their power to achieve what men had tried and failed to do. In spite of treaties, wars, and land cessions, the Sauks remained staunchly resistant to both Christianity and male-centered agriculture even after their resettlement in Kansas in 1846. Soule emphasizes that it is women who could finally convert indigenous people into obedient Christians whose power lay not in resistance but in their ability to reflect and embody the virtues of civilization. If the romances of the 1820s and 1830s suggested that the political independence of white women might be defined through their difference from Indians who were unable to break with tradition, *The Pet of the Settlement* proposes that white women and Indians willing to overcome the past could create new work for themselves by uniting their similarly spiritual natures in service of domesticity.

The Home-Boy of the Household

As in many domestic novels, the heroine's marriage to the proper fellow is not the main objective of *The Pet of the Settlement*. In spite of Margaret's reunion with and marriage to her former suitor Edward Somers, the pairing of this hero and heroine plays a relatively minor role in the plot. In fact, after the wedding that occurs halfway through the novel, Edward all but disappears, only to reappear near the end as the father of Margaret's three children. If there is a hero in the story, it is the prophet figure, White Cloud. It is he who performs heroic deeds and he whom the heroine most profoundly affects. In creating the character of White Cloud, Soule appropriates the political vision and religious spiritualism of native leaders as well as the history of enmity between the Sioux and the Sauk. She adapts both spiritualism and western conflict to her own ends, turning the power of the Indian prophets from a political force that resisted Euro-American values into an energy that restores domesticity and promotes Christianity.

The task of Christianizing White Cloud literally interrupts Margaret Belden's domestic work. A moan from the wounded White Cloud causes her to stop making corn pone and coffee so she can bathe his wounds in a scene that clearly calls up Soule's own religious proclivities. She writes that Margaret "did not know it, but that cool, fresh water, dripping down his brown neck and rippling over his brown skin, beneath which his red heart was palpitating, was a baptism to the lad. . . . The young 'White Cloud' then and there, swore in his soul that he would dwell no more with his red friends, but be as a brother to the White Dove." After Margaret utters the Lord's Prayer over him, White Cloud murmurs, "you — good; — me — glad; — me — once bad — me good now." As White Cloud feels himself cleansed, whitened, and reborn, Margaret is redefined as well, becoming "White Dove," the object of White Cloud's affections and his conduit to white culture. Margaret, despondent over her break with Edward, sees in White Cloud an opportunity to pass on a cultural inheritance, symbolized by their mutual spiritual "whiteness": "Mayhap, there is a mission for me yet on earth, though never can I bear the holy names of wife and mother, and dashing big tears from her eyes, she went bravely to her work."[34] In extending love to this new object of affection, Margaret receives a new name and a new kind of work. The work she takes on, Soule intimates, will never be the duties of "wife" or "mother," titles that blur labor roles with terms of affection, but the spiritual work of the White Dove. As White Cloud is inducted into Christianity, so Margaret, in taking on an Indian name, also embraces the spiritualism of the mission that the Prophet signified for Soule. In Margaret's literal and figurative turn from domestic work, both White Cloud and Margaret are "whitened" through their new spiritual bond.

In presenting conversion through the domestic ritual of washing the body, Soule endorses Christianization as women's spiritual work rather than as the political work of government agents. Uncle Billy crows that "I allers used to think if some one of them missionary men whom I have heard tell on, was to come around amongst the red-skins here, he'd be their first *convart*. But our darter Margaret here has done it quicker and better than one of them ar' would, for she took right hold of his heart, and when a woman gets your heart in her hands, I tell you, the game is up."[35] Redefining Sauk resistance to the assimilation attempts of the 1830s and 1840s as due to the impotence of white missionary men, Soule claims for her heroine a child that is the product of woman alone. Likewise, White Cloud rejects his "red friends" and wipes himself clean of his own history. Freed of the influence of either white men or native leaders, White Cloud becomes a palimpsest, ready for the White Dove to inscribe new meanings on him.

While Catlin, perhaps used to painting on clean canvas, believed the Indian to be a Rousseauvian "beautiful blank on which anything can be written if the proper means be taken," Soule imagines her Indian figures as having pasts; part of the triumph of the mission was in turning that past toward a "whiter" future.[36] White Cloud's childhood aspirations to domestic wealth and political power suggest Soule's understanding of native masculinity as the accumulation of luxuries, women, and glory:

> His ambition was to be a mighty chief, so fierce and terrible that the pale-faced women should still their naughty children with his name, — to have many and beautiful squaw wives — to own lodges whose sides were hung with ermine, and whose floors were of swan-down — to wear robes of the soft, white skin of the mountain-goat, all pictured over with the blood-red story of his battles, and fringed with the scarlet scalps and long black locks of his countless victims — to die on the gory field, but with his enemy in his grasp, to be buried on his favorite horse, and be known forever as the mightiest of the Sacs.[37]

In spite of these lofty and bloody ambitions, White Cloud is ripe for instruction because, according to Uncle Billy, he already favors his mother over his father and often refused to make war in order to stay home and help her. White Cloud, Billy notes, was always a "*pecooler*" Indian — he was, as historians have portrayed Tenskwatawa, more spiritual than political. Having domesticated White Cloud's past, Soule indicates that his spiritual and intellectual energies can smoothly enter a Euro-American, middle-class home. He becomes "the home-boy of the household," who, after converting his parents, eventually moves in with the Beldens. Here, he relishes his daily instruction with Margaret, with whom he disappears for hours each day in order to pore over her books. Other members of the household chip in, teaching him geography, philosophy, and math.[38]

By the end of the novel, White Cloud's ambition and religious zeal have been fully turned toward the Euro-American Christianizing mission. Resolved to become a minister, White Cloud "has become already what he aspired to be in the early days of his acquaintance with the whites, a great prophet and preacher, and is loved and reverenced by all the Indians as the great 'Ioway,' 'the Priest of Prayer.'" Margaret has helped White Cloud fulfill his dream of becoming a prophet to his people, for he has decided to erect mission houses in the "beautiful site in the northern limits of Nebraska" where his people have been resettled.[39] The goal of his prophecy is to see the Christian heaven offered by his white mother rather than to lead his people into liberation from the White Dove or to resist the takeover of lands that her Christian community also represents. Soule merges her fiction with historical reality by sending White Cloud west of the Missouri, where most of his people had been relocated by 1860.[40] Soule attempts to bring the power of pan-Indian spiritualism in line with her vision of a new unity through Christianity that would link not only tribes across the West but also white women and native men who shared an interest in religion's unifying power.

Perhaps drawing on contemporary perceptions of native prophets as the "heart" of Indian resistance who stood alongside political "heads" such as Tecumseh and Black Hawk, Soule may have seen their powers as parallel to those of white women who found authority in exerting spiritual rather than political influence on the nation.[41] In allying native spirituality with white women's moral authority, Soule bolsters the carefully created distinctions between spiritual and political concerns that characterized nineteenth-century sentimental discourse. While Soule does reference the political reality of the Sauks' precarious position, situated as they were between white settlers and their Sioux enemies, Soule domesticates this history of conflict by reimagining violence as a force that can unite mothers and their children. She rewrites the history of territorial conquest as the maternal conquest of souls and enlists White Cloud's hatred of the Sioux in service of restoring the Euro-American family. In so doing, she hints that Indian compliance with the domesticating mission will also serve white women's political interests.

One of the perplexing features of the novel is that the Prophets' involvement in acts of war seems not to be erased by their literary heir's missionary impulse; for a boy who refused to go on the warpath with his father, White Cloud is only too willing to do battle for the sake of his white mothers. Though White Cloud disavows his family early on as a result of his baptism, he does not renounce violence. The baptism scene itself is premised on a violent encounter, as White Cloud's spiritual cleansing occurs while Margaret washes wounds inflicted by her brother.

This scene invokes narratives of conversion characteristic of nineteenth-century religious tracts that legitimated imperial conquest as Christian education. Karen Sánchez-Eppler has argued that such tracts — which Soule also wrote after her return east — blurred the boundaries between acts of violent aggression and acts of religious piety. In a similar way, this scene legitimates divisions between individuals along race and gender lines in order to imagine sentimental piety as the foundation of relationships that could bridge those gaps.[42] This moment of sympathetic engagement that redefines both the Indian boy and the white woman exhibits the "tender violence" that Laura Wexler has seen as "one of the chief ideological achievements of antebellum domestic culture," for it obscures the mechanisms that upheld racial hierarchies under an aura of affection.[43] The outpouring of natural sentiment that here forges a bond of affection between a white woman and an Indian boy simultaneously acknowledges and turns away from the violence that forced the encounter. The racial order that taught little white boys to arm themselves against Indians and that legitimated taking Indian land in order to make room for white settlements forms the foundation on which such tender acts can occur. Soule's "averted gaze," Wexler's term for photographs that deny imperial racism in order to represent more benign visions of domestic harmony, allows her to present White Cloud's conversion as a consequence of Margaret's influence.[44] Soule produces that innocent or averted gaze by representing White Cloud's acceptance of civilization as an entirely internal and private process rather than a consequence of war or treaty making.

If Soule averts her gaze from Euro-American violence against Indians, she serves up a fair amount of violence between native peoples. Even as the novel valorizes White Cloud's considerable piety, it seems not to condemn his bloodier acts, including the murders of several Sioux, for these are committed in the interest of restoring familial order. White Cloud mentions several times his hatred of the Sioux, a dislike that is not surprising in light of the animosity that resulted after 1832, when the Sauk were forced to share hunting grounds with their longtime rivals. When White Cloud returns after retrieving Allie, he lets out a "warwhoop" and brandishes fresh Sioux scalps. Calling upon the direction of the Great Spirit, he vows to undertake a mission that ill fits with his newfound devotion to Christianity — a crusade to find Allie's mother and murder her captors.[45] White Cloud is at his most "Indian" when he leaves Iowa to track Allie's mother, Mary, to the Sioux chief Crouching Panther's glade in southern Minnesota. Soule relates with relish his facility in leaving signs and calling out signals for Bright-eyed and describes his actions as "Indian-like."[46] When he arrives at the glade, he slaughters and scalps Crouching Panther's tribesmen. He refrains from killing the evil chief himself, however, leaving vengeance to the Sauk man whose wife — Bright-eyed's mother — Crouching Panther kidnapped years before.[47] White Cloud's hatred of the Sioux and Bright-eyed's allegiance to her dead mother over her own father become the mechanism by which white families are reunited. Both Bright-eyed and White Cloud are allowed to be "Indian" when it serves the interests of white women.

White Cloud's deeds define a difference between the acts of white men and those of Indian men. The fact that both Margaret and Mr. Belden gently chastise Uncle Billy for his thoughts of revenge, while no one reacts adversely to White Cloud's acts, suggests that White Cloud's skin color is, as Uncle Billy calls it, a "red stain" that can be cleaned but not entirely wiped away. The novel's white men are relatively powerless in terms of the physical acts that would restore family unity. Soldiers from Fort Dodge, the men of the settlement, and even the old Indian-killer and -hunter Uncle Billy are unable to find and punish those responsible for destroying Allie's family. In fact, Uncle Billy repeatedly emphasizes his own feminine qualities, ranging from his knowledge of how to make preserves and care for the wounded to his declaration that seeing Indian heads bowed in prayer "makes a woman of me."[48]

White male power, Soule makes clear, lies in the creation of wealth. By the novel's end, Mr. Belden, Edward Somers, Margaret's brother Harrie, and Uncle Billy are all involved in their various investments in the West. As owner of the mill that has made the city thrive, Mr. Belden is the wealthiest man in town; Uncle Billy is a shameless booster for the town's progress, and Harrie's wealth tops all. Having ventured farther west, Harrie has built up a fur trade business and has "agencies not only in the Atlantic States, but in all the prominent ones of the Old World."[49] But wealth alone does not heal the rifts that afflict families in this novel; the pursuit of wealth and possessions is part of the problem that affects both women and Indians. Driven mad by their desires and cowed by their civilization to leave vengeance to God and to devote themselves to enterprise, white men cause the troubles that threaten the family and often are unable to heal them.

By weaving the Sioux and Sauk rivalries into her domestic drama, Soule channels the aggressiveness of leaders like Tenskwatawa and Wabokieshiek as well as their spiritualism. Under her pen, their fierce dedication to their tribes becomes the power, seemingly lacking in white men, to preserve the white family and to legitimate maternal power. Seeing indigenous history as integral to the acts that affect white women, she suggests that white women and Indian men will be complicit in overcoming their dependence on white men. Only after their violent acts have been reoriented to serve a narrative that restores domestic order can the two Indian characters finally find a home with the Beldens. Those who would ultimately have a place within Soule's ideal western home must be willing to turn their energies to domesticity rather than political conflicts.

The Ideal Family State

In the final third of the novel, Soule develops a kind of matriarchy in the vision of two women working and living together as teachers, models, and missionaries to a diverse collection of children. Fathers, including Mr. Belden and Edward, play such a marginal role in this household that Uncle Billy can declare of Bright-eyed that "with two white mothers . . . that child'll be a plagued sight better off than she would be with that dare-devil of a Sioux father."[50] The Indian names that White Cloud and Bright-eyed give their two white mothers, the White Dove and the White Doe, indicate that the women's familial relationship is a function of their care for their Indian wards — together, they represent a new kind of "white" family. Margaret, frequently compared to a minister or missionary, takes on the role of household manager and spiritual adviser, while Mary becomes the town teacher. Bright-eyed and White Cloud are their diligent pupils, learning not only to bow their heads in prayer but to conduct business, do housework, and understand natural history. The novel's two-woman household is an intermediary space in which characters are finally freed from the violence and insecurity of their frontier pasts and begin to adopt the kinds of work that will mark their new places in the domesticated West. The home incorporates the features of antebellum literary homes in which women exercise moral influence through their daily domestic chores and particularly through their deaths. But its more important work is to anticipate the material form of the mission household and the policies of domestic instruction, allotment, renaming, and marriage promotion through which white, middle-class women exercised authority in the assimilation campaigns of the following decades.

The ingredients of Soule's ideal mission home in the West had been percolating since before the literary reign of sentimentalism. As early as 1761, Eleazar Wheelock began sending Native American girls to work in white women's homes, a system known as "working out" that was meant to teach native girls housekeeping skills.[51] Soule suggests that this ongoing practice inspired the character of Bright-eyed, who is based on "a young Indian girl, raised in the family of a distant relative."[52] Missions to the Cherokee and Choctaw and to the Indians in the Northwest Territory in the 1830s — most famously the ill-fated mission of Marcus and Narcissa Whitman — attempted to teach Christian principles by sending missionaries to the Indians' homelands. The founding of the American Missionary Association in 1846 helped to organize these efforts. Missionary boards that served both domestic and foreign populations, however, originally sought married couples. While these associations saw women as useful tools for reaching "heathen" women, the involvement of white women in missions was often facilitated by their marriages to missionary men. Only in the 1860s, with the increasing involvement of women's organizations, did the domestic mission become conceived of as a women's enterprise — one that developed the more ethereal ideal of "influence" into the professionalized roles of missionary, teacher, and domestic scientist.[53]

It is not surprising, then, that a home analogous to Mary and Margaret's was at the center of the ideal Christian family that Catharine Beecher and Harriet Beecher Stowe endorsed in their 1869 edition of *The American Woman's Home*. Beecher and Stowe's treatise included a floor plan for the living quarters of "the highest kind of Christian family" that shows how a church, schoolroom, and family home could be combined into one structure designed to accommodate the living and working needs of two women.[54] Beecher and Stowe anticipated that the structure would find its best use in the depressed areas of the South, new settlements in the West, and on the Pacific coast, among the "pagan millions" from China and Japan. In this space, two women would not only exemplify but invite others into the "family state" by caring for the elderly, teaching young people crafts and industries, "adopting two orphans, [and] keeping in training one or two servants to send out for the benefit of other families."[55] The floor plan illustrates a home mission that is at once well ordered and adaptable to rearrangement. The upstairs consists of two bedchambers with closets and balconies; there are no separate chambers for servants. Downstairs, a movable screen separates living room from schoolroom. During worship, the screen could be moved to make one large 25 × 35 foot space. The kitchen, the focus of so much of Beecher's organizational effort, functions as the women's workspace, as an eating room, and as an entryway for visitors and students. Beecher and Stowe specified that such a home would provide a "cheering example" that would "soon spread, and ere long colonies from these prosperous and Christian communities would go forth to shine as 'lights of the world' in all the now darkened nations."[56]

The American Woman's Home reiterates the tenets central to the domestic ideology that Beecher, Stowe, and a cohort of writers had been developing in fiction and nonfiction: that ordering and morally managing the home was women's work, and that this work gave them agency in the life of the nation. Yet the 1869 treatise recognizes, as Beecher's previous works did not, the problem of women's domestic labor within the home and the nation.[57] In spite of Beecher's earlier writing, domestic workers — both wives at home and lower-class "domestics" — had failed to acquire the social status or economic remuneration bestowed on professions regarded as more specialized. Even as Beecher and Stowe diagrammed their plan for an ideal family state as represented by the mission home, they realized that property distribution in the family and in the nation endangered women, as vulnerable dependents whose labor was so easily co-opted by male heads of family. Their plan required not only that they develop domestic forms that departed from the gendered divisions of labor within the patriarchal family home but that they include racial others in the vision of ideal domesticity. In encouraging Euro-American women to extend their domestic authority to foreigners within the nation's borders, Beecher and Stowe aimed to rectify the problem of the social and economic undervaluation of domestic work. Though they stressed that woman's "great mission is self-denial," they also lamented that "especially has the most important of all hand-labor, that which sustains the family, been . . . disgraced." They argued that women need not be married in order to do this most honorable work: "Any woman who can earn a livelihood . . . can take a properly qualified female associate, and institute a family of its own."[58]

Soule assures her readers that the "maternal empire" can be passed on to Indian boys and girls through education in the mission home. White Cloud, finding his prototype in the Shawnee Prophet, turns his spiritualism to Christian mission by casting his lot with Margaret and her books, while Bright-eyed takes on the traits of an ideal middle-class homemaker. By the end of the novel Bright-eyed is "a close reasoner, an untiring student, lively and spirited in conversation and versed in all those lighter accomplishments that grace the social circle." She is also a "thorough housekeeper, capable of caring for parlor, nursery, chamber and kitchen, and can sew, knit, patch, cut and fit, crochet and embroider, equal to any *artiste*."[59] Her Sauk mother's knowledge of "medicine" lives on in Bright-eyed's care for others in the household. While Bright-eyed will never become the agriculturalist her mother would have been, Soule domesticates Indian women's caregiving knowledge, a wisdom more in keeping with Euro-American womanhood.

Soule's vision of the western mission also gives new force to the legacy of white women's influence by guaranteeing the future of Native American domesticity through private property ownership. Here again, she suggests that women might succeed where the government had failed. In 1859, for example, the government sought to assimilate Sauks in Kansas by assigning eighty acre tracts of land to family heads and by contracting to build some 350 homes and a mission among them. The effort ended in financial disaster.[60] In the novel, however, the Sioux and Sauk inheritors of white female instruction also inherit the lands of one of their white mothers. While Mary's slow death of tuberculosis is clearly influenced by the sentimental tradition of granting white women their greatest power in death, Mary's demise also a enables her to exert the more material influence represented by private property ownership. Mary wills half of the property that descended to her from her husband to her daughter and one quarter each to White Cloud and Bright-eyed. This gift of property seals the inclusion of all three dispossessed characters into the middle-class culture of security, access to property, and familial inheritance. Gillian Brown has argued that domestic novels narrated the "democratization of property" that "removes heirs and heiresses from the Gothic scenarios of imperilment by their property" only to secure these individuals within new kinds of property relations marked by affection rather than by blood.[61] *The Pet of the Settlement* follows this logic, for by replacing patriarchal property with the affective relations of the mother-child bond, it suggested the possibility of inheritance as an outcome of women's affective work rather than of paternity. Even as government attempts to assimilate the Sauks through home building failed, Soule legitimated the civilizing work of white women by allowing them to transfer property to the heirs of their affection.

Ultimately, the textual work of Mary's deed is, like Soule's novel, to incorporate Indian characters under new names and pretenses. Mary's bequest to White Cloud and Bright-eyed carries a stipulation that they be baptized and renamed Frank and Mary Mertoun after herself and her dead husband. The legacy of the white western family will live on, embodied in the two Indians, who become heirs to their property by being renamed as family. Mary's deed is also a powerful form of textuality meant to rival that of the treaties signed by government leaders and male leaders of Indian nations. Transmitting real property and individual "properties" — White Cloud and Bright-eyed's newly domesticated characters — is a textual act that white women, both as writers and as representatives of Christian, civilized culture in western homes, were prepared to perform. Replacing history's treaties, land cessions, and economic investments with unions between white women and Indian children, sealed in property, Soule is able to envision white women's domesticating work as essential to propagating Indian domesticity in the West.

Likewise, fostering marriage between Native Americans would prove key to the future of those western homes. It is not Margaret's marriage to Edward that most resoundingly confirms the ideals the novel espouses, but the double wedding forecast at the end of the novel. Allie, predictably, will marry the now-wealthy Harrie and is poised to join him in the farther reaches of the West. Like Bright-eyed, she has been groomed as an ideal woman, serving not only her own household but visiting all those in need. She is ready to be a domestic worker whose idea of family includes her entire community. And

Bright-eyed and White Cloud are to marry in a union that not only will assure their replication of the Euro-American family form but will also heal old tribal hostilities. Soule makes much of the fact that Bright-eyed is of Sioux heritage and White Cloud is Sauk, repeatedly quoting Longfellow's popular *Song of Hiawatha* (1855), in which Hiawatha, an Objibwa, marries Minnehaha, the "fair Dacotah."[62] The marriages heal old family wounds by binding Allie to the Belden family in name as well as spirit, and they heal old native rivalries by linking Sioux and Sauk in a household where such enmities are no longer of consequence.

The ideal family state, the deed, and the promise of Native American marital domesticity presaged another kind of family state that would come to fruition some twenty-five years after Soule published her novel. Mary Mertoun's fictional deed predates by a quarter century the Dawes Act of 1887, which modified earlier assimilation attempts by stipulating that marriage, renaming, education, and work should accompany Native Americans' access to real property. The law combined allotting reservation lands in homestead parcels with educating young Native Americans in industrial schools — education meant to strip those young men and women of their history and culture through tactics such as renaming and forbidding the students to speak their native languages. Indeed, indigenous people undergoing assimilation were akin to adoptees, forced to become "domestic dependents" or wards of the nation. Like White Cloud and Bright-eyed, these wards were deeded into a history that was not their own. Soule domesticates Sauk and Sioux history in order to make it complicit in rehabilitating the Euro-American family; the Indians' compliance in replicating the white family confirms its power over future Indian families. Just as the Prophets and their cohort were meant to be impressed by the throngs of white people and cities crowding the East, advocates of the Dawes Act hoped that the sight of homes and Christian women within them would overwhelm indigenous people and impress them with the power of a domestic, Christian nation.

But the fact that Soule envisions two marriages — one white and one Indian — reflects her ultimate ambivalence about incorporating Native Americans equally into her domestic vision. Like Child and Sedgwick, she recoils at the idea of mixed marriage — Margaret shudders at the mere hint of a possible love affair with White Cloud — and instead projects different homes and roles for the Beldens' white and Indian wards.[63] Part of Soule's plot entails that Indians must adapt to their new circumstances while retaining their Indianness; she thus opens up the possibility that her Indian characters cannot be incorporated into her pastoral vision in the same way that whites can. Even as the two Indians take on the roles of their white parents, relationships between the white characters and their Indian protégés are marked by difference. Looking at White Cloud's brown head bent over his studies, Uncle Billy becomes teary-eyed, proclaiming, "Ye couldn't change his brown skin into white, but ye've washed the red-stain off of that."[64] Uncle Billy — and perhaps Soule's readers, too — understands the change that White Cloud has undergone as a washing away of the "stain" itself, but the fact of his difference is one that cannot be overcome. White Cloud embraces this difference by retaining his Indian appearance throughout the novel. Even after years of living with the Beldens, he refuses to eat "white" food, wear white men's clothes, or sleep in a bed. "Can no make white man of me, if me try," White Cloud tells his adoptive family. Likewise, by the end of the novel, Bright-eyed is a fine student and housekeeper but is still "Indian" in "the color of her ornaments and the fashion of her dress" and in her retention of knowledge taught to her by her "squaw-mother."[65] Just as Uncle Billy chooses, in the end, to live outside the Belden home, White Cloud's decision to return to his own people is an ambivalent nod to Tenskwatawa's commitment to indigenous unity as well as to Soule's uncertainty about Indians' true spiritual status. Perhaps believing, like Uncle Billy, that in heaven "we'll all be white alike," she suggests that while the West may need to accommodate many races, Christian authority ultimately inhered in whiteness.[66] She hints that white women and Indians, though alike in their domesticity, must occupy separate homes that reflect their different relationships to domesticity: white women were teachers and managers; the Indians were their wards, students, and imitators.

Soule's aim is not to remove Indians or their history entirely but to force them into new contexts that bolster the vision the white middle class has of itself, even as their racial difference ensures that they will remain a mere reflection of whiteness. Following the Dawes Act, Native Americans were, like Bright-eyed and White Cloud, forced to reproduce the economic, social, and architectural features of American homes from the Missouri River to the Rocky Mountains. As civilizing pedagogy, the mission home was meant to signify the influence of Euro-American authors over the history and bodies of Native American subjects. The white, middle-class prairie "queen" was a queen indeed, as her home became the prototype for allotment homesteads meant to incorporate indigenous peoples into the American continental empire. Margaret's sons, a future entrepreneur and a budding naturalist/collector, and her daughter, the new pet of the household, suggest the mechanisms of capitalism, science, and homemaking through which the next generation would continue the project of domesticating the West. Indeed, later authors, image makers, scientists, government agents, and home economists followed Catlin and Soule in creating representations that legitimated rather than undermined Euro-American middle-class culture, thus obscuring the radical possibility that other ways of representing self might be viable.

Soule's refiguring of White Cloud as a Christian missionary was an ironic twist on the Shawnee Prophet's crusade to settle new, pan-Indian towns in an effort to combat poverty and dependency and to defend the American interior from white encroachment. Though Soule co-opted the histories of white male settlers and native male spiritual leaders in order to domesticate the conflicts that shaped nineteenth-century midwestern landscapes, her vision was ultimately, like Tenskwatawa's, prophetic. Like Tenskwatawa, too, her dream for the future was as political as it was spiritual. In channeling resistant native spiritualism into the Christianizing mission, Soule created a blueprint for future relations between white, middle-class women and the nation's Indian wards. She cast her lot with a movement, hinted at in the 1820s and 1830s, that suggested that indigenous people need not be removed but could live alongside whites if only they would turn to God and home. Only in the years following the Civil War would white, middle-class women, invigorated by the abolition campaign's success and distraught by new conflicts with Indians in the West, return in earnest to the Indian Problem. When they did, it was to advocate Soule's vision: education, homes, land, and Christianity. By 1868 Lydia Maria Child had revised her earlier indecision about the ability of Indians to assimilate in order to advocate for educating and Christianizing Indians. She lauded the capacity of Indian women for domesticity, their child-rearing practices, and their love for children, and she saw these as evidence that native women were "capable of being softened and refined, if brought under the right influences."[67]

Soule's novel took part in a broader historical shift in popular culture and government policy from regarding Indians as part of the passing West to advocating their assimilation as the nation's domestic dependents. Domestic literature performed cultural work in articulating links between nation building and child rearing, particularly in suggesting that the success of the nation would demand white women's work in raising Indian children to be coinheritors of the nation's developing lands. Soule capitalized on older ways of representing Native Americans by seizing the space of popular display cultivated by male writers and artists and by recasting struggles between male Indian leaders and the U.S. government in domestic scenarios. But in order truly to shape behavior, Soule's prescriptions for Native Americans would need to take forms other than the textual and would involve kinds of work other than authorship. Beecher and Stowe's architectural plan for a mission house; the Dawes Act, with its legal incorporation of citizens; widespread exhibition of Indian images; and more systematic Indian education would go part of the way toward achieving Soule's vision in the next fifty years. The work of other white, middle-class women would be necessary in the attempt to incorporate indigenous people and would involve the cooperation of Native Americans. Soule eagerly reclaimed the tale of the old settler in order to embody her womanhood and woman's work in a tale of frontier development. Yet as she also uneasily forecast, indigenous people would retain elements of their own cultural identities even as they became part of a story that, at first, seemed beyond their experience.

CHAPTER TWO

The House Divided

Class and Race in the
Married Woman's Home

A quarter century after Caroline Soule cast a rosy glow on the Iowa prairies she saw as a site of women's civilizing influence, feminists in that state were resolutely attempting to shrug off the veil of sentimentality that clothed women as moral civilizers rather than the household workers that they were. They argued that the prairie homestead was not necessarily a place where women could work together in harmony to promote progress; instead, they contended that it was profoundly divided along gendered lines that separated women into a lower class than their husbands. Home was clearly the site of women's labor, and prairie feminists struggled to depict the realities of women's housework in the West, infusing their claims for equal rights to wages and property with language of class oppression and wage work borrowed from eastern feminists. The voice of many Iowa women who wished to assert the economic value of housework was the *Woman's Standard*, a feminist periodical first published in 1886. Through this publication, Iowa women argued that they were not domestic dependents, but workers.

But just as Soule depended on Native American history in order to reenvision the prairie as the site of women's civilization work, Iowa feminists' attempts to recuperate housekeeping as valuable work incorporated images of racial difference that distinguished the household work of white women from the labor of women they deemed less civilized. In tracing the formation of class identity by white male workers in the antebellum years, David Roediger has argued that their understanding of themselves as workers cannot be separated from racial identity. The working class became white, he claims, only in opposition to the black slaves against whom its members hoped to define themselves.[1] Images of Native American and other nonwhite women within the pages of the *Woman's Standard* suggest that the presence of a racial other was as crucial to forming a middle-class identity for the white woman as unwaged household worker as it was to forming white male working-class identity. Promoting housework as productive work, it seems, was no less dependent on the cultural work of upholding a middle-class identity for white women than was Soule's novel-writing enterprise. Iowa feminists' market-based claims for the value of housework insist that homes did not just appear but were produced through difficult labor. Yet articles and letters that appeared in the *Woman's Standard* suggest that constructing those homes as a symbol of white, middle-class life took the effort of a multitude of writers creating a cultural context for that work. This context rejected sentimental erasures of women's household labor and instead displayed this work on a cultural stage, positing evolutionary divides between kinds of domestic workers: those who worked in "savage" domestic environments and those who worked in "civilized" homes.

These two discourses — domestic labor as economically productive work and domestic work as informed by racial difference — mingled within the pages of the *Woman's Standard*. Indeed, writers for the *Woman's Standard* shared many of the concerns that historians have identified with feminists' discussions about the status of women's household labor in other states. Most of these studies focus almost exclusively on eastern and urban areas where wage labor was the principal source of family sustenance and where the racial other was primarily a black or immigrant worker.[2] The Iowa case, however, suggests that the ways feminists explained the plight of white women working within the home was informed by continental expansion and scientific theories of racial progress as well as by comparisons to the marketplace. In the *Woman's Standard*, parallels to the degraded status of Native Americans occurred alongside analogies to slaves or wage laborers. While the wage relationship could be understood in terms of slavery's legacy, domestic dependency seemed to demand a different comparison. In this correlation, Native American women might be regarded as domestic, for they were regarded as outside the wage economy and subservient within the home. Yet defined as uncivilized persons, they seemed to provide a potent foil against which the white woman could consolidate a middle-class identity as a worker within a *civilized* home. Iowa feminists' discussions of women's domestic work show that ideas about evolutionary progress and comparisons to groups other than African Americans informed discussions about the social and economic value of unpaid household labor. Iowa women adopted the languages of both class oppression and evolutionary progress to their own ends in an attempt to gain new recognition for the economic and social value of housework.

Eastern Workers and Western Lands

When the first issue of the *Woman's Standard* appeared in 1886, Iowa feminists had long enjoyed relations with nationally renowned women's rights crusaders. Amelia Bloomer, publisher of the temperance-journal-turned-women's-rights-paper the *Lily* and inventor of the skirt and trousers combination that bore her name, moved from Seneca Falls, New York, to Council Bluffs, Iowa, in 1855. Bloomer helped to maintain contacts between Iowa feminists and leaders like Lucy Stone Blackwell, Susan B. Anthony, and Elizabeth Cady Stanton, all of whom visited Iowa in the 1860s and 1870s.[3] After the 1869 split in women's rights organizations into the National Woman Suffrage Association (NWSA), a more radical group led by Anthony and Stanton, and the American Woman Suffrage Association (AWSA), led by Blackwell, Bloomer and her Iowa Woman Suffrage Association originally opted to affiliate with neither.[4] By and large, however, Iowa women were less comfortable with Stanton and Anthony's more radical stance on divorce, support for all issues related to women's rights, and opposition to the Fourteenth and Fifteenth Amendments' exclusion of women in granting civil rights to African American men. By 1872 Anthony and Stanton's association with the controversial feminist and free-love advocate Victoria Woodhull led the Iowa group to ask the two leaders not to speak in the state.[5] In 1879 the Iowa organization voted to affiliate with the AWSA.

The founder and publisher of the *Woman's Standard* was at the center of battles between liberal and more conservative factions in Iowa. The monthly journal was founded by Martha Callanan, wife of a wealthy Des Moines businessman and philanthropist. Callanan was active in the Woman's Christian Temperance Union (WCTU) and the Des Moines Woman's Club and supported the Business Woman's Home. She was the president of the Iowa Woman Suffrage Association from 1876 until 1880 and helped to swing the organization toward the AWSA. A woman who owned some property in her own name, Callanan threw her financial support behind the *Woman's Standard*, which she called her "baby." The journal's editor from 1886 to 1888 was the less controversial Mary Jane Coggeshall, also a president of the Iowa Woman Suffrage Association and a member of the board of the National-American Woman Suffrage Association (created by the 1890 merger of the NWSA and the AWSA) after 1895.[6]

The purpose of the *Woman's Standard* was to "treat of the Home, Health, Purity, Culture, Temperance, Education, and of the legal and political interests of Woman, and of her right to the Franchise."[7] It published speeches, accounts of the activities of Iowa women's rights organizations, updates on national conventions, reports on women's legal status in the state and the nation, and household hints and tips. Iowa women regularly contributed to the paper as journalists and letter writers; the journal also reprinted reports and stories from women's rights publications in other states. The *Woman's Standard* thus reflected feminist concerns about women's work across the nation as well as the specific terms in which Iowa women saw housewives' labor in a western region and primarily farm-based economy.

Iowa's agricultural economy placed housewives in Iowa in a somewhat anomalous yet certainly not uncommon position. Farm women considered themselves to be workers, but their labor was tied to land rather than to wages. Beginning in the 1830s, most states passed married women's property statutes, which granted wives some legal rights to contract with real property — land, personal property, chattel, slaves, and sometimes even business-related property. Iowa was among these states, passing a married women's property act in 1851. After the Civil War, states began to pass earnings statutes, which allowed wives to claim rights to money they earned. In 1873 a national financial panic adversely affected many Iowa farmers, forcing mortgages and foreclosures. Not coincidentally, that same year Iowa revised its code once again, this time expanding married women's property rights even further and gaining accolades from feminists for the progressive character of its treatment of women. The statutes stipulated that a woman could sue and be sued in her own right and, perhaps most important, that married women had a right to claim their wages as their separate property.[8] Of the Iowa laws, Amelia Bloomer wrote that "the code of 1873 made a great advance in recognizing the rights of married women; and it is said the revisers sought, as far as possible, to place the husband and wife on an entire equality as to property rights."[9]

Historians have suggested that the property statutes and the earnings statutes were directed at two different classes of women. The property acts affected middle- and upper-class women, who stood to inherit property in their own right, while earnings statutes were aimed at working-class women.[10] Yet in a farming state such as Iowa, family property ownership did not necessarily give a family upper- or even middle-class status. Iowa farmers and their wives were still heavily at the mercy of creditors and the fluctuations of the market; owning property did not always translate into social power. Property connected to the farm could rarely be considered to be women's "separate" property, as the property statutes necessitated, and women's income from in-home activities — even those monies earned for enterprises such as keeping boarders or raising poultry — could not be considered separate earnings. Both the property and earnings of farmwives were so tied up in the family economy that neither statute afforded these women considerable economic liberation. The journal cited a Supreme Court case in which a woman sued for a $200 yearly wage promised to her by her husband for running the household and caring for the children; her plea was denied because the agreement "imposed no duties not in the marriage contract." The article lamented that no laws yet recognized woman's earnings within the marriage, noting that "it sounds very sweet and sentimental and vicariously altruistic to declare that love is the coin woman likes best to be paid in; but, though that is true, it is also true that when other human beings are pecuniarily benefitted by her willing service, justice demands that she be paid a certain percentage of that benefit."[11] Like theorist of housework Charlotte Perkins Gilman, the writer argued that men and women had internalized the notion of what she called "mother service"; unlike Gilman, though, writers for the *Woman's Standard* advocated legal solutions that would recognize unpaid household labor.

Contributors to the *Woman's Standard* struggled to extract women's labor from the web of sentimental relations and to stress housewives' similarities to workers in the marketplace. In 1887 Esther E. Dysart of Tama City, Iowa, described the condition of farmwives in a piece titled "White Slaves." She exhorted Iowa wives to stop denying their economic subjugation and declared that the only difference between wives and servants was that servants were paid in cash and wives "in kind."[12] Dysart's reference to the "white slave" in 1887 suggests that she identified not so much with the prewar black slave but with the white laborer, who, in the years following Emancipation, had come to symbolize oppressive wage labor.[13] Dysart compares domestic servants' paid labor to that of wives in order to make housework economically visible; wives' domestic labor, she insisted, did have a market value, but that value could only be accounted when it was done by a servant rather than a wife. Through the *Woman's Standard*, feminists in Iowa could keep tabs on eastern events such as union movements and labor struggles that had an impact on women's wages. A Mount Pleasant reader worried that women working for small wages in the East were "eking out the balance by trading in the sanctities of womanhood."[14] Yet the Iowa readers were acutely aware that many of them were denied even the privileges that workers enjoyed. In a letter reprinted from the *Leather Review*, the journal outlined the handicaps of wives: "They never revolt; and they cannot organize for their protection. . . . They die in the harness and are supplanted as quickly as may be. These are the house-keeping wives of laboring men."[15] As late as 1894, one writer for the *Woman's Standard* reformulated an analogy to chattel slavery to refer to the farm economy rather than to race: "But alas, in this state which contains our homes, our affections, the resting places of our loved and losts and all that life holds dear, the wives and mothers are, in a legal status, placed infinitely below any other human in the scale of being and classed among the live property of the husband, and perhaps this explains why Iowa is credited with possessing more live stock than any other state."[16]

The Iowa women who wrote for the *Woman's Standard* used the family farm as the basis for most of their ideas about women's access to property. Farm women regarded themselves as partners in a family business in which neither spouse contributed wages to the family economy rather than as dependents of husbands who brought home wages. They argued that farm economies were particularly destructive to women's sense of individualism, because while both men and women worked at the same enterprise, only the husband's profits were visible. Husbands' sole ownership of property seemed more egregious because it was difficult to argue that they were the sole breadwinners. Mary E. Donley of Marion County stressed that most farmers in the state hired men to help work the farm, but not many could afford to hire a woman to help with milking, poultry raising, gardening, or the odd jobs that women performed to benefit the farm.[17] Lizzie Bunnell Read of Algona addressed this issue in a letter to the *Woman's Standard*, arguing that "fully one-half the labor performed in the State is performed by women, and it would appear reasonable that they should own one-half the property, whereas, they probably own less than twenty per cent of it."[18] In looking to the farm economy, Iowa feminists stressed the physical labor of wives rather than their roles as mothers, nurturers, or spiritual guides. It was this effort, rather than some diffuse spiritual quality or need for protection, that underlay wives' property claims.

Feminists like Read believed that housework could be represented through joint property ownership in marriage. The joint property claim was raised as early as the First National Woman's Rights Convention at Worcester, Massachusetts, in 1850. Feminists decried husbands' total control over their wives' earnings and labor, arguing that male control of family earnings and property made wives completely dependent on their husbands. The spirit of the joint property claim was to emancipate the labor of the wife within the home by granting her not separate power over her property and earnings but equal control over the property a couple accrued jointly. Reva Siegel points out that joint property advocates did not necessarily want to alter gender roles within marriage but sought to make property ownership more accurately reflect the equality and partnership that they saw as inherent in the marital relationship.[19] In fact, Siegel has shown that one of the most prominent features of the joint property claim was that it preserved the notion that women's work did not have a market value. Because activities traditionally defined as women's work — cleaning, cooking, sewing, and child care — had such a low market value, feminists may have intentionally looked to the joint property solution rather than trying to give wives control over their earnings, because being paid a market value for the work they did would hardly have improved either the family economy or the economic standing of wives.[20]

Certainly Iowa feminists recognized this fact. Like earlier feminists in the East, Iowa women generally found joint property more suitable than earnings statutes to compensate farmwork. In 1860 the Reverend Antoinette Brown Blackwell had criticized the earnings statutes recently passed in New York State, declaring, "I spent three months asking the State to allow the drunkard's wife her own earnings. Do I believe that the wife ought to take her own earnings, as her own earnings? No; I do not believe it. I believe that in a true marriage, the husband and wife earn for the family, and that the property is the family's — belongs jointly to the husband and wife."[21] For Blackwell, the earnings statutes that would separate a wife's meager earnings from her husband's constituted a poor second choice to the community estate that joint property proposed. Iowa feminists were embracing this partnership model a quarter century later, as when Anna R. Weeks of Des Moines wrote to the *Woman's Standard* to advocate for partnership, rather than contract, as a model for marriage, for in such a marriage each partner would consult the other in all things, economic and otherwise.[22]

The first issue of the *Woman's Standard* included a criticism of the married women's property acts and a plea for joint property as a solution to class stratification within marriage. Lizzie B. Read of Algona wrote regarding "Equal Rights in Property" that while law allowed husbands and wives to make contracts to own their property jointly, custom prohibited it.[23] She exhorted Iowa women to be aware of the value of their labor and where it was going: "Every farm in Iowa is a bank. . . . Nearly every farm in Iowa is owned by a man, the husband of some woman. Nearly every farm in Iowa has been enhanced in value by the labor of some woman, deposited therein from day to day, and from year to year. Not subject to withdrawal on her order, but absorbed into the capital of the bank which belongs to the husband. . . . The profit of the wife's labor is absorbed into the capital of her husband."[24] Read argued that wives should be compensated; to do so, she called on the economic value of women's productive work at home. Just as the earnings statutes in other states made women aware of the market value of domestic labor, Iowa earnings statutes may have awakened women to the fact that wages earned for work other than housework could be deposited in a bank and on a woman's own account.[25] Even within the home,

Read extrapolated, a woman's tasks were valuable and contributed at least half of the necessary labor to produce and sustain a household. Constructing wives as workers, she reasoned that such work must be compensated. But Read knew that to pay a wife for her housework would do nothing to rectify her dependence on her husband; wages would merely sustain the fiction that a husband was the owner of all family property. The best method, Read concluded, was joint property. She asked, "If a man ought to be paid for plowing an acre of ground, or feeding a horse, ought not a woman to be paid for sweeping rooms, baking bread, and feeding a family?" Answering herself in the affirmative, she went on, "How much should she be paid? She should be paid the equal ownership and present control of half the joint income and property — not the possible ownership of one-third in the event of becoming a widow, as the custom now is."[26] Like earlier feminists, Read saw marriage as a partnership that must be shared jointly rather than divided. Calculating each partner's input would defeat the partnership of marriage; calculating possessions based on market value could never fairly characterize the communal relationship.

The joint property claim imagined a household in which husbands' and wives' contributions to the family economy were not evaluated by the worker's gender; such evaluations, the *Woman's Standard* noted, permeated the marketplace. Gendered labor values in the marketplace made women's wages less than men's and crowded women into limited numbers of low-paying jobs such as teaching and dressmaking. The market's undervaluation of women's labor also sustained the belief that wives were supported by their husbands. The joint property claim offered a way for women to combat the negation of the value of their labor in the household as well as the low value it merited in the marketplace. Its definition of the value of housework resisted the sentimental rhetoric's definition of women's work as purely affective; at the same time, it resisted a totally market-based conception of women as wage laborers who, in selling their labor, commodified themselves. Iowa women upheld, into the 1890s, the older conception that it was property ownership itself that would drive a wedge between women and the marketplace, thus preserving both the ideal of marriage as partnership separate from the marketplace and introducing new equality for women within marriage.

After the Civil War, the joint property claim waned in the East for two reasons. First, increasing industrialization and more women entering wage work made conceptions of earnings or entitlement without a market value harder to maintain.[27] Second, earlier attempts to posit a nonmarket value for women's work at home without challenging the gendered nature of domestic work itself lost force in the face of new feminist claims that the best way for women to gain economic equality was through liberation from domestic work. By seeking an independent income, middle-class women could take advantage of the liberties gained through the earnings statutes. Rather than attacking ideologies that regarded housewives as dependent, new ideas instead suggested that women's work itself ought to change.[28] Leading the charge against housework was Charlotte Perkins Gilman, who, beginning in the 1890s, argued that white women could seek equality by ridding themselves of confining forms of household labor and leaving the home to work for wages. She proposed cooperative housekeeping models that would radically restructure the home in order to liberate women from devalued forms of labor. The only way to liberate women from the devalued sphere of housework, she surmised, was to make housework a corporate enterprise.[29]

But this change took hold more quickly in the East than in the West. In Iowa, women were not out to radically restructure the home or to leave their farms in pursuit of wage labor or professional work. While in states such as New York and Massachusetts the joint property claim lingered after the Civil War only as a plank in the suffrage agenda, in a western state like Iowa, feminists continued to criticize the labor market's devaluation of women's work and insisted on the economic value of women's work at home to family success. Those women who continued to support joint property claims after the war were generally, like Oregon's Abigail Scott Duniway, from less urban and cosmopolitan areas. They tended to be from less affluent families, from more rural areas, and from western towns, and they did not necessarily have professional goals. As eastern journals shifted discussion of household labor to the "servant problem," western women who wrote to feminist journals suggested that their experience of housework had changed very little since the antebellum era.[30] For these women, moving out of the home to enter the wage labor force was not a possibility; furthermore, they considered themselves to be part of the agricultural labor force.

Nonetheless, these new conceptions of women's work as waged and as offering the possibility for self-sufficiency did not fail to penetrate rural western women's experience of housework. While housework itself had changed little for western women, their understanding of its value did change. Eastern women's experience with wage labor and changing understandings of women's proper place infused Iowa women's claims for the value of housework, but the western experience that Iowa women represent may also have changed the terms of the debate nationally. Offering rural homesteads as the equivalent of waged workplaces, Iowa women continued to argue that industry at home could be a source of independent self-ownership just as waged work could.

Making Home Work

Journalists for the *Woman's Standard* recast marital service as a relationship analogous to the industrial system in which humans were in bondage to wage slavery. Fictional stories published in the journal, however, were even more ambivalent about white women's status as workers. They conceived the struggle for property rights in terms that would stress the value of housework without compromising the middle-class status of women who worked in homes. The writers engaged wage-based evaluations of women's housework but, as did Lizzie B. Read, fell short of arguing that wives should seek independence by working for wages. They challenged the novelistic tradition by exposing the economic value of women's work at home; while the curtain was quickly drawn back over that labor, the relations between husband and wife were politicized in the process.

Reva Siegel suggests that many feminist stories that popularized the idea, if not the law, of joint property after the Civil War constituted a "depoliticization" of rights discourse. Rather than proposing legal change, the stories inferred that the problem of property distribution within marriage could be solved by "a species of marital therapy, rather than a claim of right" based on the "legal expropriation of women's household labor."[31] Yet these stories are more complex than the idea of emotional healing might suggest, for they, perhaps more so than the rights-centered articles themselves, engaged metaphors of industrialized labor and middle-class privilege. The shift away from legal solutions to familial change may have had more to do with legislatures' consistent rejection of joint property than with feminists' fading interest in legal solutions. These failures may have led feminists to turn to new ways of advancing arguments for the value of housework by using class- and race-based claims about self-ownership. Rather than depoliticizing claims for household labor's value, the stories published in the *Woman's Standard* suggested that household labor itself was becoming deeply politicized because it marked class and race difference in an expanding nation.

The *Woman's Standard* stories liken marital relations to industrial conditions inconveniently draped by a layer of sentiment. In 1888 the journal published an anecdote that stripped the sentimental image of marital service as a labor of love bare of its gilding to reveal the wealth-producing power of its treadmill mechanism. "A Miserable Wife" recounted a conversation between a professor and a successful farmer, in which the professor helped the farmer to see the injustice in keeping his wife destitute while he enjoyed a leisurely lifestyle. The professor calculated that the farmer's wife had earned half of the $30,000 the man had accumulated during their marriage. When asked how much his wife made for cooking, seeing to four children, and caring for the dairy herd, the farmer replies, "She, why durn it, professor, she is my wife." While he enjoyed a comfortable and social lifestyle, she was home, "going around in treadmill life."[32]

In the feminist forum provided by a suffrage newspaper, this account of household labor became overtly infused with the rhetoric of class difference. Signs of the husband's status denote the successful farmer's life: he carries a gold watch, he has a tidy bank account, and perhaps most important, he has leisure time. In short, he bears all the markers of an industrial capitalist, including monopolizing both land and assets. His wife, who "deposits" equally into the "bank" of his property, works mechanically to produce a successful farm and children but receives none of the benefits. The author is careful to note, however, that before she married, the woman had hired out for a weekly wage of $2.50. The farmer assumes that she was fortunate to be saved from a life of wage labor through a secure marriage. The farmer's claim that he protected his wife from being degraded by the marketplace echoes sentimental concerns with securing woman's place in the home but translates his sentimentalism into economic reality by calculating the investment of her labor. The fact that women's domestic labor could, by this time, be calculated in terms of a market value — $2.50 per week — allows the professor in the story to determine the real value of her earnings over the course of the marriage.

The intent, in this story and in others, was not to encourage the husband to pay the wife a salary but to recognize her contributions to the marriage economy and to pay her, instead, with his respect. Repeatedly, stories published in the *Woman's Standard* featured discussions between husbands and wives in which the goal was to make the husband realize that his wife worked harder than he did, that her work sustained the household, that she was entitled to participate in economic decisions within the family, and that she could make her own decisions about spending money. Writing on the homestead economy, feminists highlighted the permeable boundary between affective and economic values as they struggled to emphasize the monetary value of wives' household labor. These stories suggested that not only was the wife's status imperiled by her dependence, but that the family itself as a middle-class institution was degraded by the class divisions within it.

This image of middle-class women as laborers who could be commodified and consumed within their own homes was crucial to feminist reform rhetoric nationwide. Reva Siegel has found stories published in the *New Northwest* that replicate the lesson of "A Miserable Wife." Matilda Hindman's "Who Will Support You?" (1871) featured a similar comeuppance for a workingman who claimed to have supported his wife and five children for the preceding few years, even while setting aside enough money to buy a home. In reminding the braggart that his weekly wages could never have paid for the household chores necessary to feed, clothe, and care for his family, the author not only tells him that his wife "came as near supporting you as you did supporting her" but also implies that it was, in part, her labor that created the funds to purchase the house.[33] Western feminists, though, were less preoccupied with painting troubling images of the urban workingman's wife, desperate in her dependency, than with depicting images of middle-class families whose apparent well-being obscured class stratification and relied on wives' unpaid labor.

Rather than suggesting that low wages erase the identity of the worker, as some eastern writers on the condition of wage workers did, writers for the *Woman's Standard* envisioned situations in which wives used the marketplace to reveal their identity as workers. Yet they wielded the analogy to class oppression only to empower themselves within the home. The wage labor marketplace that informed so much of eastern reformers' discourse about workers' and wives' rights provided western feminists with a means for evaluating their own household labor. What the *Woman's Standard* embraced was not necessarily a market-based definition of human labor but a market-based understanding of class oppression. The wage labor market helped feminists to expose relations of dependency between husband and wife within the home as similar to, but not necessarily the same as, the relations between employer and employee. The status of wives as unwaged laborers within the home allowed feminists to retreat from completely market-based definitions of human value and to propose that the connection between husband and wife could be a partnership between equals — a relationship that the labor market rarely allowed. Rather than arguing that their labor made wives into nonpersons, these writers suggested that the marital relationship could provide alternative ways to appreciate labor value that could restore the personhood of wives as domestic workers.[34]

Even after attempts to pass joint property legislation failed in western states like Iowa during the 1870s and 1880s, the reasoning that informed such proposals persisted in the *Woman's Standard*. The story "An Eight-Hour Wife" used the metaphor of industrialized labor and contemporary debates about workers' rights in a way that empowered wives. In the tale, Mrs. Wellington announces to her husband that her housework will now conform to industrial principles. Mustering support from urban attempts to impose an hourly limit on factory labor, she vows to work no more than eight hours per day, reasoning that the limit would increase her productivity. Her alarmed husband points out that housework is not "of a nature which can be adapted to arbitrary conditions of time and season" as industrial work is. But his wife keeps to her rule. Mr. Wellington goes dinnerless for several nights when he fails to make it home before the end of his wife's workday. In the evening, their children demand care and attention, which Mr. Wellington is forced to provide because Mrs. Wellington is done for the day. He complains that the people she supervises in the home, as well as their emotions and needs, do not work "like a piece of machinery, or a climax in a dramatic production" and thus cannot conform to evaluations of women's work based on either industry or literature. The ease and rationality with which Mrs. Wellington apparently ceases her "labors of love" divorces housework from affection and temporarily turns her husband and children into "pieces of machinery." Mrs. Wellington gives up her fight only when her husband admits that her work is important to the household and finds that without her, he is unable to perform the duties that do produce income.[35]

Temporarily converting home into factory, Mrs. Wellington played on one of society's deepest fears: that the factory's economic relations would penetrate the sanctity of family life. Like eastern reformers who supported family wages for male workers as well as earnings statutes for wives in an attempt to protect women from the vagaries of the marketplace, the author toys with fears that family life could be disrupted by economic vagaries that forced the wife to labor for wages and neglect her family. But by equating mechanism with the predictable "climax in a dramatic production," the author also associates literary practice with the mechanics of production. The writer suggests that literary work was not necessarily a spontaneous explosion of genius, but a calculated and formulaic production that, like homemaking, involved the work of authorship. Nonetheless, the writer asserts, the family does not operate according to industrial rules or literary prescriptions, two nineteenth-century formulas that are here allied in producing characters who, the story is quick to point out, are unrealistic. In contrast to the midcentury domestic novels and chapbooks that opposed domestic ritual to the threatening unpredictability of the wider world, this story dramatizes the domestic sphere's unpredictability by contrasting it to the highly regulated workplace. Mrs. Wellington's transformation into an industrial worker suddenly converts her home into a factory, the products of which are food and children. By exhibiting wives' reproductive work as industrial work, the author exposes the disparities inherent in the marital contract.

But domestic work is exposed here as distinctly different from industrialized labor. The crusades for eight-hour workdays that were primarily carried out in eastern cities like Boston and New York during the 1870s pushed to the forefront connections between time, labor, and self-ownership. Highly mechanized labor, in which workers rarely saw the finished product of their efforts, suggested that what was for sale in a wage contract was not products but time itself. Amy Dru Stanley shows that those who supported the eight-hour workday argued that selling one's time, unlike selling the products of labor, was essentially equivalent to selling selfhood — equivalent to wage slavery. If a worker had to sell his or her selfhood for a period of time each day, reformers reasoned, that time should be limited in order to preserve the worker's self-ownership. Some labor theorists, on the other hand, argued that the relationship between workers and employers was more like a marriage: not a contract for service for a certain amount of time, but for a lifetime.[36] The author of "The Eight-Hour Wife" rejected this premise, asserting that while an employee might move in and out of that relationship during the course of a workday, a wife never could. Her work's character was different from that of a wage laborer in that it could not be measured by time. In this respect, a wife was more like an artisan, for her work, and thus her selfhood, was revealed in the home that she produced. Without the wife's labor, the home's character itself dissolved. While the story asserts that a wife could not limit the hours she gave her labor to her family, neither could her selfhood be sold away as could a wage earner's. In keeping the marriage safe from the complications of buying and selling time, the story suggests that a wife's domestic labor preserved self-ownership in a way that wage labor could not. In the same way, it preserved the middle-class family in a way that wage labor could not.

That the marketplace could produce subjects without selfhood — not just individuals, but a whole "mechanized family" — is apparent in *Woman's Standard* stories that celebrate a form of wives' independence that was made possible by the earnings statutes. In "Harry Brown's Lesson," the title character is a stingy breadwinner who makes his wife account for every dime that he gives her for household and personal expenses and denies her money for items he deems unnecessary. When Mr. Brown is injured in an accident, however, his wife takes over his job as a clerk and hires a housekeeper to do her work. While Mr. Brown lies uselessly at home, Mrs. Brown brings home the earnings and refuses to give her infantilized husband money for trifles such as cigars and carriage rides, indulgences that she determines would not be good for him.[37] In this economic role reversal, Mrs. Brown presumes her husband's dependency, and this dependency allows her to assume power in regulating his desires. Because Mrs. Brown wields economic power, her moral caretaking bears less resemblance to placing him on a pedestal than to policing his freedoms "for his own good." Stripped of his income-producing powers, Mr. Brown is also stripped of his masculinity. By analogy, Mr. Brown's failure to recognize his wife's labor amounts to limiting her womanhood.

In both "The Eight-Hour Wife" and "Harry Brown's Lesson," the wives return, in the end, to their lives of housework, but only after their husbands have recognized their ability to change themselves into workers either in or modeled on the marketplace. The stories suggest that the women have commodified their housework just long enough to show its value. What does it mean, here, for a wife to turn her work into a commodity and then to return to her place in the home? Both Mrs. Wellington and Mrs. Brown display their work as power, and their displays take place at home. Mrs. Wellington, ceasing to toil after her hours are over, exhibits her work through its stoppage, by conforming to the time limits imposed on factory work. Mrs. Brown displays herself as a worker by claiming the wage earner's prerogative to allocate family funds and to deny them to others. Lori Merish has posited that the identity of middle-class women as consumers afforded them a civic role in the nation; indeed, Mrs. Brown's actions show that purchasing commodities is a privilege, and that to be denied purchasing power is to be denied an aspect of selfhood, just as Mr. Brown's inability to gain access to his daily cigar emasculates him.[38] Yet this story goes beyond marking women's consumption as a sign of civic values or good taste. To consume, it suggests, is to exercise a power that is rooted in a woman's own capacity to earn wages. The right to consume also encodes her identity as a worker.

In both stories, the movements of Mrs. Wellington and Mrs. Brown in and out of the marketplace are acts of reclamation. As they define themselves as either workers in the marketplace or laborers in the home, they produce a different kind of self. Likewise, in authoring and producing themselves, they claim ownership over their own labor, challenging male authorship of the female working body and resisting male control of when and where women's labor would be visible. The stories construct a new identity for middle-class housekeepers in their ability to control their own movement in and out of the marketplace, both as workers and as consumers.[39] In so doing, they free themselves from complete correspondence with wage laborers (those who cannot escape seeing themselves as operatives) or sentimentalism (which would see women's household labor as a function of love, not of economics).

Cindy Weinstein argues that if self-ownership depends on a person's ability to maintain a self-affirming relationship to his or her work, it also "produces a version of agency in which one's own agency depends on the territorial appropriation of another's."[40] This is especially apparent in "Harry Brown's Lesson," for as Mrs. Brown takes over her husband's clerkship, she leaves her housework to be performed by a hired domestic servant. Though Mrs. Brown ultimately rejects this arrangement, more and more feminists were embracing this very solution to the problem of middle-class women's domestic labor. "Harry Brown's Lesson" preserves gender divisions, but suggests that such distinctions were tenuous, for a woman could, in fact, work outside the home as well as a man. It flirts with an organization of the family that would preserve middle-class women's independence while shunting undervalued domestic work to lower classes.

Making this claim involved complex arguments about the relative social value of women belonging to various races and social classes, distinctions embraced by the *Woman's Standard* as well as eastern feminist publications. In seeking the right to control their own self-representation and circulation between home- and market-based kinds of work, the story writers were preserving middle-class distinctions between self-ownership and dependence. The stories imply that a strictly gendered definition of independence and dependence could destroy the separation between home and market and between the middle and lower classes. They suggest that freedom to preserve an interior self distinct from the marketplace is a middle-class privilege and a product of civilization.[41] The stories provide a solution to the problem of women's property that relies more heavily than did the joint property solution on the idea of middle-class character — a trait more ephemeral than real property and more firmly based on racialized ideas about intellect, taste, and civilization.

Iowa legislators firmly denied housework's economic contributions throughout the latter half of the nineteenth century and well into the twentieth, leading to Iowa feminists' less vehement claims for a joint property act. Discouraged by these failures, Iowa feminists increasingly turned away from this property- and labor-based evaluation of housework and toward a race-based interpretation of women's value that had been prominent in the arguments of eastern feminists for some time. Perhaps because the idea of property itself was less easily defined than it had been in earlier decades, reformers turned to the new systems of order provided by civilization rhetoric.[42] Rationalizing access to home property in terms of middle-class liberties and civilization, the *Woman's Standard* suggested that the home's continuing power would rely, in part, on women's ability to justify the importance of the home to civilization in an era of expansion and empire building. These stories imagined the home through social evolution's racialized categories as well as through gender and class terms. At the same time, the stories began to incorporate the emerging professionalism of middle-class women whose work was tied neither to the home nor to the factory but to their intellectual properties and expertise.

Racializing Domestic Labor

In 1888 an article titled "Is Woman a Unit or a Fraction?" asserted woman's essential individuality by denying sentimental fictions and turning, instead, to science and the rhetoric of progressive civilization:

> Woman can neither be a slave nor an angel in the domestic relations without marring them. . . . [The idea that] home and not the individual is the unit of society [is a] sentimental fiction denied by history and unwarranted by science. . . . The home itself is obliterated the moment you ignore the sacred fact that it is made up of units whose rights are inalienable and unquestionable. That the home is the unit of the State, and that man represents that unit, and that woman must be content to shine through him as a candle through a lantern, is a doctrine that belongs to the age of the wigwam, the traveling herd, the harem and the belated Mormon. . . . We yield to no one in our regard to the sanctity of the home; but the home is made up of *man and woman*, neither of which finds his or her complement until the indestructible, globular quality of soul is recognized.[43]

The author asserts that sentimentalism contaminates the home by making woman a mere "fraction," given character only in relation to the home rather than as an individual. Sentimentality is allied with slavery's corrupt property relations and with the "barbaric" life and traffic in women associated with "the wigwam, the traveling herd, the harem and the belated Mormon." Each of the groups referenced, the author argues, degrades women into objects for sexual exchange in which their own lack of property makes them property themselves. With the exception of Mormons, each group was also explicitly non-white. Asserting that the ways of these contemporary groups belonged to a by-gone age, the author advocated more progressive forms of property ownership that would acknowledge individuality rather than partiality, self-ownership rather than commodification. The author's linking of self-possession to a racialized discourse of progress shows the very fragility of middle-class identity. Attacking ideologies of gender embedded in the sentimental and economic cornerstones of the middle-class home, the author provides a new understanding of middle-class identity by appealing to social evolutionary theory, which regarded race and class as intimately linked.

The middle decades of the nineteenth century witnessed the advent and wide acceptance of social evolution, which defined stages in human development according to increasing social complexity. Charles Darwin defined evolution in biological terms and emphasized the adaptation of organisms to their various environments. However, European thinkers Herbert Spencer, Johann Jacob Bachofen, and Sir Henry Maine argued that evolution occurred not only as a result of individual biology but also as a result of changes in a society's political, economic, and social relations. Spencer, in particular, cast social changes such as the development of patriarchy and reverence for private property as positive advancements. He defined progress as a ladder that every society must ascend, advancing along the way to ever more sophisticated systems of economic exchange, political economy, gender-role differentiation, and familial relations. Social evolution allowed nineteenth-century scientists to explain the vast differences between cultures by placing the various races along this ladder of development. European and American scholars placed their own cultures at the apex of civilization and marked them as the most socially, politically, biologically, and economically advanced.[44] The seeming inability of the lower classes to provide for themselves could be explained as a result of racial character — failures to survive in the economic conditions of industrial society.

Civilization theory had been part of discussions by women of their status in the United States for some time. Middle-class women began to compare their own situations to those of women in other lands as the mission movement of the mid-nineteenth century, in particular, brought women news of life in other lands. Joan Jacobs Brumberg has argued that, in part due to reform efforts such as those of home mission societies and the WCTU, "masses of American women, with only the slightest notions of scientific rigor, embraced the study of ethnology as early as the 1870s, precisely because they were interested in the similarities and dissimilarities in women's position in other cultures of the world." Christian reformers interested in other cultures, Brumberg notes, were not out to challenge gender divisions at home. Instead, the bulk of middle-class women who participated in mission and reform movements through contributions and subscriptions to mission journals used cultural comparisons to affirm the superiority of gender relations in the United States and the supremacy of its "home life."[45] Yet even comparisons that lauded domestic relations in middle-class homes contained subtle expressions of doubt about women's oppression. Discussing women's lack of personal and political rights in other nations seemed to confirm that white, middle-class American women enjoyed a higher status than their sisters in other nations. Fears about class divisions within the home could be mediated by appealing to the abominable conditions of women elsewhere.

Some feminists in the United States, however, embraced these comparisons in order to suggest that the oppression of American women was not so far removed from that endured by women in other nations. They suggested that women's rights were crucial to upholding the tenets of civilization that did separate Euro-American home life from the degraded homes of women in other countries. This strand of feminism, which culminated in Charlotte Perkins Gilman's vision of civilized society as one that liberated women from housework, saw wage earning not just as a mark of women's independence but as a way to measure the value of the worker herself to her society. Unlike mid-nineteenth-century feminists, Gilman did not protest the undervaluation of women's labor in the marketplace as heartily as she protested relegating all women to housework. Gilman proposed radical restructuring of the household to get rid of the architectures that contributed to women's subordination, the secluded kitchen in particular. She proposed cooperative households where professional women would be liberated from housework in order to pursue careers and where duties like child care and cooking could be parceled out to hired domestic workers. Confining women's work to the home and defining that work as, by nature, outside the marketplace, was a relic of barbarism for Gilman and her counterparts. Gilman used social evolutionary discourse to campaign for new liberties for white women, but as she propounded the theory that civilization could only come through white women's emancipation from the wageless work of the home, she suggested lines of division between women on the basis of race and class. While some white women would work outside the home as professionals, she argued, women who were less advanced could be raised up by performing the household labor that professionals left behind.[46]

The *Woman's Standard* shows that western feminists interested in theories of women's labor were using ideas of racial difference to distinguish the work that white women did from that of nonwhite women abroad and at home. In the 1880s and 1890s, new feminist plans for women's liberation from domestic labor could not help but affect writers for the *Woman's Standard*. The political investment of the journal in women's labor and property issues extended to a fascination with the status of women in other lands, and it published accounts of women's lives in places such as Hawaii, Turkey, and Cuba. "All the Rights She Wants," by J. E. J. of Salem, Iowa, chastised the American woman for denying her oppression while "conceal[ing] the secrets of her prison-house." Women's dependency, she argued, kept Christian women from acting on their moral impulses: "Should she desire to feed the hungry or clothe the naked, she must ask her husband for the means to enable her to do it." She claimed that denying women the ability to act virtuously denied them the hallmarks of civilization, for "the Turk does not lock up his wives with more jealous care, than the Christian husband his strong box from her whom he has formally endowed with all his earthly possessions."[47] Here, the language of class oppression mingles with ethnographic comparisons, equating, in Gilman-like style, the condition of women in the United States with that of women in "barbarous" lands. Articles in the journal flirted with cross-cultural comparisons in order to point out how close American family life came to barbarism; at the same time, it reinforced the idea that women in the United States were, and must remain, more culturally advanced than their less civilized sisters.

Continental expansion also informed comparisons in the *Woman's Standard* between the status of white women and that of their nonwhite counterparts. Iowa women used Native American women as a measure of their own condition in different and sometimes contradictory ways. At times their comparisons pointed out similarities between what whites generally saw as the drudgery of native women and the dependency of white wives. Native Americans seemed to provide a particularly apt way to measure white women's conditions as workers within the home. Tidbits and articles in the journal indicate that *Woman's Standard* readers were kept abreast of assimilation policies, the work of reformers like Alice Fletcher, and reformers' visits to Native American tribes and reservations. They regarded with interest the home lives of native women who were their geographic neighbors in states like Wisconsin and Nebraska, and they looked to their domestic conditions as a way to gauge the government's concern for the condition of women in general. Unlike freedmen and -women, Native Americans were largely outside the wage economy; by the 1880s and 1890s, many indigenous groups were still holding as tenaciously as possibly to hunting and agricultural economies. Like farm women, indigenous women seemed to be engaged in a "treadmill life" that left little room for activities other than home maintenance. As the government began to recognize Native American men as potential laborers and landowners in the 1880s, these feminist writers worried that Native American women would, like white women, be denied the rewards that landownership and labor within a cash economy granted to men.

These Iowa writers saw parallels between Native American women's situations and their own. One writer noted that a treaty with the Chippewas gave the women no land, "while they are the ones who cultivate the land, and do all the work. But," she continued, "justice to Indian women cannot be expected of commissioners who believe in keeping white women in political slavery."[48] Writers also suggested that civilization's supposed advancements did little to change the relationship between men and women and perhaps even retarded equality between the genders. Again citing the nearby Chippewa, an item in the first issue of the journal complained that "the ignorance of heathens is amazing. A Chippewa chief says, 'a woman can carry or haul as much as two men can.' When he learns to read he will find that women have not the strength to endure a higher education, or drop a slip of paper containing a few names into a box."[49] Tidbits in the journal also suggested that abuse of native women ought to bring all women into solidarity with one another to fight women's general submission to men. An article based on reformer Charles Hallock's visit to Alaska lamented that "Indian girls of tender years are bought by white men for concubinage and prostitution, and the cultivation and improvement which they receive at the schools only serves too often to enhance their commercial value! Outrages upon women are often committed openly, and the culprits are never brought to justice."[50] Writers worried about how introducing Euro-American economic practices would affect indigenous women's lives in a nation that still refused to incorporate white women fully into the marketplace.

Such sympathetic discussions of women's unity across races, however, coexisted with an equally strong strain of thought that emphasized the particular need to improve the class status of white women because they were white. Wives deserved more rights and respect for the labor that they performed at home, not necessarily because of their gender but due to their race. Feminists all across the United States launched this argument. With the passage of the Fourteenth Amendment in 1868 and the Fifteenth in 1870, many feminists who had supported abolition now argued for white women's suffrage, claiming that black men's right to vote made denying suffrage to white women all the more atrocious.[51] Iowa feminists echoed this sentiment in regard to suffrage, but this time in the wake of state laws that allowed property-holding indigenous men to vote. In 1887 an article announced that under Nebraska laws that subdivided Native Americans' property into homesteads, the "dirty, dusky sons of the forest" had been granted voting privileges.[52] A decade later, the paper reacted to homestead laws in South Dakota that allowed women to take out homesteads in that state by suggesting that their ability to own property only magnified the injustice of their lack of voting privileges. "We believe there are 1,800 Indian voters in that state," the author declared. While property ownership seemed to grant the rights of self-representation to native men, white women property owners were not granted such privileges.[53]

The February 1892 edition of the *Woman's Standard* included a note on the image "Woman and Her Political Peers," made by Henrietta Briggs Wall of Hutchinson, Kansas, for display at the Chicago World's Fair. The illustration depicts a white woman in profile, surrounded by the likenesses of an "idiot," a convict, and an American Indian. The woman, the *Woman's Standard* reported, was Frances E. Willard, one of the founders of the National WCTU and its president from 1879 until her death in 1898.[54] Willard was also one of the leading proponents of a feminism based on racial hierarchies. She believed that a society's advancement toward civilization was marked by its treatment of women, and that white women should be enfranchised before any foreign-born male. In her moral crusade for a "white life" (temperance, premarital chastity, and marital monogamy), Willard argued that white women should be the standard-bearers, and to do this, they needed the vote. "Woman and Her Political Peers" broadcast the message that it was an abomination that imbeciles, convicts, and American Indians might be allowed powers and freedoms that white women were denied.[55] Feminists seized on the image of the Native American warrior, just as Caroline Soule had appropriated the figure of White Cloud, to elevate their own authority. White women's concern that Native American men would wield power that the women themselves could not claim suggests their fear that Caroline Soule's domesticated Prophet was in danger of regaining his political authority.

Race played a crucial role in discussions about the value of the domestic labor of white women as well as their crusades for suffrage. Gilman helped to translate gendered division of labor within homes into evolutionary theory, arguing that if the white race were to advance, such sex distinctions were best left to those groups who had not yet reached the level of civilization that Euro-American cultures had. The *Woman's Standard* accepted this evolutionary argument for women's rights, including articles in its pages with titles such as "The Pagan Origin of Women's Subjection."[56] Iowa suffragist Carrie Chapman Catt, a protégé of Martha Callanan, the first editor of the *Woman's Standard*, framed wives' right to hold property in their own names as a sign of evolutionary progress already achieved. Suffrage, she argued, was the next step. An article titled "The Prayers towards Woman's Enfranchisement an Evolution" reprinted a speech that Chapman gave at a Storm Lake, Iowa, convention in 1898. "The effort to give the ballot to woman is not a movement carried on by women disappointed in love, or by men who are cranks," Chapman declared, "it is a movement brought about by evolution." Chapman argued that each culture was characterized, in its early stages of development, by enslavement of women and by their status as the property of their husbands. She asserted that progress began in the fourth century, when philosophers decided that women did have an immortal soul. Recognizing that women had souls eventually led to acknowledgment of their individuality, and Chapman exulted that "now [woman] can hold property on equal footing with man."[57]

Not all Iowa feminists shared Chapman's conviction that women had achieved equality with respect to property rights. Many, in fact, believed that the movement had failed. Writers for the *Woman's Standard* continued to argue that the property laws to which Chapman referred were deeply unsatisfactory because they did not recognize housewives' contributions, and several essayists continued to champion the joint property cause in the name of civilized society. In 1899, the year after Chapman's speech at Storm Lake, one writer lamented the continuing rift between the letter and the practice of the marital property and earnings statutes. "If the wife had an equal share in the joint earnings of the family during her married life it would be in fact what it seems to be in theory and law," she maintained. "But the wife has no equal share in the joint earnings of the family. These earnings are all considered the estate of the husband."[58] One of the tragedies of women's lack of access to earnings, the writer suggested, was not only that women were unable to will homestead property but that they could not give freely to churches or charitable associations. The inability of women to distribute family earnings as they wished, the author implied, limited their access to the organs of moral authority that characterized "the white life." In the pages of the *Woman's Standard*, writers and advocates of the joint property claim theorized that selfhood inhered not in the workplace but in the home. They desired to make family property, as the shared property of husbands and wives, the foundation of moral, civilized, white life rather than a site of intrafamilial market relations.

Unlike Gilman, who suggested that the gendered division of labor within families was more suited to "primitive" cultures and ought to be rejected by whites, feminists in Iowa used arguments about racial advancement to assert that the work that white women performed in the home, though nonwaged, was still valuable to the cause of civilization. They adapted Gilman's crusade to free women by allowing them to exercise self-ownership to the context of work performed *within* the home. They accepted Gilman's claim that white women's housework needed to be seen in light of its value to civilization in order to be properly evaluated, but they rejected her claim that no marriage that operated on a gendered division of roles could be considered as a partnership.

In Iowa, writers proposed a clear link between women's work at home and racial progress, for they could argue that pioneer women's work had helped to transform the prairies from wilderness to civilized farmland. H. F. C. contended that it was obvious that women who helped to settle new lands should be entitled to joint ownership of lands they had transformed.[59] Margaret Campbell of Des Moines stressed wives' roles in the settlement history, declaring that in the "half a century . . . since Iowa became the home of the white man . . . women have shown as much moral courage and zeal as their husbands in settling and building up a State. The men and women worked together, suffered together, and were ready to die together, if need be, for the protection of their homes and their children." Yet, she went on, "the vilest wretch that walks the earth" is the "political superior" of woman.[60] Writers in the *Woman's Standard* argued that the hard work involved in wresting lands from the native inhabitants and settling new communities justified the equal access of wives to the property that they had helped to improve. Rather than using wage work to measure the value of domestic work, these articles privileged white women's role in western expansion and civilization.

Precisely because discussions of Native American assimilation revolved around questions of property ownership rather than enfranchisement, Iowa women found that their own inability to claim rights in family property was made more distressing as the government distributed property to those very people whom they regarded as having less of a claim over the land than they did. H. F. C., who, along with Iowans Lizzie B. Read and Grace Manchester, was one of the *Woman's Standard*'s strongest voices in support of joint property ownership, warned that the progress achieved by Iowa's pioneering men and women could be lost if legislators failed to recognize women's legal personhood. In "Property Rights of Married Women" she argued that work done by women in settling in new lands should entitle them to joint ownership of property in life, not just one third dower right upon a husband's death. Elsewhere she asserted that "the Indian mortgage upon [Iowa lands] was set aside by the aid of fire-water and fire-arms. . . . Throughout the struggle with the Indians, and of that for the 'inherent right of mankind,' man involved woman in care, toil, privation and sorrow" but had failed to allow women equal access to the property rights that men enjoyed. H. F. C. invested men's political conservatism with an evolutionary quality, stating that their failure to change the laws would pass on to "each generation a lowered standard of right and justice. This lowered standard reproduced in both sexes, retrogression is constantly accelerated."[61]

If property ownership by Indian men distressed white women who were not fully granted that freedom, Native American women provided examples of the kind of retrograde housekeeping that middle-class women wished to avoid. Moreover, writers submitted that the domestic work that middle-class women performed could be the highest achievement of civilized culture. In "The Indian Problem Solved," the author demolished the romantic vision of the wild, free Indian woman, painting instead a picture of a life marred by physical ugliness, weakness from childbearing, loss of children, and lack of religious knowledge. "Teach the women, young and old, that their highest, holiest duty is the intelligent management of the home and the children, that

God has given them," the author exhorted at the end. "Not until the Indian women become good nurses, good cooks, good housekeepers, in a word, intelligent Christian women, will the Indian problem be solved."[62] The journal was equivocal, though, about whether native women were truly capable of becoming "good housekeepers." One curious anecdote questioned what it meant for Indian women to do domestic work. The article reported that "the Apache squaws who remain at the agency since the removal of Geronimo from their social circle, are rapidly advancing in the arts of civilization, and spend much time in sewing and quilting the scraps of the former's victims into fancy work for home decoration."[63] The tale suggested that while Apache women were perfectly capable of learning "the arts of civilization" as symbolized by sewing, quilting, and home decoration, their essential savagery prevented them from truly understanding their work as more than a kind of rote labor, devoid of its higher function as a marker of civilization. The story implied that domesticity had an essential character that Native American women could not learn merely by performing its tasks.

The image of Apache women expressing their "savagery" by way of needlework seems jarring in a forum that was dedicated to championing the economic value of women's housework. Yet even as they fought with the male establishment — lawmakers and husbands — for the ability to represent women's selfhood, feminists suggested that the security of the middle-class family depended on its distinction from the lives of white women's evolutionary inferiors. In 1894 *Woman's Standard* writer Lucy Mallory invoked a class-based understanding of wives' status, only to replace an image of home divided by class with an image of home as the center of civilization and the mechanism of evolution. Rejecting quantitative evaluations of women's work that would evoke comparisons to wage labor, she offered a more qualitative interpretation that represented home as the center of learning and taste — an image that drew as much on racialized visions of home as economic ones. In "The Home of Injustice," Mallory suggested that "industrials" stop protesting in Washington and begin to seek justice at home. Even as idle men raised their voices against capitalists, their wives were working at home, and if women's work "should be rewarded with just wages, these women should be entitled to two-thirds of the income of their husbands, for they work, at the least twice as many hours as their husbands do." More important than this economic recognition of wives' work, however, was the understanding that "woman is the heart or center of the home." Here, though, woman's position at the heart of the home was not likened to the bonds that joined a wage worker to his employer, but to the machinery of evolution. Even the wives of "industrials," she suggested, can make middle-class homes. Mallory used the term "evolve" conspicuously to discuss the home's importance to maintaining civilized culture: "All the masterpieces of light, liberty, love, art, science and literature are evolved in the home, in the quiet of one's own chamber. . . . Growth in study of all that is good and true have never been evolved in crowds. Noisy gatherings and great crowds are but the froth on the silent waves of Infinite Progression. Justice, liberty, and light must be evolved in the restful peace of the harmonious home; otherwise they will never have an inception and be cultivated, finally, to external realization."[64] Mallory was ambiguous about woman's role in cultivating home as a site of evolutionary progress. On one hand, she seemed to argue that equal rights might free women to participate in creating culture in rooms of their own. On the other hand, the article suggested that men retreat from the public places of class protest to their homes, where they might identify with the arts and sciences that mark the middle class, and where wives, recognized as men's equals, would be content to provide such spaces of "cultivation."

The moral imperative of keeping the home free from market relations did not fade from either feminists' discourse or legal discourse by the end of the nineteenth century, even though feminists attacked the sentimental home as an economic prison for women. In spite of, and in fact because of, the Iowa legislature's refusal to acknowledge the economic value of housework, the *Woman's Standard* continued to protest the gendered class division caused by unequal property distribution. Writers argued that more equal property relations would eradicate gendered divisions at home and thus protect the family from dangerous economic oppression of some of its members. The movement for joint property challenged beliefs in the fundamental character of domestic labor as economically valueless; but it did not significantly challenge woman's role as guardian of the home, and by the turn of the century, that position had been bolstered by new discourses of race, progress, and evolution. In the face of both continued failures and the new emphasis on women's work as informed by race rather than class, feminists' agitation for the joint property claim waned by the turn of the century. The *Woman's Standard* decreased in size and moved its production site from the capital city, Des Moines, to Sutherland, Iowa, in 1897 and then to Waterloo in 1899. More preoccupied with moral reform than with changes in property legislation, the writers spent less time discussing women's legal status at home. Instead, concern for the lack of time and space for self-cultivation dominated discussions of farm women's lives.

In Iowa, arguments that proposed class divisions within the household existed alongside racialized discourse that made women's access to family property a requirement for progress and evolution rather than evidence of proletarian discontent. Drawing on the racial arguments of the national suffrage movement, the *Woman's Standard* validated the home as both the space of women's work and the site of civilization, thus suggesting that in acknowledging women's rights to family property, legislatures would be sanctifying the work of civilization itself. Central to this argument in Iowa was the idea that women's unpaid, domestic labor at home was crucial to civilization. Rather than championing paid labor outside the home as a sign of evolutionary progress for women, Iowa women's arguments show that the rhetoric of progress and self-ownership was as important to discussions about the value of women's work at home as it was to feminist proposals that women be liberated from domestic work. What faded in this turn to civilization theory was the radical argument that housework was economically valuable and that women's lack of access to family resources amounted to class oppression. In claiming that the privileges of white racial superiority belonged to women workers at home, the feminist writers for the *Woman's Standard* also endowed these workers with a middle-class identity rooted in evolution rather than economics.

The *Woman's Standard*'s emphasis on Native American women as a standard for comparison suggests that feminists understood women's domestic labor not only in terms of the marketplace or slave labor but also with respect to the home lives and status of their Native American neighbors. Defending the value of civilized work at home provided non-economic legitimation for women's domestic labor; this idea also underlay national discussions of Native American women's work in the context of assimilation. Like the joint property proposals that Iowa women advanced, the Dawes Severalty Act of 1887 imagined that access to property would stimulate progress. Debates about the benefits of the act, however, privileged racial concerns over considerations of the devaluation of domestic labor. As white women became involved in the crusade for Native American assimilation, they would take their self-images as preservers of middle-class interiority with them as they embarked on professional careers in reform. Those who promoted domestic work as an agent for civilizing Indian women left this legacy of class concerns behind.

CHAPTER THREE

Object Lessons

Domesticity on Display in Native American Assimilation

In 1885 the Women's National Indian Association (WNIA), a reform group dedicated to Native American assimilation, instituted a new committee to provide funds for Native Americans to build homes. Sara T. Kinney, head of the WNIA's Home Building and Loan Committee, emphatically believed that homes were object lessons that stimulated Native American women to work at home. To illustrate the positive effects of the loan program, she described one woman who refused to "live and dress more like white people" or to make "white women's bread" as her husband desired. Kinney reported that the woman "did not like white people, nor their ways, and she would have none of them." For this woman, refusing to accept white women's domestic habits and work amounted to a refusal to be "whitened," not just by the flour of white bread but by the utter change in ways that domesticity would produce. Yet a loan from the WNIA prompted a chain of events that Kinney regarded to be as evolutionary as it was revolutionary. Kinney noted that the woman's husband hoped that even if his wife would have none of the white woman's ways, she would enjoy some of the white woman's things. He applied for a WNIA loan to add a kitchen and buy a stove for his wife. Kinney told how the man constructed his addition and then "watched for the effect" on his wife:

For a time the woman seemed perplexed by this unusual magnificence and scarcely knew how to regard the new condition of things. But the right influence had reached her at last. She soon began to feel disturbed because of grease spots on the new pine floor, and a scrubbing brush was brought into requisition. Then, of course, she began to notice the difference between the clean floor and her own face, hands, and clothing. The scrubbing brush was again called for and worked wonders along those lines. By degrees she has lost many of her slovenly ways, and at last account she was learning to make "white woman's bread." Here, then, is an instance of one Indian woman who has been civilized through the medium of a pine floor and a scrubbing brush.[1]

Kinney credited the house for the woman's new habits of industry, emphasizing that architecture itself could be a transformative influence. Acknowledging the woman's housework only in a roundabout way, Kinney stressed the power of objects associated with civilization: pine floors, scrub brushes, and white woman's bread.

Middle-class Indian reformers appealed, in publications and at national conferences, to already potent beliefs in domesticity's centrality to civilization. Feminists in Iowa had mingled pleas for new legislative definitions of women's work with evolutionary ones; the WNIA, however, defined women's domestic work almost exclusively as a barometer of civilization. Distinguishing itself from male reform organizations, the WNIA stressed women's capacity not only to bring about new legislation but to enact progress through practical work in the very homes where Indians lived. In doing so, the association called on anthropological theories that lent scientific credence to older beliefs in the moral power of the home and homemaking by positing the home as evidence of evolutionary status. In the context of Indian assimilation, domestic work became not just the work of maintaining home and family but was scientifically legitimated as an engine of civilization itself. White women activists, teachers, fund-raisers, and fieldworkers celebrated the model home as a space in which civilization could be attained by way of women's work.

These reformers turned from the economic divisions that plagued gender relations within the white woman's home, instead putting the Indian home and Indian women's work on display in the national theater of assimilation opened by the Dawes Act. Those who, like Kinney, extolled the model home's civilizing power looked at women's work as part of what Tony Bennett has described as the "exhibitionary complex." Model homes were analogous to museums and exhibitions, where everyday objects and even bodies are displayed as object lessons meant to impress viewers with the system and order validated by the creators of the display. Model homes, as object lessons, were meant to sway Native Americans to accept the domestic order that the homes represented and to convince white women that their work was crucial to evolutionary progress.[2] Carrying the model home's message to wider audiences through journals, books, and photographs, reformers publicized "women's work for women" as the labor necessary to transform assimilation's political and scientific objectives into concrete reality — to ensure, for example, that the goals of assimilation policy would come to fruition through the "medium of a scrubbing brush." The WNIA shifted the focus of assimilation from property acquisition and forms of work coded as male to domestic work: cooking, cleaning, sewing, and child rearing. In so doing, it validated the household labor that white women had been doing for centuries and that held little power in an industrializing world. Moreover, reformers suggested that the civilized body could be female as well as male.[3]

But by emphasizing model homes as object lessons that incorporated white and native women into a new evolutionary order, reformers were defining these homes as workplaces and thus integrating both groups into the industrial order that the model home also legitimated. Neither middle-class white women nor their indigenous sisters were able to ignore that model homes were subject to economic and cultural forces that challenged assimilation's agenda and made it difficult to uphold the order that anthropological science and, increasingly, domestic science, required. The economic transitions that accompanied assimilation, the lack of financial support for white women's work in the field, and indigenous resistance all destabilized the easy equation between homemaking and racial progress that reformers had sought to establish. WNIA reformers responded to the instability of reservation homes by shifting support from Indian homes to homes for female fieldworkers; field matrons, in turn, responded by entrenching themselves in a professional ethos that stressed management of Indian women workers within model homes. Furthering civilization by "making home" became a series of quantifiable skills and activities that white women sought to perform and to teach. In trying to empower both themselves and indigenous women by adhering to scientific rationality and domestic industry, they advocated a more industrialized version of the model home where progress was measured not in domestic accomplishments but in adherence to system, order, and wage work.

Mother-Work

The idea that the moral power of women could justify their action and work outside the home had motivated women's secular and religious organizations since before the Civil War.[4] That the WNIA should take up the assimilation banner wielded by women like Caroline Soule is no surprise, as the group developed out of the Women's Home Mission Circle at First Baptist Church in Philadelphia in 1879. The organization originally called itself the Woman's National Indian Treaty-Keeping and Protective Association and included primarily wealthy women brought up to regard charitable work as women's province.[5]

In turning to the Indian question, however, the group distinguished itself from charitable societies that aided immigrants, freedmen and -women, and cultures abroad. The WNIA saw missions to the Indians as a more pressing moral duty, and a specifically American one. Because the United States occupied native lands, members of the WNIA believed a debt was owed to natives — a debt that a Christian nation was particularly situated to repay. "The question of our duty to these, though numerically a small one, is morally greater than that touching any of the new-comers upon our soil," read one editorial in the WNIA's journal, the *Indian's Friend*. For these women, the existence of dishonored natives on American soil seemed to distinguish the Indian problem from the problem of helping freedpeople and immigrants, for they believed that Indian men had been forced into idleness and women and children still stood at the mercy of rapacious white Indian agents and settlers. Reservations floated like blighting "islands of darkness" in the midst of an otherwise industrious, Christian nation.[6]

For the first several years, the association combated this blight by petitioning and lobbying the government to uphold treaty rights. In 1882, however, the male-dominated Indian Rights Association (IRA) formed and took over much of the political work that the women's group had begun. In that same year, the organization changed its name to the Women's National Indian Association and shifted its focus to a more woman-centered definition of Indian work as "the Christian motherhood of the nation obeying its instincts toward our native heathen." While the group never embraced woman suffrage, it was feminist in its condemnation of the oppression of all women, regardless of race. The group started branch societies in each state, communicated to its members information about the "Indian problem," and set to work "thundering out appeals to Christian consciences" for the protection of native peoples.[7]

WNIA members spoke frequently at the annual Lake Mohonk Conference of Friends of the Indian, started in 1882 by Albert Smiley, a member of the Board of Indian Commissioners. The WNIA also counted among its members Indian school teachers and missionaries who published frequently in school papers such as Carlisle's *Red Man* and the Hampton Institute's *Southern Workman*. But the WNIA's primary organ of communication was its monthly journal, the *Indian's Friend*. It contained information about missions and educational efforts, updates on legislative matters, and appeals for financial support. It published accounts by women who traveled to or worked in the field among native peoples, framing the work of white and Native American women in diverse geographical spaces as part of a widespread movement toward progress and the achievement of a domestic ideal. In so doing, the *Indian's Friend* offered its readers a vision of a nation managed by women's expertise, and it encouraged its readers to regard homes — and women's work within them — as insistently visible and, in fact, crucial to Native American uplift. While the IRA made it possible for these women to leave policymaking to their enfranchised brothers, the WNIA developed a civilization policy that relied heavily on uniting moral values with evolutionary beliefs by focusing on the home. The IRA and other male-directed Indian reform initiatives emphasized male property ownership and wage labor, but the WNIA's vision of the model Christian home, like sentimental novels such as Caroline Soule's and feminists' accounts of the value of work performed at home, focused on the moral power of women as well as their domestic work.

The WNIA carved out a niche for itself by stressing the need to address Indian women in particular. "The women are harder to reach than the men, for they stay at home, mind their children, chop the wood, get the meals, and pull the harness off the horses when the men come home from visiting," wrote one missionary. Indian women needed to be shown the "better way," and this was a task for which white women were better equipped than white men. In missives printed in the *Indian's Friend* and the *Southern Workman*, reformers stressed the particularly degraded condition of Indian women and their homes. Women were "domestic drudges," and a man had "absolute power over his wife and children"; they were also often at the mercy of white soldiers, miners, and traders. Their homes were described as "rude huts" or "burrows" little better than the homes of animals. In 1881 the editors of the *Southern Workman* pressed women to answer the call of duty, arguing that "the condition of women is the test of progress. The family is the unit of Christian civilization. What girls are, mothers are, and mothers make the home. Shall we help the Indians to homes? Indian girls have been drudges, slaves. They are not so bright and responsive as the boys of that race. Is not an effort for them wise and timely?"[8]

The WNIA staunchly believed that this effort should be concentrated on individual homes for Indians and regarded the agency system as an utter failure because it did not address the home life of the Indian. Changing the home was a woman's mission. In 1889, WNIA president Amelia Stone Quinton confidently declared that the group, "in the hands of the Christian women of the nation is perfectly able to supply what is needed and to do this mother-work for the Indian race. . . . Let us women then give to the destitute tribes Christian homes and missions, for without these no race can rise."[9] Like other middle-class women's reform groups of this era, the WNIA had answered a national question with a woman-centered solution and so provided a field ripe for women's cultivation.[10]

Morality, Evolution, and the Model Home

By the late nineteenth century the "Christian home" had already enjoyed decades of prominence in print and visual culture as a symbol of Euro-American civilization and its attendant virtues: morality, industry, and domesticity. Architectural treatises, pattern books, novels, and women's magazines all offered versions of the model home in its physical, moral, technical, and commercial aspects, turning domestic space into an exhibition of national character. Mid-century architectural theorists such as Andrew Jackson Downing and Catharine Beecher developed plans for houses that would outwardly indicate the moral sentiments, cultural values, and class status of their occupants. Downing asserted that through its architectural style and exhibition of taste, the ideal home would "show, at a glance, something of the daily thoughts and life of the family that inhabits it."[11] Women's virtuosity in creating interiors was an important part of middle-class womanhood and conferred upon women the responsibility of making an environment that would display the virtues of civilized, moral life. Women's magazines and housing designers believed that homes had the potential to influence and even transform the habits of those who viewed them. The right home could help a nineteenth-century family to counteract successfully the urbanity, immorality, tastelessness, competition, crass consumption, and dependence that threatened the family in an industrializing world.[12]

Though most nineteenth-century domestic advice was directed at white women, using domestic display to transform those regarded as less than civilized had long played a role in assimilation. Educators stressed the importance of homes as models for Native Americans as early as 1761, when Eleazar Wheelock opened the doors of Moor's Indian Charity School in Lebanon, New Hampshire, to female students.[13] Because Wheelock himself was not able to instruct girls in the domestic arts at his school, he paid white women to teach them. The idea behind this practice, known as "outing," was that Euro-American homes would function as examples for indigenous girls with no understanding of domestic economy. Women's domestic work was at the heart of this form of exhibition, as household labor became a form of education — and a source of income and household help. Like later model homes for immigrants and African Americans, the outing system bound morality and civilization to the home environment even as it emphasized wage earning as a virtue.

A century later, anthropologists validated the civilizing power of homes and housework through the new language of social evolution. Lewis Henry Morgan, an anthropologist who was also a lawyer, railroad investor, and New York state senator, made homes the focus of scientific inquiry. In 1851 he published the *League of the Iroquois*, followed in 1871 by *Systems of Consanguinity and Affinity of the Human Family*, a kinship study that proposed that a society's evolutionary status could be measured by its progress toward a monogamous, nuclear family secured by private property ownership. Private property was an essential characteristic of a civilized race, according to Morgan. He asserted that the increasing control of a society over the sources of subsistence was the force behind its social evolution. Morgan's colossal work *Ancient Society* (1877) was a sweeping history of the evolving complexity of political, economic, and domestic systems. Like other early ethnologists, he labeled cultures with the states of savagery, barbarism, or civilization. Savage societies lived in a state of "communism in living" characterized by matrilineality and extensive kinship networks, while civilized society's "passion over all other passions" for property explained its establishment of "political society on the basis of territory and of property."[14] Morgan proposed that domestic architecture indicated a culture's social, economic, and political organization; so important was it that Morgan developed what was to be the final section of *Ancient Society* into a tome of its own: *Houses and House-Life of the American Aborigines* (1881). He argued that the growth of civilization "can be traced from the hut of the savage, through the communal houses of the barbarians, to the house of the single family of civilized nations," a dwelling that symbolized the monogamy, private property, and political society of civilization.[15]

Morgan's crucial contribution to social evolutionary theory was his belief that progress need not be a slow march to civilization but that it could be stimulated by deliberate changes in property relations — the basic social system that influenced all other aspects of culture. To Americans looking for a way to deal with natives within the nation's borders, Morgan offered a rational solution to the Indian question. Reformers surmised that communal property ownership and extended kinship relations undergirded Native American cultures and that breaking up these practices would destroy tribal identity in favor of the sense of individualism fostered by property ownership. Though Morgan himself did not espouse Native American assimilation through property ownership, identifying private property as the key to evolutionary advancement suggested a way to step up the process, transforming Indians from hunter-gatherers into yeoman farmers, secure in the possession of familial property.[16]

In 1881 Alice Fletcher decided to put Morgan's theory to the test and, in so doing, helped to transform the civilization question into a matter that hinged on domestic design. A visit to the Omahas in Nebraska convinced her that evolution by design could work, and Fletcher went to Washington, D.C., to lobby for the allotment of reservation lands as individual homesteads. She advised assimilating Indians through a land policy that would enact new forms of property and domestic relations among them, erasing communal ownership of property and vesting individual ownership in the heads of nuclear families. The plan would break up extended kinship ties and tribal subsistence systems; new property lines were meant to increase the social and physical distance between individual tribe members and force them to conform to American economic relations in the marketplace and in the home. In 1881 and 1882 Fletcher lobbied vigorously in Washington for an act that would assign homesteads to individual Omahas. Her petitions, information gathering, and calls on politicians eventually resulted in the Omaha Severalty Act, which arranged for the sale of 50,000 acres of communally held Omaha reservation lands in exchange for funds to help the people develop their own homesteads and begin life as landowners. Fletcher herself was assigned the position of federal allotting agent, and between 1882 and 1884 she worked assiduously to assign homestead tracts to each head of family on the reservation and to explain to the Omahas that conforming to Euro-American habits of industry and domesticity was their best hope for survival.[17]

Fletcher, with the support of the WNIA and IRA, continued to lobby for a statute that would enforce allotment nationally. In 1887 the Dawes Severalty Act endorsed, as official government policy, dissolving collective tribal land-ownership and replacing it with individual property ownership. Alice Fletcher echoed many reformers' beliefs when she announced that "allotment means for the Indian pioneering," arguing that like the pioneer, the Native American must work the land or die. Fletcher also justified the Dawes Act's provision that lands left over after allotment had been completed would be purchased by the federal government and opened for settlement by non-Indian homesteaders, explaining that their white neighbors' "object lessons of working and farming expedients will be of untold advantage. The Indian must have the air of civilization all about him if he is to become a useful citizen and fulfill his own manhood."[18] For Fletcher and for other members of the WNIA, home building was the linchpin of the allotment plan. Without homes that could provide the necessary influence, the policy would fail. Fletcher believed that the government alone could not "meet the necessary work demanded in order to enable the Indian to successfully meet the change that is upon him." For this, women were needed.[19]

Yet the government's attempt to enforce assimilation could not help but cast into relief questions about women's status and the value of women's work in the late nineteenth century. Morgan had surmised that political and economic progress cost women their freedom, as matriarchy gave way before the consolidation of property under male heads of families. Progress, for women, was supposedly marked by seclusion in the home and powerlessness in the political society that was the prize of civilization. If Native Americans were to be assimilated through private property ownership that concentrated economic power in the hands of men, what place would be accorded to women in this legal transformation? Morgan himself offered a solution. Though he conceded that civilization was detrimental to women, his theories also justified reformers' claim that the home was the apotheosis of civilized life, and that civilization could be learned through changes in the home environment. In homes, not in the ability to own property or to vote, lay the key to progress — and making homes was women's work.

Morgan's theories bolstered moral imperatives with evolutionary science, seemingly proving Catharine Beecher's assertion in her 1841 *Treatise on Domestic Economy* that "as society gradually shakes off the remnants of barbarism, and the intellectual and moral interests of man rise, in estimation, above the merely sensual, a truer estimate is formed of woman's duties, and of the measure of intellect requisite for the proper discharge of them."[20] White, middle-class women reformers interested in assimilating Native Americans seized the idea that a civilized home was one in which women were the moral authorities. They downplayed the patriarchal control of property that the IRA and anthropologists saw as central, envisioning woman-centered homes. Without criticizing the family as an institution, these reformers suggested that it was less male ownership of the property than female direction of and influence on it that would ensure Native American progress.[21]

Seeing Is Believing

In 1885 Philip and Minnie Stabler, both "thoroughly honest, trustworthy, and industrious persons," erected a modest frame house near Bancroft, Nebraska. Having assured his creditors of his character and motives, Philip secured a loan and gathered estimates from various lumber dealers in the area. He modified his house plan to fit his budget and engaged a carpenter to help him build the house; the two men completed the structure in less than two weeks and for under $400. Philip insured his home against the calamities of fire, lightning, and tornadoes that plagued Nebraska settlers and went about working his farm in hopes of paying off the loan as quickly as possible.[22] In the meantime, Minnie Stabler received gifts of a cook stove and rocking chair and undertook the duties of a housewife in earnest.[23] She set aside the morning hours for her own education, and in the afternoon she worked at cooking, washing, ironing, sewing, and cleaning. She owned a sewing machine, and she prided herself on her three-year-old son's articulateness. On Sunday evenings Minnie and Philip hosted prayer meetings at their home.[24]

Funds for the Stabler cottage were provided by the Connecticut branch of the WNIA, which noted that just two years earlier, Philip had been "a 'wild, blanket Indian,' roaming over the prairies, sleeping in a tent and hunting buffalo for a livelihood."[25] The WNIA believed that Stabler's decision to give up his tent in favor of a permanent home signified his desire to revoke his "savage" ways and live "like white men." Just as important, however, was the WNIA's conviction that the home itself would function as an architectural catalyst for social progress on the Omaha reservation. The national leadership of the WNIA praised "those civilized Christian Indians who now at various points are planting among their red brothers model Christian homes with the purpose of making the latter centers of civilization, object lessons of instruction and inspiration, and beacon-lights of hope to those more needy than themselves."[26]

The potential of the home to function as a metonym for the cultural ideals of civilization was not lost on Alice Fletcher. In 1881 the Stablers, with Omahas Noah and Lucy La Flesche, came to the Hampton Institute at Fletcher's instigation.[27] Fletcher was convinced that model homes could function as educational tools for young couples, and she raised $400 for materials with which Philip and Noah would construct the "Omaha Cottages" that were raised behind the women's lodge at Hampton.[28] The *Southern Workman* reported that the houses "furnish an effective object lesson to the students, and teach them how comfortable and attractive a house can be got up at small expense. At the same time they also give such an insight into true housekeeping, as cannot fail to do good."[29] The houses were furnished with upholstered wooden boxes that served as "miniature sofas; corner shelves answer for a what-not, while a wardrobe and wash-stand have been manufactured out of a few boards and draperies of coarse burlap, trimmed with maroon cotton flannel." The La Flesches' house was adorned with "some strips of red carpeting, gay Christmas cards tastefully arranged on the walls, and a few plants near the window," all of which made "the wee house look very inviting."[30] Clearly, Hampton instructors believed in the civilizing power of domestic objects, an effect that Lori Merish calls a "feminine proprietary relation" that refines and comforts even as it signals productivity and the containment of brutish desires.[31] Indeed, educators at Hampton anticipated effects far in excess of the dimensions of the cottage; one staff member wrote of hopes that the home's "light will shine far off into many a crowded cabin and comfortless teepee, and transform them likewise into pure, sweet, Christian homes."[32]

At the second Lake Mohonk Conference for Friends of the Indian in 1884, Fletcher promoted the Omaha Cottages as security against returned students "going back to the blanket," arguing that students should be encouraged to make their abodes "centres of civilization" at home.[33] Sara T. Kinney, leader of the Connecticut auxiliary of the WNIA, was present at the meeting and was deeply affected by Fletcher's proposal that cottages could function as object lessons. At the WNIA's annual conference in 1889, Kinney, now head of the Home Building and Loan Committee, remembered Fletcher's Lake Mohonk speech as "a really wise, practical plan by which Indians might be helped to help themselves . . . based upon the fact that the organization of the Indian tribe, is such as to make of prime importance, the rearing of homes in the midst of the people." Kinney enthusiastically incorporated social evolutionism's terminology to create a new image of the home as an anthropological object lesson in which "home conveys to us the picture of one roof sheltering father and mother, and their children, secure in the sharing and inheritance of the property resulting from the toil of the family." Tribal relations, she explained, could "only be broken by giving to the members of the tribe individual ownership of land and homes. . . . Wherever this has been done by allotting land in severalty, the grip of the 'tribal relation' has been loosened, and the way opened for the founding of the family and the upbuilding of the home."[34]

WNIA reformers repeatedly stressed the visual power of model homes on reservations. They referred to such dwellings as "beacon-lights" and "centers of civilization," emphasizing that every home built on a reservation would create a domino effect by influencing the behavior of reservation inhabitants. In 1893 the new leader of the Home Building and Loan Committee, Philadelphian Mrs. E. P. Gould, declared that "the picture of this unpretentious home with its plain but civilized furnishings is familiar to you all. There is no need I think to speak to this audience of Christian mothers and sisters of the elevating influences that must necessarily emanate from every one of these object lessons that we can possibly put before our Indian friends. Seeing is believing, and one such home, it seems to me, is worth more than volumes of instruction setting forth how the white man makes his home."[35] The almost mystical power that Gould ascribed to the home suggests that domesticity was less effort than emanation and could be transmitted best by way of exhibition.

The nineteenth-century exposition provided a site where the anthropological order of nation and world might reach the hearts and minds of the popu-

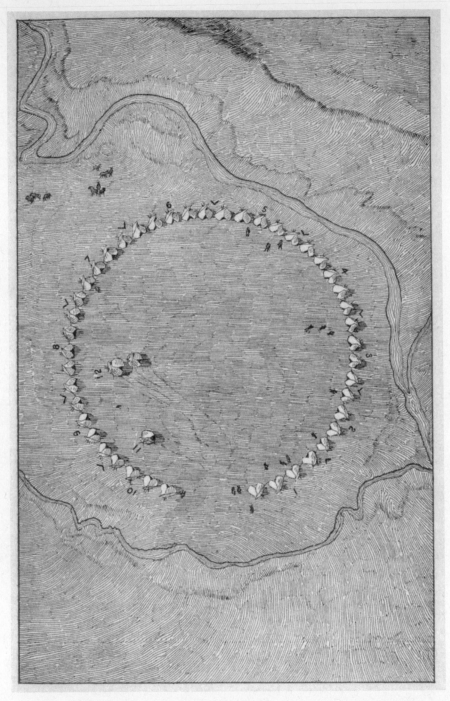

Figure 3.1. F. W. Miller, drawing of an Omaha tribal circle. 1885. From Fletcher, *Historical Sketch of the Omaha Tribe*. Reproduced by Library of Congress.

Figure 3.2. F. W. Miller, "Village of the Make-Believe White Men." 1885. Drawing after a sketch by an Omaha man. From Fletcher, *Historical Sketch of the Omaha Tribe*. Reproduced by Library of Congress.

lace; Gould noted that the "picture" of home was already firmly embedded in the hearts and minds of women nationwide. Alice Fletcher's anthropological exhibit on Native American assimilation at the 1885 New Orleans Cotton and Industrial Exposition played on this vivid picture, shrewdly translating scientific study into popular form through photography. As an ethnologist, Fletcher respected the traditions and lifeways of the Omahas. Yet her exhibit clearly indicated that these traditions were untenable in contemporary society; it focused on the deterioration of the Omahas' traditional domestic life and the evolutionary possibilities that allotment offered. Sixteen photographs, two drawings, and a map depicted the transformations that resulted from the Omaha Severalty Act of 1882.[36] Her display of benign, everyday activities and structures depicted home building in a before-and-after sequence that linked land use, labor, and gender relations through the iconography of domestic architecture.

Two images in particular illustrate the transformation in housing that Fletcher hoped would bring the Omaha people into civil society. One (fig. 3.1) depicts a one-dimensional, bird's-eye view of a traditional Omaha tribal circle. Rather than each tent appearing to be a discrete, individual home, the teepees, seen from above, form a unified circular design. A second image (fig. 3.2) shows

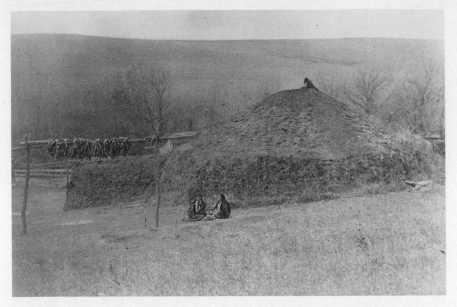

Figure 3.3. Omaha sod dwelling. Photograph by Mr. Hamilton of Sioux City, Iowa, for Alice Fletcher, 1885. Courtesy President and Fellows of Harvard College Peabody Museum, Harvard University.

a reproduction of a sketch an Omaha man made for Fletcher and represents a new Omaha village, complete with cottages, roads, and a steamboat landing. In contrast to the bird's-eye view, this image has dimensionality and is dominated not by one large circle but by a number of squares in the form of cottages and garden plots. Houses are numbered and labeled to indicate private ownership, and roads lead someplace — to the mission, the agency, or village shops. This transformation, the exhibit implied, would include positive changes for women. Another image (fig. 3.3) depicts two women in traditional dress working in front of an Omaha earth lodge, a dwelling that, in its resemblance to the landscape itself, would hardly have been recognizable to audiences as a home.

The final image in Fletcher's 1885 photographic display shows a young Omaha woman and her son in a tiny cottage (fig. 3.4). The woman is probably Minnie Stabler, and the house is one of the diminutive Omaha Cottages erected on the Hampton school grounds. In contrast to the image of the sod house, clean lines define this home. Unlike the photograph of two women working in front of the earth lodge, this picture elevates the familial and domestic roles of women over their labor. While fairgoers would have seen the earth lodge photograph as evidence of native women's drudgery, the image of the Omaha Cottage stresses that this woman's place is within her home, directing the activities of her son,

Figure 3.4. Omaha Cottage at Hampton Institute. 1885. From Fletcher, *Historical Sketch of the Omaha Tribe*. Reproduced by Library of Congress.

who is poised at the doorway as if to enter his new role as an assimilated man. Relegated to the interior but looking directly at the audience, Minnie Stabler embodies the understated authority of the middle-class Victorian wife. Her husband, Philip, is absent from the image.

By emphasizing domesticity in these "after" scenes, Fletcher successfully played on the sympathies of fairgoers, who could now read the signs of evolutionary progress as confirmation of familiar and even sentimental ideas. The display showcased ownership of private property, the productive labor of men, and the roles of women as housekeepers and children's caretakers. Translating abstract scientific principles into potent images that culminated in the triumph of domestic life, Fletcher bridged the gap between government policy and a world order legitimated by its conformity to beliefs in the sanctity of home, family, and moral womanhood.

Fletcher's translation of social evolution into a home-centered narrative allowed Sara Kinney to claim social power on behalf of middle-class women as custodians of the household, and she began to organize support for the assimilation effort by raising funds to erect model homes for Native Americans. In 1885, based on the Stablers' success, the WNIA voted to accept the Home Building and Loan Committee as a permanent department of its work. The group connected its own activities to the work of legislators pressing for reform in Washington, arguing that "all the success of this work for freeing, elevating, and Christianizing our native American Indians, . . . promises to be permanent because to be based upon the creation of the Indian home."[37] In its first years the department was extremely successful. State auxiliaries as well as individuals clamored to finance cottages and loans to native couples; in 1888 the department's funds exceeded $2,000 and meted out over $1,600 in loans.[38] Reformers lauded this effort at "colonizing young couples in congenial communities of their own, apart from degenerating influences."[39]

Three years after the Home Building and Loan Department was established and a year after the Dawes Act was passed, the WNIA leadership attributed the success of home building to its appeal to the "hearts and sympathies" of local members.[40] Kinney and the organization's national president, Amelia Stone Quinton, called on rank-and-file WNIA members to envision themselves, their homes, and their domestic work as crucial rungs on the evolutionary ladder, rather than as part of the restricted space that Morgan had regretfully conceded to be a byproduct of progress. As Quinton traveled the states giving speeches, raising funds, and helping to found local branches during her long tenure as president, she paid little heed to cultural differences among tribes as diverse as the swamp-dwelling Seminoles of Florida, the southwestern Pueblos, and the mission Indians of California whose social systems, work patterns, and habitations responded to different geographical situations and beliefs. For Quinton, the route to civilization was the same everywhere, and the path lay directly through the Native American home: "The work which is being done in the homes among the women and children, is that which will lead the tribe in the shortest way to civilization. . . . In our women's work we are striking at the very root of things."[41] A teacher at the Santee mission school expressed similar sentiments about the value of women's work: "When you get a woman to understand that it is her highest duty in this world to take care of her family and home in a Christian and intelligent manner, you have got near the heart of the matter."[42]

By 1900 Quinton could celebrate the end of what government critic Helen Hunt Jackson called the "century of dishonor" by attributing the success of the assimilation mission to the tireless practical and spiritual efforts of Euro-American women.[43] Linking Christian duty, democracy, and womanhood, she replaced histories centered on legislation, the military, and property with one that vested authority in the inspiration and activism of women: "The land in severalty idea was one of President Madison's, we are told, and of others all along the years; but it was also from a divine inspiration that the women's association, first as a society, planned and began a popular appeal and combined movement to secure it. . . . Ideas have wings, and they nest in minds and hearts;

and what a singing of birds follows in the fullness of time!"[44] Quinton suggested that while men had wrangled violently for centuries over land, the conversion of the Indian question into a domestic subject, a matter of "minds and hearts," was accomplished by women who transformed a political problem into a movement with "popular appeal." The exhibitionary complex lay at the heart of the movement. As president of the WNIA, Quinton promoted the physical structure of home as an object lesson, a metonym for civilization that would at once mobilize the support of middle-class women and serve as an educational tool for Native American women who would create new "nests" in which to lodge the ideals of civilized culture.[45]

Working for Progress

The WNIA and its mission workers constantly referred to their efforts to exhibit the tenets of civilization as "work" and "labor." Alice Fletcher, in particular, stressed that making assimilation a practical reality would take a tremendous amount of effort by women working in the field. Moreover, much of the burden of making these nests took labor on the part of Native American women, and this burden created a divide between the exhibitionary quality of "women's work for women" that the WNIA leaders celebrated and the day-to-day labor of housework. The location of Fletcher's Omaha Cottages on the grounds of the Hampton Institute suggests that model homes, as object lessons, were aimed at ordering the nation's subjects through a structure that was, like the school itself, dedicated to producing workers. Reformers' plans for native girls clearly articulated the exhibitionary complex's potential for organizing individuals as workers. The process of civilization was contingent not only on their seeing and believing but on their working and producing. Model homes were meant to reproduce the educational structures that encouraged Indian schoolgirls to be industrious domestic engineers.

A crucial part of the Dawes Act's plan to "set [Indians] coveting Christian homes instead of a tent" was to send children to schools where they would learn "the trades and employments of civilized life, and then send them back to their homes."[46] Indian school administrators believed that the order that the industrialized world was built on necessitated an equally orderly environment. Students who entered Indian schools found themselves confronted with a new architecture that stressed straight lines and rectilinear order rather than the circular forms that often structured life at home. Students underwent a transformation in physical space much like that illustrated in Fletcher's photographs: from the circular layout of the teepee and earth lodge to the square lines of the schools. The schools often featured rectangular malls with orderly plantings surrounded by buildings in straight lines. Classrooms, dormitories, and dining rooms were dominated by rows — of desks, beds, and chairs. David Wallace Adams notes that like the lessons students learned in class, the ultimate lesson of the schools' architecture and landscape was that "in the interest of symmetry and order, the wild must be tamed, just as the Indian must be civilized."[47]

Educators also believed that ritualized learning, routinized labor, and close monitoring of behavior were the best methods for ridding students of their old ways. Students were forbidden to speak their native languages or to engage in traditional religious practices. While schools claimed to create a "homelike" environment that would replace the homes from which the students came, they not only upheld a social order that valorized Euro-American ways of life but stressed work as the best method of training students. Students spent half the day in school and half the day in industries such as carpentry, agriculture, and smithing for boys and cooking, sewing, and laundry for girls — labor that kept the schools running. While schools offered literacy and economic power to Native Americans and promised to incorporate them into American society as equals, many students were channeled into trades and domestic industries that were not only economically devalued but difficult to find on reservations, where few such opportunities existed. The skills students learned at schools were not necessarily those that were needed in their homelands.[48]

Yet proponents of home building surmised that if just a few young men and women created these exhibits of culture on reservations, this group would become leaven to the rest. Both the *Indian's Friend* and the *Southern Workman* enthusiastically reported such incidences of leavening, especially among students who had returned from school to make their homes into object lessons. Reformers relied particularly on girls to effect this transformation. Girls, they argued, needed to be educated along with boys, in order that they might display "a gleam of enlightened Christian sentiment . . . in the Indian home." If girls learned domestic arts, such as knitting, sewing dresses, making frames for pictures, and otherwise decorating the home, they would influence the whole family, for it would "make their homes better, and more permanent, besides preventing much gadding about and gossip, by keeping young mothers at home and industrially employed."[49] The project would also prevent transience in the tribe and keep these girls from becoming the sharp-tongued gossips their mothers seemed to be. Implicit in this condemnation of gossip and transience is the suggestion that isolating women in their homes would keep them from speaking out in tribal councils, preserving rituals and stories, and maintaining kinship ties.

Teachers impressed on girls the importance of performing domesticity as a component of home ownership; they also impressed on both boys and girls the importance of domestic labor to civic identity. At annual performances held at Hampton on the anniversary of the Dawes Act (which instructors there heralded as the Indians' own Emancipation Day), students displayed, through the performance of home-building and homemaking activities, the values of the nation into which they were being assimilated. The boys at Hampton celebrated the second anniversary of the Dawes Act by miming at building as they sang the "Carpenters' and Painters' Song":

> I am building me a house and I pound, pound pound
> Brush, brush, brush, now I'll paint it all so fine;
> Brush, brush, brush, for this handsome house is mine.

The girls, acting out the motions of washing clothes, sang the "Laundresses' Song":

> When our work is done,
> They'll be clean and smooth and white.
> A civilizing power is the laundress with her tub;
> We are cleaning more than clothes, as we rub, rub, rub.[50]

These lyrics were crucial to the racial implications of the exhibitionary complex as it was instituted at schools that were invested in "cleaning more than clothes." At a sweep, the lyrics link domestic industry and its companion values of cleanliness and cheerful labor with civilization and, most noticeably, whiteness. The domestic values to which girls at school were exposed each day and that they were expected to exhibit at home were explicitly associated with whiteness and were meant to "rub away" all traces of native culture. The songs suggest that native girls' access to civilization, symbolized by whiteness, would come as they literally worked their way up the ladder of progress; doing laundry afforded girls "civilizing power." Through their domestic labor, the songs assert, women would be producing not just homes but an ideology of civilization that required the subordination of their tribal identities.

In her 1891 novella *Stiya: A Carlisle Indian Girl at Home*, Marianna Burgess, a white instructor of printing at Carlisle, elaborated on the uses of the architectural object lesson in stimulating work.[51] The story, written from the point of view of a returned Pueblo student, was first published in 1889 in the Carlisle

School's newsletter, the *Indian Helper*, and was later published, together with eight "strange pictures of real life among the Pueblos," by Houghton Mifflin and sold to the school's patrons.[52] Designed for distribution to Carlisle students who returned home, it was meant, as Native American writer Leslie Marmon Silko has asserted, to "'inoculate' them against their 'uncivilized' families and communities."[53] *Stiya* explains how one girl's exposure to Carlisle's cleanliness, careful attention to personal appearance, and pious Christianity stimulated the cycle of civilization at home. After returning to her pueblo, Stiya compares her parents' home and her mother's work with the methods of housekeeping she learned at Carlisle. Disgusted by her mother's cooking and washing, Stiya vows to continue keeping herself and her house as tidy as she did at Carlisle. When she and her family are stripped, beaten, and locked in a room for refusing, at her urging, to attend a village festival, Stiya gains strength from thinking of Carlisle: "In the midst of the fearful agony and excitement, thoughts of dear Carlisle came to me, — my duties in the school-room, in the dining-hall, in the laundry, in the cooking-class, in the sewing-room, in the quarters, — the whole beautiful picture of sweet content on the faces of the boys and girls, as they went their daily rounds, loomed up before me and gave me courage."[54] Suffering scorn and humiliation in front of her village, Stiya is comforted by the memory of Carlisle's systematic architecture — its rooms segregated for various purposes — and of highly regulated tasks, of "daily rounds" and "duties." *Stiya* suggests that pueblo life is barbarous and its political systems tyrannical; the story offers as its replacement a commitment to routinized labor governed by architectural order. Stiya's incarceration in the pueblo's prison causes her to entrench herself in self-discipline; her memories of Carlisle's organizing principles steel her to face the trials ahead.

The book details Stiya's attempts to re-create, as best she can, the architectural and behavioral model of Carlisle. Loath to sleep on the floor with her parents, Stiya uses money earned from her "outing" work at Carlisle to purchase chairs and a bedstead. She also buys a washtub and board, flat irons, a dishpan, dishes, cutlery, and a suit of "white man's" clothes for her father.[55] Stiya's dedication to her new civilized lifestyle and the architecture that literally supports it eventually causes her father to change his ways. To build a frame home for his Carlisle daughter, her father finds a job shoveling coal at the train station. Stiya works for the storekeeper's family in order to purchase furniture for her new home.[56] Thus, Stiya's simple desire to escape her pueblo and create a model home of her own stimulates a new cycle of civilization at home and brings her father into the same habits of industry that she has embraced. Her commitment to routine results directly in her father's proletarianization.[57]

Figure 3.5. *Indian School, Carlisle, Pa.* 1891. Illustration from Burgess, *Stiya*. Reproduced by Cumberland County Historical Society, Carlisle, Pa.

Stiya is so intent on reproducing Carlisle's architecture that she decorates her new home with pictures of the institution; her incorporation of Carlisle's visual order into her domestic space exemplifies the exhibitionary complex at work. Stiya reassembles Carlisle's architectural order as part of her own home's interior, affirming her allegiance to the ordered spaces of the school and thus making her home an extension of its cultural order as well. Bennett describes the "exhibitionary environment" as one that incorporates the "display of things" into "supra-national constructs" that reproduce a social evolutionary racial order.[58] Burgess cleverly prepared the book to be a material artifact to be incorporated into the domestic and evolutionary order that she described, since the final page is a photograph of Carlisle, showing its white frame buildings surrounding a grassy, tree-studded quadrangle (fig. 3.5). Its straight lines emphasize both perspective and order, inviting the viewer to enter the image — and the very heart of Carlisle's civilizing space. Burgess supplied her readers with the image that Stiya displayed in her home as an example of the architectural and industrial order of civilization, and she invited student-readers to display it in their homes as well.[59]

The closing image of Carlisle echoes an image of Carlisle's refined and pious product: opposite the title page is a photograph titled *Stiya* that depicts a Native American woman in a dark, high-necked dress (fig. 3.6).[60] She stands stiffly

Figure 3.6. *Stiya, Carlisle Indian Girl.* 1891. Illustration from Burgess, *Stiya.* Reproduced by Cumberland County Historical Society, Carlisle, Pa.

behind a chair, her hair is pulled back, and she wears a small cross around her neck. The photograph of Stiya provides a model of womanhood analogous to the architectural model represented by the image of Carlisle. Like the campus, she embodies an orderly and carefully constructed cultural ideal. Interspersed in the text are six other photographs; these are of traditional pueblo life and people, including an image of a sun dance, children, and pueblo women at work. Thus the woman and the architecture that produced her emerge as images that physically contain their less civilized counterparts within a narrative of evolutionary progress codified as the reproduction of civilized domestic models. No longer a Pueblo, Stiya is now a "Carlisle Indian Girl" — still clearly an Indian but also clearly a product of a new culture and an exhibit herself.

Though she carefully re-creates Carlisle's order on the reservation, Stiya never gains the professional status that her teachers acquired by doing the same work. By assimilating as workers within the community outside the pueblo, Stiya and her father simply exchange racial difference for class difference. The domestic ideology she absorbed from her Carlisle teachers upholds a class ideology that not only supports local business but bolsters the professional status of her teachers. At the end of the story, Stiya's accomplishment as a homemaker is sanctified by the arrival of two Carlisle teachers who "came out to New Mexico upon business for the school." The teachers stay in her home, sleep in her bed, eat her bread and pie, and admire the pictures of Carlisle that ornament the walls.[61] The exhibition of self and home that Stiya presents constituted their "business" in two ways. First, observation of Stiya's labors was part of the teachers' work in New Mexico, for school authorities regularly journeyed west to check on returned students and to scout for prospective pupils. Second, Stiya's work confirmed the teachers' professional legitimacy. By adhering to the precepts of Euro-American life, Stiya represented the continuing influence of lessons that translated the exhibitionary complex into a way of ordering potential laborers.

Resistance at Home

Burgess's novella implies that white women's professional sensibilities were shaped by images of Indian women. The photo of Stiya as a "New (Indian) Woman" on the frontispiece, followed by the image of Carlisle, where Burgess herself worked, confirmed the growing sense that middle-class white women had of themselves as participants in the work of social uplift. White women reformers found in model homes, and in the laboring bodies of Native American women, the structure of a professional identity founded on the twinned efforts of managing others while exhibiting self. Photographs of Pueblo life that Burgess included in the book suggest another important component to this self-fashioning, for middle-class white women promoted, exhibited, sold, and purchased native women's arts and crafts as part of their crusade to promote progress. Increasingly, the WNIA associated progress with wage labor, as students were taught that producing arts and crafts for sale was as crucial to supporting their families as housework. The work that white women did for the government and their encouragement of "traditional" arts and crafts facilitated their own goals for public recognition on the national scene while they engaged in uplifting indigenous women.

By the mid-1890s, reformers were realizing that the influence stimulated by home building and education was failing on reservations. In spite of increasing numbers of government-built log and frame homes, people clung to traditional domestic patterns and community rituals. They pitched their wickiups in their new yards and left their allotments for summer camps according to traditional cycles.[62] On the Omaha reservation, which had given Fletcher and the WNIA so much hope, women continued to decorate their faces and bodies, and men adorned their hair. Marriages were still conducted in the old way, and extended kin groups resided together in the new homes as they did in the old, often organizing the items in the house just as they did in the lodge, placing their possessions around the walls. People wore "white" dress but slept in their clothes. Women were anxious to own sewing machines, and men wanted to drive buggies; but rather than spending their time farming, according to a report, the Omahas continued to "group together and talk of neighborhood news." Although allotment on separate and often distant homesteads made communication more difficult, oral culture persisted. The Omahas now used lumber and shingles, but they continued to build structures for traditional activities and even, in the case of one "Fire Chief Lodge," in traditional form. In an attempt to approximate the earth lodge, the Omahas had built an octagonal wooden building.[63] Even the drawing of an Omaha town that Fletcher had displayed in 1885 bore the mark of native skepticism; her informer called it "Village of the Make-Believe White Men." All signs suggested that tribes were adopting the new architectures but not the ideology it symbolized.

A law passed in 1891 facilitated the resistance of Native Americans to assimilation and contributed to their poverty. Congress approved leasing of tribal lands and any allotments owned by persons unable to farm them due to "age or other disability." In 1894 the government changed the terms to read that anyone who had an "inability" to work the land could lease, a change that left women particularly vulnerable, for their gender alone could render them "unable" in the eyes of the law.[64] The number of leases approved by the Commissioner of Indian Affairs skyrocketed, from 6 between 1887 and 1894 to 2,500 by 1900.[65] Fletcher had argued early on that not all people would want to work the land, as Indians, like whites, aspired to different kinds of employment. But more often than not, the people leased their lands to eager white settlers and lived in ways that allowed them to continue their cultural traditions but cost them land and resources. In 1894, 223 leases were approved on the Winnebago and Omaha reservations; by 1900, more than 500 farming and grazing contracts allowed white farmers to take over acres of Omaha and Winnebago lands, often by bilking their holders out of allotments.[66] As the number of leases grew, the number of home-building loans that the WNIA gave out began to falter; in 1899, the Home Building and Loan Department failed to find any qualified applicants, and in 1900 no one applied. The group began to redirect home building funds to home industries, and soon the department was abolished.[67]

The demise of the home-building department cannot be attributed to leasing alone, for Native Americans continued to build homes. Schooling, allotment, and the continuing strength of indigenous cultures show that leasing was just part of larger patterns of change that indicate that individuals selectively adopted Euro-American ideals and that new and old patterns were difficult to maintain in the face of change and conflict. The fates of Philip and Minnie Stabler and Noah and Lucy La Flesche, who received WNIA home-building loans in 1885, are emblematic. Omaha Rosalie Farley was an unofficial agent in the business transactions between the Stablers and the WNIA, advising both Philip and Minnie and keeping accounts for the WNIA. Rosalie and her husband, Ed Farley, continued to help the Stablers, but their role on the reservation became increasingly conflicted as land-leasing disputes split the tribe. Philip passed away in 1894, after which Minnie leased out the Connecticut cottage and eventually sold some land.[68] The La Flesches managed to maintain financial security, farming and leasing out some land, while still participating in traditional patterns of kinship exchange and in a group that kept alive tribal songs and dances. An 1895 report noted that the La Flesches had rented out their cottage and were living elsewhere. Later reports held that a white man was working the land and that Noah had sold most of his allotment.[69]

Changes wrought by allotment made some traditional practices more difficult to maintain; as Fletcher had suspected, women suffered from weakened kinship ties and losses of social power due to their changing work roles. Susan La Flesche, whose education as a doctor was financed by the WNIA, had a WNIA-sponsored office on the reservation (to be "object lesson" and "in every sense a home") from which she conducted her practice. Her professional life was rhetorically domesticated by the WNIA as "a home for the sick and careworn women and children of her tribe."[70] In 1892 La Flesche wrote an article for the *Indian's Friend* titled "The Home-Life of the Indian." She stated that in spite of her own efforts, "the home life of the Indian of to-day is essentially the same as the home life of the Indian thirty years ago." She noted that while the people lived in frame houses rather than teepees and farmed rather than hunted, the "internal workings" of the home had not changed. Her story was a curious blend of praise and criticism, for she looked back fondly on the earth lodges she knew as a girl, where she used to play on the grass-covered roofs, where stories were told by elders, and where dances and councils were held. In nodding to the WNIA and their home-building efforts, she recognized that positive environmental changes had taken place since the cottages were built. At the same time, she criticized the home cure as superficial, noting that whether a family lived in a teepee, a sod house, or a frame home, the life inside was the same because the Omahas remained in poverty. Moreover, the women of the tribe had lost social power, for "the houses on the reservation are far apart and the women cannot very well pass away the time by gossip with the neighbors as some of our white friends have the *privilege* of doing." She argued that though the women stood more equally with their husbands than they did in the past, the change had been incomplete.[71] Native women were falling victim to the same devaluation of domestic labor and its attendant spatial separation of home and work that plagued white homemakers. In the capitalist economy that took little heed of women's domestic labor, the women had lost as much as they had gained by becoming the moral guardians of their homes.

While La Flesche criticized the system that advised a visual and architectural solution to deep economic disparities, the persistence of traditional culture among Native Americans served to reinforce growing sentiments among reformers and the general population that Indians were simply less civilized than whites. Reformers retrenched themselves in paternalistic and maternalistic ideas that portrayed natives as unruly children needing to be led forward into the light of legal personhood. The WNIA despaired over the damage to homes that selling and leasing Indian lands caused. Letters and articles in the *Indian's Friend* relate the literal destruction of homes due to leasing. Field matron Helen Tompkin reported that Michigan Indians were being defrauded of their homes and lands due to their inability to understand or read legal papers. She described visiting a woman in dire straits who told her, "'A white man keeps coming here and telling us that he has bought the place and we must move off. I cannot sleep nights for fear of losing our home.'" Native American women who embraced the new methods of housekeeping in hopes of keeping their lands were thwarted by the legal and economic realities of reservation life. Fieldworkers found their own work frustrated by these same circumstances, for it was difficult to exhibit domesticity on reservations where home ownership was so tenuous. Referring to her duties, Tompkin concluded, "There was not much opportunity here to 'adorn the house with rugs and pictures.'"[72] There was little comfort in a chromolithograph hung on the wall when the homes themselves were in danger of slipping away.

Regular and Systematic Work

Tompkin's telltale quotation marks around one of her official tasks reveal the irony of domestic performance in spaces where a tasteful home was little protection against the powers of speculators and politicians maneuvering for possession of Indian lands. Nonetheless, this was the official duty of the field matron, according to the program that started with one position in 1891: creating Anglo-American domestic order in places that had none.[73] An article that originally appeared in the *Philadelphia Ledger* and was reprinted in the *Indian's Friend* contained a list of duties comprised of complete care of the house (including, as Tompkin so ironically noted, "adorning the home with pictures, curtains, home-made rugs, flowers, grass plots and trees"), yard, fences, and animals, as well as the supervision of games and sports and religious observances and the organization of social and educational societies. It was, according to the article, a full-time job, and one for which the salary was so low that "the field matron cannot always procure the little house of her own, and the horse for making her visits."[74] Indeed, the $720 yearly salary approved in the Indian Appropriations Act for 1891 allotted no funds for anything but wages.[75] To combat the lack of financial support or official regard for this work, the WNIA offered its aid in constructing homes for matrons. In addition, the organization, which already employed several matrons on its own missions, hoped to influence the Department of the Interior to employ WNIA matrons as official government agents when that position became part of the Civil Service in 1896. Just as the Home Building and Loan Department began its decline, then, the WNIA began to bolster its support for field matrons and their homes.

While the duties of a field matron could be daunting, the rewards, according to the *Indian's Friend*, could be great indeed. The office could offer to "a simple, plain, honest woman" an opportunity to be "a powerful civilizing influence in all her neighborhood."[76] When the domestic duties were transplanted from everyday life to a location in which domestic work was the object of attention on all sides, a white woman could suddenly become "powerful," exerting a tangible influence on the people and landscape around her. The WNIA determined that white women were needed on all reservations; they and their homes, not necessarily the native people themselves, must be catalysts for change. The field matron became an institution in the symbolic force of her domestic womanhood and the government-sanctioned civilization policies that she represented. The field matron was not only to be an example of domestic womanhood but a skilled professional.

The Bureau of Indian Affairs instituted the field matron program, in part, at the behest of the WNIA, which sought professional legitimacy for women working in the field. The field matron program was part of a wider late nineteenth-century movement that brought middle-class women into newly created professional fields first cultivated by charitable work. College-educated women trained in social work and home economics, in particular, helped to turn domestic labor — cooking, cleaning, and child care — into work that, practitioners believed, demanded more than just the "natural" qualities of womanhood. Theirs was a domesticity infused with scientific credibility. Social science and domestic economics programs applied chemistry, medicine, architectural science, anthropology, sociology, and nutrition to attempt to rectify some of the problems facing, in particular, the working and immigrant classes.[77]

Many of these new professionals were particularly concerned with the spatial design and technology of the home. These women — whom Dolores Hayden has called material feminists — often departed from moral arguments about women's worth to society in favor of claims that rooted the power and influence of women in their material conditions: their control over household space, their access to wages and property, and their physical and economic integration into public life.[78] Material feminists believed that social evolution could be prompted by environmental change, and that bettering the condition of women would effect a more civilized society.[79] At the heart of their crusades for social change was a reinterpretation of women's roles. They claimed that rather than a source of moral uplift, housework was difficult labor performed by often uninformed, ill-prepared, and underpaid women in restrictive environments. As more and more immigrants arrived in the United States toward the end of the century, the problem intensified. Settlement houses, most famously Jane Addams's Hull-House, began to provide cooperative living for women attempting to balance domestic life with self-sufficient living. Hull-House and its descendants not only addressed the housing and child care needs of working women; they provided classes and events that helped to educate women about health issues, labor reform, and the arts.

Model homes and domestic training were part of reform efforts directed at the working classes. The Freedmen's Bureau stressed the purchase and care of consumer goods for the home in order to promote a work ethic among black men and women and to encourage marriage and family feeling. Early model homes for blacks in the Reconstruction Era were meant to curb the bad habits that reformers believed had been cultivated during slavery.[80] Because African Americans, unlike Indians, were already regarded as hard workers (reformers believed that many black women financially supported their husbands), homes and housework were meant to instill in them a sense of the virtue of labor that was supposed to have been lost in slavery. Reformers also concentrated their efforts in urban areas. For example, Katherine Bement Davis directed the New York State Workingman's Model Home at the World's Columbian Exposition in 1893, showing how an Irish immigrant family could fill nutritional and household needs on a limited budget.[81] Candace Wheeler, a professional interior designer who directed the Applied Arts Division of the Woman's Building at the same world's fair, elaborated on Downing's ideas, asserting that "good surroundings are potent civilizers." Well into the twentieth century, housing reformers and settlement house workers were offering classes and model homes as methods of training immigrants in the care and maintenance of moral, sanitary homes. As Eileen Boris argues in her study of middle-class women's immigrant reform efforts, "These missionaries of the beautiful offered more than useful information to wage laborers and the immigrant poor. They presented the dominant culture through housekeeping courses and home decorating guides; they would Americanize by design."[82]

Field matrons and women who worked at Indian schools were part of this growing body of professional women. Though less well known than some of their urban, eastern counterparts, teachers and missionaries to Native Americans shared some of the same core values. Teachers such as Elaine Goodale Eastman and Cora Folsom and fieldworkers like Grace Howard, Julia French, Sibyl Carter, and Mary Dissette shared a generally feminist vision in that they believed that the bonds of womanhood united them with their native sisters and called them to use their femininity to train other women in the domestic arts. More so than the generation of wealthy clubwomen who founded the WNIA, who were largely involved in charity work, these professional women were keen on the power that working for wages could offer to women who were, they often believed, degraded as a class. They were stimulated to work for Native American progress both by the social crisis on reservations and by their own desire for independence and authority. Like other professional women in developing fields, matrons carved out new areas of expertise for themselves that specifically focused on women and children. They depended on the support of the wealthy, as in the funds offered by the WNIA, but aimed ultimately for the legitimacy of a government post. And like those women who ministered to the poor in urban areas, field matrons and their patrons felt the need to educate rank-and-file women about problems on reservations in order to garner more widespread support.[83]

Though model homes for Indians predated slightly the early twentieth-century boom in model homes for city-dwellers, the field matron program developed concurrently with urban efforts to alleviate the condition of the working poor. But the situation field matrons found on the reservation was different in several ways. First, though field matrons were responsible for conducting activities similar to those at urban settlement houses, they were without the urban geography, resources, and cooperative opportunities that even settlement houses in the urban areas of the West offered. Field matrons were often isolated in pairs or even singly on reservations where medical care, playgrounds, and wage work opportunities for native women were rare or nonexistent. Second, field matrons were combating not only what they saw as domestic disorder and ignorance, but an entire cultural system that they believed to be far less advanced than their own. In spite of ongoing assimilation attempts, their clients held to older cultural patterns, such as migration, festival dances, and even polygamy, that field matrons believed to be deeply antithetical to domestic life. They were attempting to implement a domesticity that was forced upon Indians by government policy; they often faced a resistant clientele who had not always chosen to join the body politic. Finally, field matrons and Indian educators were rarely invited into the upper echelon of policymakers in the Indian Bureau. Policies that were developed to help women and children in cities were part of women's issues over which urban reformers could claim ultimate authority. The specific problems of indigenous women, however, seemed to remain first and foremost part of the Indian problem.[84]

Facing these obstacles, field matrons seized the power of domestic display on reservations, and thus exhibitionary theory was at the heart of the field matron program. Reformers genuinely believed that by simply seeing the accoutrements of civilized life, Native American women would be inspired to keep house in the Euro-American way. As the WNIA began to change its focus from the Indian home to the more centralized presence and influence of the matron, it extolled the power of the field matron to create order by awakening moral sentiments among the people around her: "[Her] home, so different from theirs, will be a forcible object lesson. To make it an effective one, the Indians must know that she whose home it is is their true and sympathetic friend in all pertaining to their best interests. Assured of this, they will come to her home to gain all the help, physical, mental, and moral, that a true friend can give. By sharing her home with the people, and occasionally sharing in their home life, very practical help may be given."[85] The need for a matron's influence to enter all spaces, both spiritual and physical, stressed a domestic reciprocity in which the matron, as a "friend," initiated sharing and visiting between her home and the homes of the people. The passage also hints, however, at the limits of reciprocity: she is "true friend" only in that which pertains to "their best interests" — what was practical, efficient, and moral by official standards. It was the field matron who was to determine those interests, and she could withhold or grant her loving friendship accordingly.

Grace Howard, working in North Dakota, took solace in the work that her Indian employees performed for her. Girls in her house sewed, cooked, swept, dusted, set the table, and did the washing and ironing. Men worked for her, too, haying, hauling timber, and working the fields. Howard's satisfaction was triple. The $30 she paid monthly to her workers went to the improvement of their own homes. Those who worked for her often stayed to hear Bible lessons, and some were baptized. But perhaps most satisfying to Howard was the sense of proprietorship and power she gained as a result of her ability to employ and influence her workers. "My home has a wide influence," she declared. Women made dresses on "my machine"; girls and boys she referred to as "mine" attended "my school." She stressed that while missions should employ Indian women, "a white matron should have charge." In spite of all trials, she argued, there was a great need for "regular and systematic work" such as her own.[86]

Though the exhibitionary complex suggests that civilization by systematic influence was as benign as moral influence, women like Howard were acutely aware that domesticating homes and bodies was arduous and did not occur by some more diffuse process of moral suasion. Julia French, a matron in Agua Caliente, California, seemed to mock the very notion of influence when she asked, "But what of the field matron? Sent into the open field, without a weapon, she is expected to carry with her some unseen influence by which all crooked things shall be made straight, and order and harmony brought out of the chaos of Indian wretchedness!"[87] Emphasizing that their duties constituted a form of work rather than feminized influence, matrons attempted to raise their status in the eyes of the government. Matrons seldom enjoyed the support of Indian agents and frequently suffered from lack of supplies. They lamented that moral progress itself was impossible to chart and quantify except by enumerating their own and native women's labors. Matrons could count how many homes they had visited and how many women had attended their sewing and cooking classes; they knew how many women had cleaned their homes, whitewashed their walls, or baked white bread. Yet such measurements were the only way to calculate moral change, and those calculations were not as easy as systematized forms of learning by seeing might suggest. Matrons often complained that they had attempted to teach women to sweep floors, yet the women had no floors; they were charged with teaching sewing classes and running Bible studies, yet the women often migrated away from mission homes as part of seasonal cycles. Helen Tompkin, working in Mount Pleasant, Michigan, laid bare the facts: "All these things ought to be done, but where is the material coming from? Actual suffering, hunger, nakedness and want of proper shelter meet me at every turn." After recounting a litany of disasters, as if to convince herself of her legitimacy, she added, "Last month I rode 490 miles, made eighty-eight calls, saw seventy-six families, and put in twenty-seven days' work of eight hours each."[88]

Like the household labor that white feminists illuminated, the realities of life on reservations defied the carefully scripted moral order that white women in the field were charged with upholding. Overtly, matrons celebrated their homes and the influence that their work had on reservations, but the subtext of many of their letters contains a lament similar to those of Iowa housewives and the domestic writers Jeanne Boydston has studied. With so much need on the reservation, so many daily visitors and duties, and the complications of intertribal politics, matrons sometimes were hard pressed to find time to cook, clean, sew, or finish the other responsibilities that were so necessary to their mission. The more chaos white women encountered on reservations, the more they stressed the need for financial support of the system they embodied. One woman wrote that "visiting among Indian families in their homes, seeing the abortive attempts to perform the necessary duties of home life, seeing the discouragements, and failures attending efforts to attain 'white people's ways' of living, impresses one more and more with the importance of industrial training, and domestic economy."[89]

Reformers pressed for more women to be appointed field matrons and for women to be appointed as official government inspectors of tribes and homes. One matron expressed her desire to work for the government rather than for a benevolent society, for "if employed by the government it would give me a backing and an influence which no society could give." She complained that white men anxious to buy up Indian lands had no reason to respect or listen to her when she protested their practices of duping people out of their property and homes. She hoped that if the settlers "knew I was employed by the government they would be induced to right these wrongs, fearing prosecution." The matron found that in order to promote domesticity, she needed to have the knowledge and authority of an agent, lest she have no homes in which to instruct. Her complaints hint at her knowledge that domestic labor held little in the way of legitimacy; thus her domestic imperatives shade into professional ones as she argues, "These Indians need some one to do their business for them. I could save them hundreds of dollars."[90]

Quite a Business Woman for the Indians

Increasingly, field matrons found a niche for themselves as managers of Native American women laborers. Not only did their homes encourage native women to create homes that reproduced the cultural values of civilization, but they also suggested that object lessons made space for two kinds of women workers: those whose superior domestic knowledge suited them to be managers and those who had less control over the products of their labor. Field matrons' cottages doubled as cottage industries, and the physical space of their homes was divided between living and working areas. Mary Eldridge, whose endeavors in New Mexico won her the designation "model matron" from the WNIA, received funds from the organization for the construction of a "small house" to accommodate a loom, a knitting machine, and sewing machines. There she would instruct Navajo women in producing the "famous Navajo blankets . . . thus introducing among the women for whom nothing has yet been done industries that may be extended to give self-support to those eager for it."[91] The idea that instructing Navajos to produce goods that they had made for years would bring them civilization by introducing "systematic work" and "regularity of living" did not seem incongruous to supporters of the enterprise. In fact, they believed that it was the industry itself that would uplift; wages would be a side benefit.

White women's support for cottage industries drew on a context that adapted international forms of uplift to a specifically national condition. Eileen Boris, in her study of the arts and crafts movement in the United States, has argued that middle-class women seized on the movement as a way to elevate women's traditional work — such as needlecraft, lace making, and weaving — to the status of independent artisanship.[92] The Woman's Building at the 1893 Chicago World's Fair, for example, displayed the arts and industries of women around the world and presented the revival of ancient arts and crafts as a sign of women's technical expertise. Several displays, those of lace making and its products in particular, exhibited industry as a method of uplifting the lower classes.[93] The exhibits at the Chicago fair suggest that promoting and managing others' labor was a crucial element of the conception that American women had of themselves as participants in the modernizing world. Just as feminists crusading for property rights had turned from unpaid domestic labor as a legitimate source of power in an industrializing society, white women reformers began to advocate paid employment for themselves and for indigenous women. Keeping house had not afforded white women economic and political clout, and they suggested that native women would be served best by focusing more of their energies on wage labor. Reformers also surmised that indigenous women were even more in need of financial independence, because they believed that the young women needed wages to escape their families, culture, and what reformers saw as the oppressive tribal environment. Yet native women were generally denied access to the professional roles that white women enjoyed and instead were encouraged to produce craftwork that could be sold for the "primitive" qualities that consumers desired.

Reformers' views of what kinds of crafts would capitalize on already existing forms of Indian women's work were often misinformed. The craft work that women were responsible for in tribal societies varied widely. Drawing on Euro-American traditions, reformers assumed that women produced useful goods for daily life — clothing, pottery, and baskets — while men produced items for ceremonial use. Reformers believed that by teaching women skills that would elevate them to the status of artisans, they were giving them new access to prestige and income. Yet work role divisions were not always so clear-cut in many indigenous societies; men made textiles, and women were involved in doing quillwork or painting for ritual and religious ceremonies. Moreover, some societies already had well-developed women's guilds or artisanal groups, and women sometimes received remuneration for the tasks that they did, as well as prestige within their tribes.[94] The industries reformers chose to foster among the women were a combination of those kinds of indigenous crafts that they associated with household products, such as weaving, basket making, beadwork, and pottery, and new domestic tasks such as lace making and quilting.

In categorizing Indian women's industries as a new phenomenon promoting self-improvement, white women workers transformed the idea of native women's labor into a symbol of women's economic and political progress — an idea to which they themselves subscribed through their work as uplifters. Margaret D. Jacobs's study of white women's participation in the arts and crafts movement among Pueblos in the first decades of the twentieth century found that white women who supported assimilation were less "concerned with reviving a 'traditional' and 'authentic' craft [than] with supplying the Pueblos with a viable means of making a living." The image of Indian women held by white women was shaped by the view white women had of themselves and by their own aspirations for professionalizing themselves by advancing through the ranks of government employment.[95]

For Sibyl Carter, who worked in Minnesota with Sioux, Oneida, and Ojibwa tribes, the image of Indian women as workers was concretely linked to her own professional identity. Her image of herself as a worker was marked by loss of the domestic space. "What is the difference between an Indian woman and me?" she demanded at the Lake Mohonk Conference for Friends of the Indian.

> I was brought up on a Louisiana plantation, and I had not the least idea that I was ever to be cut adrift. But the Civil War came, and the Northern soldiers burned down my home, and I lost my father and home on the same night. What happened? Christian women gathered round me, and got me a school to teach. I shall never forget the first money I received, sixty dollars a month, for teaching that public school in Chicago. I felt as rich as Vanderbilt. . . . I have had all the work I could do, and have always been able to pull up some other woman. For thirty years I have earned my own living, and am proud of it.[96]

Because Carter's home had been destroyed and she was forced to work for her living, she saw in the plight of Indian women a reflection of her own experience. Carter's tale begins with the destruction of the patriarchal, pastoral home of the slave South that catapulted her into a world of work, wages, and other women. Carter, who had lived in Chicago, might have been familiar with the progressive politics of that town, particularly the emerging philosophy of Addams and the settlement house movement. Hull-House addressed impoverished women's experiences with pragmatic solutions. Its brand of social justice espoused women's cultivation of themselves as workers and thus encouraged them to experience the dignity and self-fulfillment that labor offered. In 1894 Carter announced a credo that the WNIA would come to endorse as well: "Work is power. Work ought to be the foundation stone." Wage work, not the unstable home space, marked independence and participation in civil society.[97]

Lace making was Carter's chosen industry, and she endorsed it because it capitalized on indigenous women's skills in making beadwork and because it was a relatively inexpensive industry to start up. She also reported that making snow-white lace promoted cleanliness and good hygiene. Lace making literally and figuratively whitened her employees, for in order to produce clean lace, a woman needed to have clean hands; to have clean hands, she needed to have a clean house. Once again, labor is subsumed under the rhetoric of civilization that linked whiteness with progress. Carter presents Indian women's creation of clean, white lace as a marvel; in her case, however, it is less their class than their race that makes their ability to act white a sign of progress.

Carter stressed lacework as labor that, unlike some of women's other duties at home, created value appreciable on the market. Carter and other reformist women hoped that wage earning would lead to independence for all women as it had for themselves. "Let Indian women have all fair opportunities," the *Indian's Friend* pronounced, for "among Indians as among whites there are many women who must be the bread-winners of a family, and we rejoice at the growing opportunities of these to prepare themselves for honorable self-support. Among ourselves the number of women in business has more than quadrupled during the last ten years, and in New York City alone there are 100,000 self-supporting women."[98] The WNIA's journal used the language of professional empowerment to explain women's growing participation in the wage economy; like the wage labor of their urban counterparts, however, that of native women often arose out of need and led to a new kind of dependency in the marketplace.

The value of Carter's cottage industry lay in its civilizing influence, but the items the women produced were in demand in a marketplace stimulated by the arts and crafts movement. The WNIA's annual reports reveal that promoting arts and crafts created a market for native women's goods, particularly in eastern cities. By 1902 the organization reported that sales of Indian women's products in New York City had reached $18,000 and that "their baskets, rugs, etc. were now to be found in many of our leading cities." By 1903 Carter had cottage industries at ten different locations in the United States, including Minnesota, South Dakota, and New Mexico. She employed 550 women and girls who earned a total of $6,000 in one year. She traveled to Europe to study lace making in Italy.[99] She acquired funds for the construction of the industrial cottages, bought and distributed materials, sold the lace and pottery that the women made, and distributed wages to them. Even Marie Ives, editor of the *Indian's Friend*, felt the effect of industrial education from her post in the East when some missionaries asked if she could sell some crafts for them. At a meeting in New York, Ives sold beadwork, baskets, and copies of the *Indian's Friend* to comers who were drawn to the gathering not by missionary zeal but by the chance to purchase crafts. For a moment, at least, Ives seemed more motivated by entrepreneurial enthusiasm than by moral reform: "I do not know but what I shall open up these little places wherever I can get people to take the Indian industries and take the Indian's Friend. . . . I really became quite a business woman for the Indians."[100]

Carter argued that cottage industry was the best way for Native American women to capitalize on their artisanal skills. Yet Ives's comments reveal the tendencies of cottage industries to reinscribe the relations of production common to the factory system. Eileen Boris points to lace making shops for immigrant women in New York City to show that "despite the goal of training self-sufficient artist-artisans, what the shop actually created was a workforce to execute designs copied from old Venetian lace." Like these shops, model cottages on reservations were sites where indigenous women were taught to copy designs and perform repetitive and monotonous work. Carter and others stressed the home environment over the process of production, "picturing the outworker as a true woman contributing to her family's welfare" and thus eliding "the reality of piecework performed in the home."[101] As white feminists who lobbied for joint property acts well knew, domestic labor was both difficult and economically undervalued.

It is also true, however, that many Native American women embraced the opportunity to earn wages. Jemima Wheelock, an Oneida woman educated at Carlisle, wrote to Carlisle's *Red Man* regarding women's work and extolled the progress being made by women breaking into professions such as law, medicine, and ministry. She mentioned the advancements of native women who had been given opportunities to become more than "drudges merely." Yet Wheelock also drew examples of strong, working women from her own heritage. She described meeting an elderly Oneida woman in Wisconsin who announced that she had "toiled for many, many long and cold winters in this world." She worked her own land and announced, "Everything you see inside of my fence is mine and no one else's." Wheelock described another woman who did all her own farmwork, hauling hay, planting crops, and harvesting. Wheelock did not count such work as drudgery but noted that these were examples of women's strength and industriousness, drawn from the agricultural traditions of her female ancestors.[102]

Because she had been educated at Carlisle, no doubt, Wheelock subscribed to a feminist vision that shared some traits with the feminism of middle-class white women, celebrating wages and denigrating domestic work as drudgery. Wheelock may be an exception; thousands of Indian women worked for wages but often for reasons other than those propounded by white women reformers. Jacobs notes that field matrons and other reformers promoted wage earning among native women as a way to "make them independent and capable of leaving their homes."[103] Native American women, however, did not necessarily wish to leave home, and they sought independence from the government rather than from their families. While it is difficult to assess most Native American women's reasons for working for wages, most likely their work was selective; they chose to work, and seasonal work allowed them to support themselves and their families while still maintaining aspects of their culture. Carter and others assumed that if Indians worked, they would become "just like white people" in their ways, but in fact many Native Americans created "multicultural" labor patterns that combined old subsistence strategies with new ones.[104] Carter found that women were not always willing to come to the cottages to work, and she indicated that they would often work selectively for a period of weeks and then return to their own homes, perhaps incorporating the new work into older patterns of migration and labor. By maintaining some of their familiar forms of work, such as seasonal foraging, women were helping to supplement a new economy that was insufficient for their families' needs. Just as white urban women often supplemented the deficient family wages their husbands earned, indigenous women kept up old patterns of work in order to bolster government rations and their husbands' loss of economic stability as a result of acculturation. Remaining at the margins of capitalism actually helped women to maintain the kinship systems and trade patterns that empowered them.[105] Matron Maryette Reeside saw the patchwork of Kiowa women as a "great power for good" in civilizing their ways. One woman, however, used the quilts she produced to pay a white man for helping her till her land, an arrangement that suggests that her domestic work found its way into exchange economies that were a hybrid of old and new ways.[106] Learning to quilt allowed her to keep her land and uphold her traditional role as cultivator. This mixed economy, one scholar of Indian labor suggests, allowed Native Americans to resist "full commodification of their lives."[107]

Having begun with a faith in domestic work within the home as an agent of transformation, reformers had come to believe that Indians stood little chance to assimilate on equal footing with whites, for most areas of wage labor were, as the WNIA regretfully acknowledged in 1900, "already too full for Indian competition."[108] Because many Native Americans were selective about the wage labor they performed; because indigenous women's domestic labor, like white women's housework, was not classified as real work; and because the move toward arts and crafts as wage labor for natives further set indigenous people apart as artisans rather than modern laborers, many whites concluded that indigenous people were unable to perform many of the kinds of work that would have garnered them more economic power and authority.[109] The growing professional culture that encouraged matrons and other workers in the field to exhibit Euro-American cultural traits in a highly systematized fashion worked against the economic success of many Indian workers. While the efficiency of the new system reinforced punctuality, industriousness, cleanliness, and rules above all, field matrons failed to take into account the local economic strategies that Native Americans had been developing for centuries. Reformers stripped many older forms of work of their legitimacy, replacing them with industries meant to acculturate but that ultimately created a relationship between middle-class reformers and Native Americans that was based more on an industrial model of managers and laborers than on the domestic model that reformers originally envisioned.

Model homes on reservations made room to redefine native women as wage laborers while creating a physical space in which white women, giving home an ethnographic history, capitalized on the exhibitionary power of the home as an object lesson. But the model home was a flawed object lesson. By the 1880s, women's place within the industrial order that assimilation ultimately sanctioned already had been called into question. In the capitalist economy that Indians were to be incorporated into, women's domestic labor held little economic clout. Only by calling on ethnographic science could white women link household labor to patterns of order and a system that legitimated their work, a move that allied them with the rising professional class. They were able to make this move by building on an exhibitionary complex that contained the seeds of women's professionalism and the notion of dependent underclasses in need of domestic management. Middle-class identity, as Morgan himself hinted, was not built into the structure of the home but into systems of relations that granted some groups power over the labor and property of others. The shift that white women attempted to make from seeing women as a dependent class to a racialized understanding of dependency marks a shift within definitions of domestic work and the home itself. Encounters with natives and the chaotic spaces of the reservation convinced white women that only by accommodating their work and that of Indian women to an industrial model could they make a place for women's work within the exhibitionary complex.

CHAPTER FOUR

The Cook, the Photographer, and Her Majesty, the Allotting Agent

Unsettling Domesticity in E. Jane Gay's *Choup-nit-ki*

etween 1889 and 1892, Alice Fletcher spent four summers in Idaho, allotting lands on the Nez Perce reservation. Accompanying her was the equally headstrong E. Jane Gay. Gay, who had behind her a varied career as a teacher, a nurse, a poet, and a clerk in Washington's Dead Letter Office, had taken on the roles of the allotting party's unofficial photographer and, just as important, its cook. During the Idaho summers, the women crisscrossed the reservation with their wagon and Sibley tent. Fletcher mapped the terrain and settled land disputes, while Gay snapped photographs and kept an eye out for fat prairie chickens to serve up for dinner. While Fletcher sent official reports back to Washington, Gay sent lively letters to friends describing the women's escapades. Some of those letters, sent to Captain Richard Henry Pratt at the Carlisle School, were published in Carlisle's *Red Man* between November 1889 and November 1891. In 1909 Gay and her niece transcribed and bound all the letters, together with nearly half of the 400 photographs Gay took during her travels, in a two-volume book she called *Choup-nit-ki, With the Nez Percés*.[1]

Overtly, Gay's photographs seem to endorse the goals of the WNIA and its cohort by implying that assimilation could be achieved by turning Native American hearts and minds to the virtues of Euro-American domesticity. Many of the images show domestic scenes that depict allotment work and its outcome: Fletcher and the surveying party at work at a campsite, towns, schools, Nez Perces posed in cabin doorways, and young Nez Perce girls at play. Fletcher's matronly body, a central figure in the survey photographs, seems to legitimate allotment as a benevolent, domestic project, while photographs of Nez Perce homes, farms, and families suggest the ease with which the Nez Perces could take on the new roles that the government pressed upon them. In keeping with the WNIA's vision, Gay's letters describe allotment as a process akin to homemaking, stressing the similarities between Fletcher's work of surveying and assigning homesteads and Gay's own job of overseeing the household and providing for the nutritional well-being of their party.

Though Gay's chronicle of Nez Perce allotment privileges domestic scenes, her vision is far from innocent.[2] One of her domestic scenes, titled *Reservation Chairs*, an abstract image of three chairs grouped together, whimsically situates the grandiose ideologies of imperialism, evolution, and nationalism in what appear to be the most benign and broken-down of domestic objects (see fig. 4.1). The titles Gay bestowed on these chairs — "Seat of War," "Survival of the Fittest," and "Arch of Triumph" — rely on potent nineteenth-century terminologies of power, difference, and hierarchical ordering that were used to legitimate the Dawes Act. Yet as household objects, the chairs evoke domesticity and familial parity.[3] Gay's ironic equation of domesticity with imperialism intimates that the gendered power structures inherent in Victorian domesticity were crucial to the formation of empire. Indeed, imperialism, Anne McClintock argues, was imagined as "coming into being through domesticity," an assessment that is borne out by U.S. assimilation policy in the early 1890s.[4]

Yet Gay's photograph, which she refers to as an "object lesson," unsettles that dynamic, for the chairs are broken and the familial relationships they symbolize parody imperial authority and the patriarchal order of evolutionary theory. *Choup-nit-ki* indicates that the vacant chairs represented the three members of the unconventional household to which Gay belonged while living and working on the reservation. The backless "Seat of War" is that of allotting agent Alice Fletcher. The "Survival of the Fittest," divested of all but one upright, almost vicious-looking post, belonged to the Cook, Jane Gay herself. And the "Arch of Triumph" was the seat of the party's Photographer — also Jane Gay, in a role she playfully constructed as male. While the impulse to order individuals according to race, class, gender, and sexuality underlay the imperial and evolutionary ideas to which the titles allude, Gay's object lesson plays with the links between persons and the descriptions that define their places and implies that the connections come from the image's creator rather than any material reality.[5]

Her photographs and letters document social and governmental insistence on organizing the nation's household during the early allotment era, but they question that insistence by exposing the absurdity of the whole enterprise. In Gay's narrative, domesticity fails to function as a gloss on the imperial project because domesticity itself is problematic and often deceptive. Instead, civilization policy, with its strict reliance on evolutionary science, gender differentiation, and systems of ordering, influences Gay's interpretation of the household

Figure 4.1. E. Jane Gay, *Reservation Chairs*. Idaho State Historical Society (63-221-184: *Nez Perce Chairs*).

that she shared with Fletcher and of the work that she, Fletcher, and the Nez Perces did between 1889 and 1892. Indeed, in this case in which the two-woman household that Beecher and Soule imagined became reality, domestic tasks did not appear harmless but, instead, were marked by the same systems of ordering and hierarchy that characterized imperialism. In her ironic take on Fletcher's allotment work, Gay herself defies the classifications so crucial to domesticity, representing herself as male and female, philosophical professional and oppressed domestic laborer, authority and outsider. Focusing on the divisions and deceptions common to allotment and to her own domestic life, Gay highlights the dissonance between words and images, between organizing narratives and daily life. Gay's focus on Fletcher's domesticating enterprise and her own domestic efforts shows that both rely on deliberate work, suggesting that the natural order of things is not natural at all, but consciously — and sometimes painfully — made.

Tumbling into the Valley of Paradise

On 30 May 1889, the *Teller*, the newspaper of the burgeoning mining town of Lewiston, Idaho, announced the arrival of Alice Fletcher, noting that she was an easterner and "an efficient agent for the business." The newspaper bid the townspeople and local settlers to provide all necessary help and courtesy to the government agent to allow her to do her work as quickly and efficiently as possible.[6] The newspaper portrayed Fletcher as a woman of power, intellect, experience, and organization who would quickly complete her work and return to the East. Its praise for Fletcher, however, was a not-so-subtle disguise for the townspeople's hope that her appearance signaled the opening of new land to homesteaders. Within a month of Fletcher's arrival, the newspaper reported, 100 "intending settlers" arrived to encamp on the borders of the reservation, make preemption claims, and "keep posted on the development and progress of the reserve" so that when "the bars are let down these people will be on the spot to locate their homesteads on the most fruitful soil on the continent."[7]

Mentioned only once in the newspaper as Fletcher's "companion," E. Jane Gay was nonetheless part, albeit unofficially, of the surveying party. Gay had begun sharing Fletcher's Washington home a year earlier, and their domestic partnership would last until 1906. Having known each other as girls in the 1840s, Gay and Fletcher probably ran into each other again at a public lecture in New York City sometime in the mid-1880s. Gay shared Fletcher's sense that assimilation was the best way to incorporate Native Americans, but she was also drawn to this woman whose professional drive was sometimes compromised by her physical weakness (Fletcher endured several bouts with depression and physical ailments, one of which had left her partially lame). Fletcher's diary began including references to Gay in 1888, when reports of "Miss Gay's" almost daily calls gradually gave place to descriptions of their home life together that simply began "Miss Gay and I." Gay, whom Fletcher addressed in letters as "Lassie," admitted that her "admiration . . . for any sort of pluck took the form of protection" and appointed herself Fletcher's moral compass and domestic comforter, to counterbalance Fletcher's busy professional life.[8]

Like many female Boston marriages of the nineteenth century, Fletcher and Gay's relationship may have been encouraged in the single-sex environment of the female academy, which "represented the first time in U.S. history that women were encouraged to be independent, and to explore the public and private pleasures of being together" in a social and intellectual environment.[9] Both Gay and Fletcher attended the Brooklyn Female Academy after its founding in 1846. Eight years older than Fletcher, Gay was one of the senior students, while Fletcher was one of the youngest. Fletcher likely continued her education there while Gay went on to finish her schooling at Emma Willard's seminary at Troy, New York. Willard, a leader in crusading for a well-organized and well-funded system of education for women, argued that the aim of women's education should not be to teach women to be the "pampered, wayward babies of society." Neither should it, however, encourage women to aspire to absolute social parity with men: while women ought not to submit unconditionally to men's will, submission and obedience by women was the social corollary to men's economic support of them. The seminary's curriculum included courses in geometry, geography, algebra, and religion as well as regular domestic instruction and adherence to a strict schedule meant to encourage women's careful management of themselves and their homes.[10]

The education that Gay and Fletcher received at midcentury fostered middle-class women's sense of independence and illuminated the joys of sororial partnerships, but it stressed the social necessity of the role of women as their husbands' domestic helpmeets. Schools encouraged women's interests in fields such as science, medicine, and law yet did not advocate and, in fact, could not facilitate changes in society that would allow women substantial access to these fields. Gay's education may have fueled her professional ambitions but nonetheless taught her that women's talent, virtue, and service lay in domesticity. Some women still found ways into the professions, and Fletcher was one of them. A reform-minded feminist, her passion for science and her curiosity about the origins of American women's social position led her to the emerging discipline of ethnology; in the early 1880s, she became one of the first ethnologists to do fieldwork, and she supported herself through her work at Harvard's Peabody Museum, her duties as a government allotting agent, and later, by a lifetime fellowship at the Peabody.[11]

Fletcher recognized that the anthropological theories to which she subscribed could be detrimental to the status of Native American women. The accumulation of resources by male heads of families enabled progress, but it reduced women to dependency on men for their subsistence, confined them to home, and stripped their housework of economic value, for the value of a woman's work in the home was regarded as her husband's property. Gay shared Fletcher's belief in civilization's march from its matriarchal origins. She remarked that their society had "been built up largely upon the altruism of the woman, at the cost of her independence; and is still an expensive luxury to her." Gay compared the white woman settler's difficult life to the freedoms of Indian women, arguing that the Indian woman "can jump upon her pony and ride away whenever she chooses. . . . She will tie the cradle-board to her saddle and gallop off as free as her husband; freer, indeed, for she *owns* her children, her horses, her home and all its belongings."[12] Gay, it seems, was well aware that what the government regarded as a primitive, unacceptable way of life was, in fact, empowering to the Nez Perce women.

Moreover, Gay and Fletcher rejected heterosexual marriage, the crowning institution of civilized life. In the 1890s, when scientists, policymakers, and social theorists were fervently classifying individuals according to racial characteristics, ideas about social and physical development were also fueling curiosity about the homosexual as "invert."[13] Although Carroll Smith-Rosenberg has shown that romantic female relationships were an acceptable part of nineteenth-century middle-class culture, other historians have suggested that because the diaries of professional and literary women who were part of this culture focus on emotional and intellectual support, researchers may have overemphasized the nonsexual nature and thus the acceptability of such relationships. During the late nineteenth century, in fact, the possibility of a woman desiring another woman suggested a dangerous assault on the tenets of civilization. According to social evolutionary theory, progress was predicated on increasing differentiation between the sexes, and a woman's masculine desire was associated with primitivism. The more civilized a race was, theorists posited, the more the genders developed distinct biological, emotional, and behavioral traits.[14] By the turn of the century, inversion and primitivism were defined alongside each other as deviant and dangerous to progress.

Fletcher and Gay's encounter with the harsh landscapes and different culture of the Idaho Nez Perces was, in several senses, a venture into an inverted world for the two women. Escaping the male-dominated political and economic institutions of eastern society for the rugged campsites of northern Idaho, Gay may have sensed an opportunity to create, in this place that seemed to lack civilization, a new space where she and Fletcher would be social allies, intellectual companions, and authorities over the processes of assimilation. At home in Washington, Fletcher shared her professional life more closely with her co-ethnologist, informant, and adopted son, Omaha Francis La Flesche. In becoming the allotting party's photographer, Gay may have seen herself as taking on a crucial role in furthering Fletcher's latest professional work.[15]

By 1889 the Kamiah Valley in Idaho, where Gay sought this merger of professional and private life, was the home of the "progressive" group of Nez Perces, those who had been most influenced by the Protestant missionaries who had come to the valley as early as the 1830s. Gay noted that Kate McBeth, the missionary who, along with her sister Sue, was engaged in the work of instructing Presbyterian Nez Perces during Gay's stay, described the valley as a "Paradise."[16] Indeed, in photographs of Kamiah and the Clearwater, Gay often depicts the valley using traditional artistic conventions that depict landscape as view. In *Entrance to Kamiah*, the hills divide to provide a view from above, and the horizon line emphasizes the expanse of sky as well as the breadth and depth

Figure 4.2. E. Jane Gay, *Entrance to Kamiah Valley.* Idaho State Historical Society (63-221-19).

of the landscape. The topography almost seems to suggest an ideally feminine landscape, the hills opening to provide a vision of a fruitful valley, ripe for cultivation (see fig. 4.2).

The Valley of Paradise, however, was no pastoral retreat, and entering Kamiah proved to be a treacherous descent into a disordered world. In 1889 Gay and Fletcher literally tumbled into the valley for the first time, their horses and wagon skittering over a rough mountain path in the midst of a thunderstorm. Fletcher arrived there "wet and mud-stained, her eyes . . . dimmed with congestion" to join the "disjointed members of her party" who had made better time down the steep canyon. The Cook, upon reaching the bottom, "grumbled something about the 'descent of man'" but resisted the surveyor's suggestion that conquering the Idaho landscape would necessitate a "reversion to type." The valley, like the Nez Perces Fletcher could not see, was silent and physically resistant. Gay emphasized Fletcher's vulnerability and undermined her authority by stressing her longing for home: "Her Majesty was oppressed," Gay announced, "and she closed her eyes to the beauty of the landscape. Its loveliness did not compensate for what it lacked. There was no soul in it for her and she reached back for the clasp of the hand of a far-away friend." Both Fletcher and Gay retreated into their respective interiors. Fletcher forgot about the Cook entirely to retreat into thoughts of home, and the Cook, predictably, withdrew into thoughts of food, querying as to whether there might be fish in the river to fry up for dinner.[17]

Gay coyly suggested that while the sisters McBeth may have seen the valley as a sort of female paradise (neither Kate nor Sue McBeth ever married), for Fletcher and herself it was much rockier. The descent into Kamiah is, in a figurative sense, a descent into a more primitive place, inhabited by those whose culture and tradition were foreign in the eyes of the women and the government. Their tumble metaphorically suggests what the scientific establishment had already begun to argue: that just as it was unnatural for two ladies to ape masculine roles by exploring unknown valleys, it was pathological for two women to reject marriage and to seek unnatural pleasures. The Cook, in fact, did find the valley beautiful, but in the letters, Fletcher failed to see what the Cook saw or even to recognize that she shared her sense of anxiety. In a mysterious passage, Gay wrote that Fletcher sought the hand of a "faraway friend," which suggests that Fletcher sought comfort from someone back home in Washington — someone who was, significantly, not Gay.[18]

Miss Fletcher's Companion(s)

The Vale of Kamiah proves to be deceptive, and the landscape suggests that it will be no real paradise. Fletcher was responsible, however, for arranging it and its Nez Perce inhabitants through legal descriptions that would order them according to civilized patterns of private property and nuclear family life. Fletcher's survey implemented a system meant to project a new, rationalized, national order on tribal spaces that had not traditionally been ordered by private property. Historians have characterized this kind of scientific mapping and ordering as masculine and even militaristic, a war waged against alternative ways of seeing the landscape.[19] Photography was a visual corollary to the surveys, as professional photographers aided in mapping landscapes and keeping records of tribes that were thought to be disappearing before the engine of development. Together with surveyors and scientists, photographers helped to legitimate the idea that western landscapes could be crossed, settled, and exploited and that their native inhabitants could be tamed and ordered.

Participating in Fletcher's survey as a photographer provided Gay with a meaningful way to capture the landscape as well as to bring her work closer to Fletcher's. Gay visited Fletcher in Nebraska when Fletcher allotted the Omahas in the early 1880s and experimented with photography there. When Fletcher suggested that a photographer would be a useful and productive addition to her ethnographic and official work in Idaho, Gay enthusiastically took on the new role. She went to Massachusetts to study with her journalist brother, learning to take photographs and to develop them herself. Joan Mark argues that photography was a "near-perfect choice" for Gay, in that it allowed her to "cope with her status within the allotting party" by playing both a "professional 'male' role" and a "supportive 'female'" role in the group.[20] Nicole Tonkovich also points out that the camera, as a tool of empire building that was analogous to the survey itself, gave Gay power to counterbalance Fletcher's insistence on law and order by recording moments of Nez Perce resistance.[21]

Because Gay not only made photographs but represented herself as the male Photographer, she simultaneously questioned the allotment enterprise and the gender conventions that undergirded imperialism. As the male Photographer, Gay acknowledged the masculine in herself; she constructed her maleness, however, in terms of social and professional rather than sexual behavior. Gay acknowledged gender difference by creating discrete personalities for the rational, philosophical Photographer and the impulsive, emotional Cook. At the same time, she called attention to gender as performative rather than biological, in opposition to social evolutionary definitions of gender. Indeed, readers of Gay's articles in the *Red Man* may not have known that the Photographer was not male.

In the guise of the Photographer, Gay appropriated a traditionally male occupation. Nineteenth-century western survey photographers had a reputation as hardy explorers and geographers whose images of landscapes helped to survey unmapped terrain. By the late nineteenth century, the Kodak hand-held camera (one of the cameras that Gay used) made outdoor photography much more accessible to women.[22] Rather than portraying the Photographer as a rugged outdoorsman, however, Gay painted him as a professional, a philosopher, and an artist. He is given to uttering thoughtful, almost clichéd pronouncements, indulging his artistic soul, and lounging under trees. It is the Photographer who records the landscapes they traversed in Idaho, who snaps portraits of the Nez Perces as they come to listen to Fletcher explain the process of allotment, and who aids Fletcher by taking ethnographic portraits of Nez Perces with traditional tools.

The Cook, on the other hand, is a forthright and practical woman whose primary concern is with the alimentary satisfaction and domestic comfort of the allotting party. She is preoccupied with "digestive forces" — her party's never-ending need to eat and, less directly, the nation's tendency to consume any individuals who stood in its imperial pathway. The Cook is concerned with her "hopeful but untired stove, her tin and her wooden ware, our canned tomatoes and our coal-oil can, our corn beef and lucifer matches, flour bags and groceries, our axe and umbrella, our potatoes and salt."[23] Her attention to household labor forms the basis of a series of metaphorical comparisons between the agency system and domestic appliances, supplies, and even livestock. Speculating on her faulty stove leads her to regard the government as a similar "one-sided machine" that has "succeeded in gelatinizing the Indian's backbone until he lies limp and inert in his degradation." Learning that the family hens had been eaten by a coyote causes her to lament, "We had been acquainted with the Agency system long enough to have learned how to protect helpless creatures."[24] While the Photographer engaged primarily in mental and imaginative work, the Cook's chores were physical: she drove to town for supplies, she kept the campsites and cottages tidy, she plucked and boiled the chickens, and she made the meals.

The Photographer's calmness and philosophy exemplify the objectivity associated with photography and with professionalism in general. Through the medium of the Photographer, Gay could disassociate herself from the Cook and her domestic labor. A true "genius," according to the Cook, the Photographer is speculative and possesses "vivid imaginative powers which served him in lieu of physical activity—which even went so far as to convince him that he had actually performed onerous duties to the verge of bodily exhaustion." In this case, Gay consigned her own domestic toil as the Cook to a corner of the Photographer's imagination and foregrounded his mental work over the Cook's demanding duties.[25] The Cook often remains a "silent observer" of the survey and attempts, whenever possible, to choke down her feelings of frustration when her party ignores her efforts: "She chopped her emotions into hash; she baked, boiled, and fried them, but they would not down."[26]

Conversations between the Cook and the Photographer play with conventional characteristics of maleness and femaleness, and Gay often places the two personae at odds with each other. The Photographer accuses the Cook of lacking the ability to read maps; the Cook accuses the Photographer of lacking "moral perpendicularity." In the banter (and often arguments) they share, they articulate the gendered traits that social evolutionism defined as crucial to the survival of the race. When the Cook wistfully wishes that "'things were more equal in the world,'" the Photographer philosophizes on the mutual exclusiveness of equality and progress: "'heights and depths, discords and antagonism, good and evil are all forces working towards the world's development: equality would be the dead level of no progress." When the Photographer announces that the "primal germ" of the human race was "natural affection," a trait learned from the mother, he seems to reinforce some of Jane Gay's own matriarchal leanings. But when the Cook asks about the father, "What is the primal germ of his whole spiritual development?" the Photographer "unblushingly affirmed" that it was "selfishness."[27] The Cook is often agonizingly impatient, but the Photographer, perhaps due to his trade, is preoccupied with the slow measure of time. As the Cook and Briggs, the surveyor, wrestle with the cook stove, "the Photographer viewed the situation with his ordinary calm exterior. He never allows himself to be flustered; it interferes with his profession. He is a philosopher. 'Everything,' he asserts, 'is largely a matter of *time.*' 'All the ills of life are simply ill-timed good.' 'Everything will correct itself in *time.*' 'All mischief is brought about by under- or overtime.' 'True philosophy is to keep cool and take things as they come.'"[28]

The Photographer's artistic acuity, rationality, and acquisitiveness, defined against the Cook's morality, explosive emotionalism, and domestic work, exhibit in microcosm the moral, intellectual, and social differences that social evolutionists outlined. Yet in reality, these distinctions are undermined by the fact that both characters are Gay, who exhibited male and female tendencies. She was simultaneously the detached Photographer who was tempted to snap a photo of Fletcher clinging to the tail of a horse as the agent was dragged down a steep incline, and the Cook, whose love and respect for Fletcher prompted her to acknowledge that such a picture would be a "gross libel" upon a woman so dedicated to her benevolent mission.[29] The categories of maternal love and acquisitiveness necessary to progress emerge as false distinctions legible only as performance. Separating and naming her two selves according to work roles, Gay suggests that the feelings and behaviors of "He" and "She" arise in response to what they do, not because of their biological blueprints.

Gay effectively used photography to undermine gender categories as well. Some time after her return from Idaho, Gay made several portraits of herself as the Photographer and the Cook and inserted them as illustrations in *Choup-nit-ki*. Two of the images, in particular, construct the Photographer and the Cook in reference to what they do, yet in both photographs the model is Gay herself, her face hidden from the camera. *The Photographer* (fig. 4.3) appears early in the first volume of *Choup-nit-ki*. The image is of Gay, her hair cropped short and topped by a straw boater, facing away from the viewer toward her camera. She holds a stopwatch in her hand to indicate the importance of time to the Photographer's profession — and, most likely, to his philosophy. *Behold the Cook* is situated early in the second volume and shows Gay standing at a stove in a dress, her face obscured by a white bonnet (see fig. 4.4). Both the Photographer and the Cook are posed with the tools of their respective trades.

Figure 4.3. E. Jane Gay, *The Photographer*. Schlesinger Library, Radcliffe Institute, Harvard University.

It is clear, moreover, that both roles are equally constructed, performed by Gay herself and equally suspect as a depiction of reality.[30]

Gay does not just play with the features that constitute maleness in order to rationalize an attraction to Fletcher; in fact, she plays with constructions of both masculinity and femininity as she questions the whole system of differentiation and ordering that underlay the assimilationist project. Historian Anne Herrmann has called the "illusion of a 'masculine' subject" a "necessary deception" in women's writing about female partnerships. The implication that one of the partners is more mannish than the other, Herrmann argues, makes their female love possible.[31] In the context of Gay's chronicle of Nez Perce allotment, such a conclusion would be reductive, for private life and national agendas are

Figure 4.4. E. Jane Gay, *Behold the Cook*. Schlesinger Library, Radcliffe Institute, Harvard University.

intertwined. The Photographer is only one of the "deceptions" necessary to define progress. Gay's commentary and photographs together undermine constructed distinctions between the kinds of imperial and domestic work that the Photographer and the Cook seem to embody and reveal both kinds of work to be equally as problematic, deceptive, and even violent.

Her Majesty, the Allotting Agent

Gay expressed the folly of Fletcher's endeavor by portraying both landscape and natives as elusive and tricky and by denying masterful vision to herself and to Fletcher. Upon their arrival in Lewiston in 1889, Gay and Fletcher found that the landscape was deceptive and did not lend itself easily to the idyllic vision of western freedom that Gay had constructed for herself as they spun "along over the green illimitable prairies." Gay expressed a feeling of mastery as she gazed out upon the celebrated open spaces of the West, passed through Yellowstone, and first glimpsed a cowboy. The openness in the West contrasted sharply with her more regulated New England existence, and she remarked that "I began to feel as if I had already a new lease of life in this open, free land of breath and sun. It is superb, wonderful, and makes one wish he could begin all over again and work out a new term of existence, wider from the very start."[32] Gay, as the Photographer, immediately accepted this vision of the West, translating the landscape into a settler's paradise. After talking to the residents, he learned that Idaho was the "garden spot of the earth," where anything will grow, and moreover, "Chinamen do all the work!" Yet the vision of paradise that Gay and Fletcher strained to see turned out to be a mirage, for even as the Photographer recited his tale of bounty, "a dust storm broke upon the town and for an hour we gasped and struggled to breathe the clouds of alkaline dust which surged up against our hotel and penetrated to our room."[33]

The two women's quest for the suspected 800 to 2,000 members of the Nez Perce tribe was thwarted by a landscape and a people that denied visual appropriation:

> Now the reservation comprises nearly 800,000 acres; is crossed and re-crossed by cañons, cut into by gulches, broken by hills and buttes and rocky wastes and traversed by a confusing network of cattle and pony trails. . . . We climb over weary miles of almost impassable country, scrambling over sharp trap rock, broken like the refuse from a quarry, and we do not come upon an Indian. He may have a local habitation and a name, but the man himself is peripatetic. You may see his cabin perched far up on a bench or bluff, but two sticks leaning against the door will tell you that the owner is not at home. . . . If the Government furnished balloons, we would feel encouraged as we contemplate the other side of yawning abysses, and the towering mountains beyond. If it permitted pontoons, we might hope to triumph over the treacherous fords of unreliable mountain streams which must be crossed, but we lie awake at night trying to solve the problem.[34]

The resistance of the Nez Perces and the landscape to visual ordering only seemed to provoke Fletcher's determination to allot acreage to each head of family. Akin to the power of seeing is the textualizing power that Fletcher also held. Her task was not only to survey the land but to identify individuals and record their names in conjunction with the plots of land they chose. Gay described this task as an attempt to "square the circle," stressing Fletcher's obsession with lines and order and the difference between the gridlike national order and kinship-based tribal organization.[35] Fletcher's squaring involved a fundamental re-presentation of reservation space, and to do so required the all-encompassing vision of a monarch and the abstracting eye of a scientist. Gay suggested the violence implicit in both kinds of visions in a passage that presents Fletcher's activities as inquisitorial: "The Special Agent has set up a blackboard in the office. It is the blackboard used long ago by the Missionary and, over the ghostly substratum of gospel texts, lessons in elementary surveying are given and sections are drawn and quartered and driven like wedges into the Indian brain by the Interpreter."[36] Gay noted that the spiritualism of earlier mission work had been replaced by the force of allotment. Using metaphors that stress violence and invasion of the body, Gay implied that the allotment mission penetrated Nez Perce identity as thoroughly as surveyors have penetrated the land.[37]

Fletcher took considerable time to register each member of the tribe and attempted to translate kinship relationships into the Euro-American family form. Fletcher's imperial work was to query each Nez Perce who came to be registered and to find "the suppositious head of the family who is to have 160 acres thrust upon him *nolens volens* when found." Allotment practice dictated not only that the head of the family be named but that inheritance lines be established. In a tribe structured by a village kinship system rather than by patriarchal lines of inheritance, this was no mean feat. Moreover, Fletcher's inquisition into the names and identities of the Nez Perces constituted a violation of traditional practice, for names were considered to be the property of the individual and his or her family and were carefully guarded. Determining an individual's name was "a triumph of diplomacy": "Does her Majesty say to the man or woman, 'What is your name?' She knows better than that; such a direct method would not only fail to produce the desired result, but would insult that man, who must not speak his own name nor utter that of his wife." In naming, Fletcher made the first move toward capturing the individual Nez Perce and abstracting him or her from the home landscape.[38] Gay emphasized this abstraction in a sample allotment description from Fletcher's plat book: "Kolkartzot. South half of south east quarter of North half and South East quarter of Lot 15, and the North East quarter and North half of South East quarter of North half of Lot 18; and the North west quarter and north half of south west quarter of north east quarter; And North half and North half of south half of North west quarter of Lot 17."[39] The long excerpt is meant to befuddle readers, just as the Nez Perces themselves must have been confused by the scientific code that replaced familiar landmarks.

The photograph *Consultation on Land Allotment* (fig. 4.5) shows in less technical terms the power of Fletcher's plat book. A Nez Perce family — Charley Adams and Louise Kipp and their children — gathers in a family portrait: the girls stand close to their mother, who holds a baby on her knee, and a young boy slumps against his father. All are in western dress, and mother and father gaze squarely at the camera. A half-smile crosses Louise Kipp's face. The family divides to reveal a matronly woman sitting at a table, household goods scattered around her — a washboard, a tin cup, a pail, and a food can. The woman, however, is not doing household chores but writing in a large book. The relatively benign pose of the subjects in the photograph belies the consequences of the Adams-Kipp family's visit. The image records their registration as citizens-to-be and the denial of their tribal heritage. The family's clothing suggests that Adams and Kipp had already adopted some new lifeways and were perhaps already farmers; their visit may have been prompted by an attempt to protect the lands they had already improved.

At first, the photograph appears to be a simple domestic portrait of a family posing proudly at the moment of their incorporation. Yet a closer look at Gay's composition reveals a structure ordered on her perceptions of Alice Fletcher's power and its impact on Nez Perce subjects. Mary Pratt has termed eighteenth- and nineteenth-century European explorers' and surveyors' colonizing vision of the Americas the "monarch-of-all-I-survey."[40] That way of seeing is reformulated here in a context specific to late nineteenth-century assimilation, representing "Her Majesty's" survey of the Adams-Kipp family from her position above and behind. Fletcher, although in the background, commands a good deal of the photograph's compositional space and splits the conventional family portrait. She sits above the family, and the space her body occupies divides the family, seemingly along gendered lines, as Adams, with his son, sits apart from his wife and daughters. Opening the space necessary to include Fletcher forces the oldest daughter into the foliage at the right, and her left arm is cut off.

The image complicates both domesticity and the allotment mission. The photograph itself is domestic in its content and presents Fletcher as a maternal figure. It is overt in its suggestion that allotment was a process of domestication. Yet it is equally overt in implying that this process could easily fracture families

Figure 4.5. E. Jane Gay, *Consultation on Land Allotment*. Idaho State Historical Society (63-221-71).

or, as in the case of the unsmiling daughter on the right, inflict damage on individuals. Nicole Tonkovich has noted the frequency with which Nez Perces "exceed the contents of their frames" in Gay's photographs. Certainly Gay's lack of experience contributed to these photographic flaws, but Tonkovich argues that this positioning is only partly unconscious. Gay's remarks about Her Majesty's inquisition show clearly that Gay saw allotment's "drawing and quartering" as one that could leave some individuals — particularly women — at a loss, for family property and marital customs did not fit neatly into the boxes that Fletcher drew for the Nez Perces.[41] It was clearly important to Gay to split the family in order to leave a wide opening to reveal not only Fletcher but her book and a nearby washboard and bucket. In fact, these cleaning implements are more visible and prominent than Fletcher's plat book, thus emphasizing not necessarily what is imperial about Fletcher's work but what is domestic about it.

Gay took immense, ironic pleasure in depicting Alice Fletcher's matronly, eastern body in the rugged western territory. More than once she derived amusement from the unlikely picture of Fletcher's frumpy hat, plump frame, and partially lame leg in the midst of landscapes first described for eastern audiences by Lewis and Clark. "Her Majesty's hat," Gay wrote, "would cool the advances even of a mountain lion."[42] Though Fletcher often appears in authoritative situations in the photographs and the narrative, holding her plat book

Figure 4.6. E. Jane Gay, *Carrying Wood*. Idaho State Historical Society. (63-221-248: *Woman Carrying Bundle of Wood*)

or conducting meetings, Gay's sense of irony was not above equating Fletcher's work with the kind of domestic labor that even Nez Perce women performed. A photograph of Fletcher with her reports and one of a Nez Perce woman with her bundle of wood are striking for their similar composition. In *Carrying Wood* (fig. 4.6), the woman trudges away from the camera, a pile of wood slung on her back. *Final Report* (fig. 4.7) shows Fletcher in the same pose, dragging her paperwork behind her. The reports of the survey, Gay implies, are the results of efforts as intense as the work of wood gathering that traditionally fell to Nez Perce women.

Many of Gay's photographs are of the campsites where she stayed with Fletcher, the surveyor Edson "Joe" Briggs, and the Nez Perce men who rounded out their allotting party. Her narrative derives its structure from the physical locations that Gay and Fletcher claimed as temporary homes — "Squirrel Camp," "Camp Desolation," "Camp Bearing Tree," "Camp Lily." Gay's photographs of campsites conflate household space and imperial space, placing Fletcher's national housekeeping alongside her own household chores and blurring the boundaries between the two kinds of work. Tonkovich notes of Fletcher's presence in many of the images that "each photograph of Fletcher in

Figure 4.7. E. Jane Gay, *Final Report*. Idaho State Historical Society. (63-221-50: *Starting for Washington with Reports*)

camp carries a reassurance that this woman carried civilization with her."[43] Because Fletcher's body and the temporary homes she shared with Gay are central in so many photographs, Gay's compositions imply that civilization intrudes upon the environment and that domestic scenes, as created both by herself and by Fletcher's survey work, are achieved only through effort and even illusion.

Fletcher's tent appears in nearly every camp image as a landmark in the sometimes visually barren spaces of the Clearwater Valley. The tent, stenciled with Fletcher's name and official business above the flap, was Gay's way of marking Fletcher's presence at various locations; at times, the tent seems to stand in for Fletcher herself. Though the tent, as a testament to civilization and government power, gives some kind of order to many of the images, Gay's photographs of the tent also represent it as unable to anchor the landscape or to bring order to the members of the survey party. In *The Damp Thermopylae* (fig. 4.8), for example, Fletcher's tent is pitched rakishly to the left, while the landscape itself seems to slope precipitously to the right, the wagons, horses, and survey party alike in danger of tumbling out of the frame. The whole image seems to slip away from the Nez Perce cottage at the upper left. The slant of the image may well be due to the position of Gay's tripod on a hillside, but the effect is one

Figure 4.8. E. Jane Gay, *The Damp Thermopylae*. Idaho State Historical Society. (63-221-209: *Survey Camp (Camp Thirsty)*

of precariousness, suggesting that the best housekeeping efforts — imperial, photographic, or otherwise — could not create a straight line where one was not meant to be.[44]

Wati-Wait-Houlis' Tent (fig. 4.9) depicts a much more tranquil domestic scene. The survey camp is transformed into a pastoral image by the presence of two children in the foreground. Gay took photographs to remember the site that they shared with a camp worker, Wati-Wati-Houlis, and his wife and daughter Lily. Gay wrote that it was "pleasant, when, in the morning, we drew aside our door flap, to see Wati's tent all in order, thrown open to the air and sun, and Lily playing beside her mother who sat on a mat, sewing and crooning softly to the child. It was a picture of peace and contentment."[45] Wati-Wati-Houlis helped the Cook in her labors, and the Cook took great enjoyment from three-year-old Lily. But the picture of domestic bliss that Gay illustrated here was to prove illusory, for some time later Wati-Wati-Houlis and his wife returned to report that Lily had died. As a photographer, Gay was able to capture a domestic scene, but her narrative reveals that the most tranquil vision of home could be thwarted by harsh conditions in which children sickened and died. Neither the aesthetics of the image nor the order of the survey could remedy difficult realities on the reservation. Family life, as the tears of Wati-Wati-Houlis and his wife testify, is as harsh as it is affirming. All that remained of Lily was a photograph of her that Gay gave to the grieving parents.[46]

Figure 4.9. E. Jane Gay, *Wati-Wati-Houlis' Tent*. Idaho State Historical Society (63-221-35: *Camp Robusto*).

The tenuousness of the very idea of family that allotment was meant to uphold structures other photographs. In *Family Umbrella* (fig. 4.10), Fletcher and Briggs appear as comfortable and proper as a husband and wife on a Sunday picnic in the park. In the image, what is envisioned as a Sunday picnic is actually the work of allotment, in which the two collaborated in consulting plat maps, marking corners, and labeling plots. The task of housekeeping, however, is equally prominent in a still life of frying pan, washboard, and bucket that occupies the right foreground. This highly conscious arrangement may have been Gay's way of marking the Cook's presence and role in the camp. Other camp workers are included in the image in the two Nez Perces who recline at the edge of the frame, both part of the work and, like the Cook, excluded from the domestic circle of the collaborating surveyors. The man on the right holding the map appears to be James Stuart, who helped both women as the party's interpreter, surveyor, civil engineer, driver, supplier, and general handyman. The man on the left was likely one of a number of Nez Perces that Fletcher and Briggs employed as chainmen. Together with the cookware, the two men represent the labor necessary to support Fletcher's and Briggs's professional civilizing work. Not privy to Fletcher's and Briggs's power as surveyor and adjudicator of claims, Gay and the chainmen were nevertheless crucial to the work that Fletcher performed there.[47]

Gay simultaneously conflates domestic and imperial labors and divides them

Figure 4.10. E. Jane Gay, *Family Umbrella*. Idaho State Historical Society (63-221-11: *Camp Sunday*).

by separating the support workers from the family that the imperial vision upheld — significantly, a vision of family that was both heterosexual and white. Her use of the term "family" in the title can only be ironic. While Briggs, who was married, was an integral member of their party, he and Gay sparred frequently, and Gay often made snide reference to Briggs's prototypically male habits of smoking and whistling. Gay played with the notion of family by including her frying pan and James Stuart in the image, for this arrangement mimics the family, composed of herself, Fletcher, and Francis La Flesche, that they were members of at home in Washington.[48] In a drawing made from this photograph, *Briggs and Her Majesty* (fig. 4.11), only the allotting picnic remains, and both the Nez Perce chainmen and elements of the landscape are missing. In remaking the photograph to isolate Fletcher, Briggs, and her map-making activities, Gay also erased Stuart, who holds up a map in the original image, and thus the realities of the Nez Perces' authority and knowledge of the landscape that was their home.[49] The washboard, pan, and pot, however, remain resolutely in the foreground, proclaiming that even the most domestic scene harbored elements that could expose it as illusion.

Figure 4.11. E. Jane Gay, *Briggs and Her Majesty*. Idaho State Historical Society (63-221-104).

Wrestling with the Problem of Dinner

The Cook's tools appear in a number of photographs and testify to her understated presence in the allotting party. In her letters about camp life, however, the Cook is a prominent personality for whom civilization theory provides a lens on her work and the workings of the household. Each day at their home was a reenactment of ethnologists' understanding of the struggle to emerge from barbarity to civilization. Battling mud, dust, and rain, Gay strove to keep clean and do her work in the temporary lodgings of the campsites and their cottage at Kamiah. Moreover, petty squabbles between members of the allotting party led to confrontations that Gay reframed as momentous occasions in the battle for power and survival. On one occasion, the Cook struggled with Briggs over a pair of chickens, and the claim that each of them staked to the property led the Cook to call on her knowledge of Morgan's theories in order to explain their desire for possession of the birds: "The Cook says that it is the manner of appropriating the goods of this world that differentiates peoples and the Cook is a keen observer."[50] Gay's depictions of home life intimate that home life and reservation life were equally problematic, for both were often based on false distinctions, misleading assumptions, and lack of clear vision. Her own work and Fletcher's, in fact, took place in a household characterized by irony, defectiveness, and downright deception.

In what may be the only photograph of their time in Idaho that shows Gay and Fletcher together, the two women are doing housework (see fig. 4.12). This photograph, titled *Monday Morning*, emphasizes racial difference over gender-role differentiation, as James Stuart's seeming willingness to participate in Fletcher's imperial whitening duties brings him into the picture. Here, imperial ordering is cast as domestic work: work that was the province of white women and was based on their ability to recast a native body — a male native body — as a domestic worker like themselves. *Monday Morning* shows domestic work to be visible, influential, and part and parcel of assimilation work. As in the image of the reservation chairs, imperial imperatives are cast upon domesticity, but here domesticity is portrayed as bodies working toward a specific national product: a transformed native subject. The image implies that the incorporation and production of new people that imperialism is based on is not a function of heterosexual relations in the interest of patriarchy but is a product of women's domestic efforts and their management of foreign subjects.

Gay and Fletcher might both be housekeepers, but the kinds of housekeeping work they do affords them different access to power. Gay's description of life in their cottage challenges the gendered division of work within the home, for the fact of their two-woman household parodies the separation of spheres along gender lines. Gay was well aware that progress was supposed to mean sex-role differentiation, but in her take on their domestic life, Gay questioned the basis of such distinctions. Often referring to her companion as "the Special Agent," she stressed that Fletcher's work placed her much closer to official power and to the acquisitiveness associated with male authority in the nation and in the heterosexual household. Upon their arrival at Kate McBeth's former cottage at Kamiah in August 1889, Fletcher set up her office while the Cook conducted her explorations in the pantry. Her paltry conquest narrative was a nuisance to Fletcher, for "the labors of Her Majesty were interrupted by bulletins from the Cook who was developing a mine of treasures left by the blessed little missionary." While the Cook mapped out her terrain and articulated her discoveries, Fletcher was "deep in abstruse calculations." The Cook's "shout of triumph" upon unearthing a white crockery washbowl was the last straw for Fletcher, who groaned at the Cook's insistence on glorifying her quotidian discoveries in the face of the agent's far more crucial work.[51] After more than one battle with a resistant household appliance or difficult dinner preparation,

Figure 4.12. E. Jane Gay, *Monday Morning*. Idaho State Historical Society (63-221-27).

the Cook lamented that "Her Majesty has all the lions in *her* way. The Cook beats the air and has no trophy to show how many are her slain."[52]

In spite of the power difference between them, the juxtaposition of seemingly inconsequential household matters and the business of imperialism structures Gay's narrative. In a passage in which her own activities provide a counterpoint to Fletcher's, Gay finds irony in the coexistence of imperialism and domesticity as embodied in Fletcher and herself, respectively:

> Here is a new day, and we rise to meet it. Indians straggle in to look after their land. Reports are to be written, weekly and monthly and quarterly statements to be made, savings to be gone over, quarrels to be settled, rival claims to be adjudicated.
>
> Behold her Majesty, triumphant over the hardships of life, seated at the board table, like a queen on the throne, pen in hand, writing her decrees. Behold the Cook! attired in a long calico apron, and not much else; for the thermometer reports 102° in the shade. . . .
>
> I am devising ambrosia for the goddess, the materials for which still lie in sundry bottles and tin cans. Briggs's stove has an oven that has no bottom. It had a backbone once: but it has sagged since it came on the Reservation, naturally enough. The plates are broken transversely, and dip horizontally an inch or two or more or less, trying to fit the warped backbone. . . .

The stove had legs once. When it arrived at the agency, they were able to stand alone. Now they lie in a heap in the corner of the kitchen. Strength has gone out of them.

The joints of the pipe fit each other just as the coats and shoes furnished by the Indian Department fit the children. The style is particular to the Institution.

I stand before this stove, wrestling with the problem of dinner.

Her Majesty sits day after day, with an aggravating persistency, listening to the stupid, advising the vicious, stiffening up the weak, forgetting to rest, studying how to help those who won't (she says can't) help themselves, unmoved under abuse, steadfast under calumny.

It is enough to drive a looker-on to madness. There is not an Indian with hair so long, and blanket so dirty but that can claim her attention, be she ever so faint with hunger and the cook ever so impatient.

There she stays, while I am mounting guard over the box top, whereon are spread the results of a long struggle with Briggs's stove.

Victories, to be satisfied, should be taken advantage of at the moment of completion. I am sorry to say that the flavor of some of the cook's victories is lost while her Majesty is holding court in the outer room. And the exasperating part of it is that she never knows what she has lost.[53]

In this extraordinary passage, Gay presents a vision of domestic space that is at once the seat of imperial power and the site of domestic toil. Her own struggle with dinner preparations parallels Fletcher's struggle with allotment procedures in an environment where household appliances — in this case, the camp stove — are like the Nez Perces who "straggle in" to make their claims. The stove's weak construction functions as an ironic analogy to the weak construction of the reservation system, which had reduced the Nez Perces to dependency and rendered them, like the stove, "unproductive." But just as Fletcher perseveres in her allotment work, Gay presents herself as valiant in her own unacknowledged struggle. While Fletcher endeavors to create a functional map out of the diverse stories and individuals who staked claims on the land, Gay is engaged in creating a domestic "spread" out of the "sundry bottles and cans." The meal she prepares is her own "decree," her own claim to authority. Her assertion of authority over her domestic environment and her consequent "victory," however, is less powerful because Fletcher pays no heed to it.

Gay also described the way that Fletcher's ordering impulses affected the Cook at moments as mundane as mealtime. Fletcher insisted that Gay place the entrée (even if it was a pot of tough chicken) squarely in the center of the table; Fletcher would scrutinize its placement until "Her Majesty's scientific soul is appeased with so much order as is attainable with the means at hand." Gay also "devised little fictions" to conceal the "blighting truth" about their meal, renaming corned beef hash, for example, as quail on toast. Her efforts, she reveals in her letters, are all in an effort to bolster Fletcher's confidence lest she lapse into "moral turpitude" in the atmosphere of conflict bred on the reservation.[54] Like a good wife, Gay tried to sustain her professional partner by indulging her needs and keeping up morale, but part of performing this role involved concealing the truth of their circumstances.

Domestic life was riddled with hierarchies that separated domestic labor from professional work as clearly as they separated canned goods from ambrosia or corned beef hash from quail on toast. In a household where gender could not figure as a category of difference, work roles emerged as the single factor constituting difference; at the same time, Gay depicted those roles as performances played by Her Majesty and the Cook. Language and scientific precision were only a gloss on the realities of cottage life. Far from suggesting that domestic life was a soothing response to imperial manipulation and power, Gay asserts that domesticity and domestic labor were shaped by the same brutal systems of order and hierarchy. In the chain of command within her household, however, Gay was anxious to maintain her own control over subversive elements — namely, the Nez Perces who worked for them. She discussed at length the Cook's frustration when John, a Nez Perce hired to help around the house, refused to scrub the floor because he would rather read *Harper's*. Perhaps because of her own preference for literary endeavors over household labor, she was doubly irked by his resistance. In another incident, the Cook could barely contain her frustration when James Stuart disappeared for six days, shirking his duty to finish painting the new church belfry. When Fletcher fretted that he might have been killed, the "Cook remorsefully recalled the many times when her wish had been father to that thought, and was silent."[55]

Gay's less-than-charitable thoughts about Stuart testify to a violent streak in the Cook, who confessed, "From the first day of our arrival upon the reservation, she had been possessed by the desire to own a gun," ostensibly to kill prairie chickens. Purchasing a gun in Chicago on the way to Idaho for a second season of allotting work may have been another attempt at exerting control over her surroundings. The Cook went to a shop on State Street and asked for a gun: "anything that will kill," she insisted, and she bought one that the clerk claimed was a "sure thing." Gay described Stuart's and Briggs's inability to assemble the three-piece gun and her own pride when she took it and "triumphantly snapped the pieces together." Rationalizing her gun as a defense against pests and a way to provide game, she used the gun with the relish of an outlaw — or an ornithologist. The Cook listed the things it killed, writing down the names of birds with scientific precision.[56]

Gay's urge to act the scientist even as she mocked Fletcher's attempts to "catch" the Nez Perces, record their names, and pin them onto allotments belies Gay's desire to be Fletcher's professional partner as well as her domestic companion. On one occasion, the Photographer and the Cook set out on an archaeological dig, hoping to find some Nez Perce skulls to show the ethnologist. The Photographer quickly lost interest and wandered off, while the Cook continued to dig fervently. Her quest, however, turned up nothing but James Stuart's amusement and lip-smacking recollections as the Cook uncovered an old pit used for cooking camas.[57] The Cook's fervor had been sparked by a desire borne of "pure science" and of a wish to "spring a triumph on Her Majesty. . . . She would like to show her that the labors of amateurs, outside of culinary operations, were sometimes productive of results which commanded respect." Yet her excavation only returned the Cook to a remnant of Nez Perce culture that represented the domestic duties she had tried to escape and left her without any theory besides that supplied by Stuart's superior knowledge.[58] Unable to position herself as the most powerful member of the household, Gay attempted to exert some kind of command of Nez Perce history. Failing that, she would turn toward their future in an attempt to exercise authority.

Necessary Deceptions

At the time of the allotting party's arrival, the Nez Perces were in a state of transition that created internal divisions. Nez Perce society traditionally was arranged by kinship systems but also by social class, which divided the Nez Perces into three groups according to wealth and power. Most of the group fell into the middle class, while slaves and powerful, wealthy leaders formed the other classes. Upper- and middle-class men generally married within their class, but more wives might be taken from the lower class. This simultaneous stratification and interpenetration of classes set the stage for some of the later conflicts over polygamy and landownership that plagued Fletcher. The arrival of Presbyterian missionaries Eliza and Henry Harmon Spalding at Lapwai in 1836 upset some of these hierarchies and created new ones. While the missionaries preached equality, offered instruction, and enforced rules that affected all classes, they also introduced Euro-American ideals. As the Nez Perces chose to accept or reject those ideals, they split into two new groups: the "progressives" or "loyal Nez Perces" and those who resisted white culture — the "Heathens." Historians Allen Slickpoo and Deward Walker indicate that while the Nez Perces embraced the opportunities for education that the missionaries offered, many of them balked at the church's insistence on a total change in lifeways. Their resistance was read as laziness, and church strictures became more severe. By the 1870s, both Protestant and Catholic missionaries had significantly re-organized the social space of Nez Perce territory. People settled into "church-village complexes" or "mission contact communities" that linked residential and political alliances to religious ones.[59]

By the late 1880s, a new class system had developed on the reservation, a division that Kate McBeth celebrated. Her sister left the valley after being ac-cused of fomenting antagonism among the Nez Perce, and Kate defended Sue's behavior, writing that one of the agent's "complaints against us is that we were creating an aristocracy among the Indians, and that he couldn't manage them as he chose. Christianity *was* then uplifting a class, although they were alike poor." Nez Perces who accepted Christianity often did so because of a lack of power and status in Nez Perce society. Native American Presbyterian ministers could raise their positions and grasp some of the power that had belonged to hereditary chiefs, for native ministers also held leadership positions in tribal government. In 1889 a power struggle involving old and new leadership led to the establishment of the Second Presbyterian church in Kamiah by Archie Lawyer, who took with him half of the church's membership.[60]

When Fletcher and Gay returned to the reservation in 1892, the Nez Perces were embroiled in this conflict, and the two women worried that internal divisions would keep the Nez Perces from accepting their allotments, thus leaving them vulnerable to land losses. At one point, Gay's frustration at the encroachments of white cattlemen and squatters on Indian lands led her to counsel a Nez Perce named Te-le-pah to resist. She then became implicated in her own counsel. "'You must stop quarrelling among yourselves and com-bine against — against,'" the Cook stammered. "What is she saying? Against *what*, against *whom*, must the Indians combine if they would be saved?"[61] Gay's confusion stemmed from her recognition of a predicament that she and the Nez Perces shared. Like them, she was discontented with the place she had been assigned in the evolutionary paradigm that insisted on female submis-sion in the name of progress. Like them, the demands of progress had divided her against herself, splitting her identity into male and female elements just as the Nez Perces had divided into progressive and traditional factions. Gay recognized that for them to rebel would mean rebellion against the forces of civilization — against white people and their ways — and this was a rebellion she could not endorse.

In spite of her failure to wield the power that Fletcher exercised on the reservation, Gay shared Fletcher's belief that civilization was the only way for the Nez Perces to save themselves from the inevitable onslaught of greedy white settlers. In spite of her own sense of rebellion, Gay believed that submission was necessary to civilization. Indeed, she represented herself and the Nez Perces as marginal elements that must be contained. Gay satirized her past instruction in proper womanly conduct through the vehicle of the Cook, who suppressed her emotions according to her "New England education, which had taught her that salvation was to be obtained only in doing what she did not want to do, and that human happiness, for the most part, consisted in cheerful martyrdom."[62] The element of revolt she harbored within her was another source of her self-mockery: "Clearly the Cook tho indispensible [sic], is a dangerous member of our party."[63] Yet by acknowledging and then containing her own desires, Gay assured herself that her imagined counterparts, the Nez Perces, would do the same. "What do you suppose would happen if the world's cooks once suspected their omnipotence?" she asked her readers. "Suppose they should 'strike' some Sunday morning before breakfast, where would our spiritual development be before bedtime? The only weak point of the situation would be the appetites of the cooks themselves. So you see it is the weak points that save the world."[64] Calling on feminists' arguments about the importance and value of labor performed by the cooks of the world, Gay stressed the power of the nation's invisible working women. Rather than arguing that household laborers were held down by a patriarchal, capitalist system, however, Gay submitted that the cooks' submission came from within: they are contained by their own desires.

She compared her resignation to the "powers of Nature" to that of the Nez Perces, misreading their ambivalence and silence as the placid acceptance with which she struggled. "I no longer scorn the soul that cannot fly steadily towards the sun," she wrote.

I see virtue in a vigorous jump; it also is progress. All cannot be eagles, some must be crickets. The Photographer says, "The balance of life must be maintained." I do not know exactly what he means, but there is comfort in what he says. I suppose it is another way of saying that whatever *is* is right, an aphorism never disputed by our red friends. They never rebel against the powers of Nature and seldom against the powers that be. The powers that be are ordained of God — so are the crickets. A New Englander would go stark raving mad, and dance frantically over the things that produce a soporific effect upon those to the manner born.[65]

Thus Gay rationalized the Nez Perces' containment within Euro-American domestic structures by rationalizing her own containment as part of the "balance of life," the natural order of things as "ordained of God." Significantly, Gay used the photograph *Monday Morning*, with its image of both women and Indians engaged in domestic chores, to illustrate this passage (see fig. 4.12). Gay, like Fletcher, hoped that the building of homes would aid the Nez Perces in keeping their land and in elevating them to the rights and privileges of civilization and citizenship. Her acceptance and belief in assimilation required that she accept social hierarchies that seemed undesirable and unfair.

Perhaps because Gay recognized that identity was, in many cases, a matter of role playing, submitting to the "order of the world" led her to channel her desires for power and recognition into acceptable modes and prompted her to react rather more violently than Fletcher to the ways the Nez Perces performed identity and wielded power on the reservation. The most conspicuous method that Gay chose to order those around her was by acting the role of the Photographer, a technique that allowed her to fashion the civilizing mission as a monumental endeavor that endowed domestic order with national importance. While many of her photographs are of Fletcher's allotting work, nearly as many record the results of that work in images of Nez Perces in their new homes. Several photographs arrange homes as backdrops to Nez Perce family groups; one powerful portrait of a Nez Perce couple seems to emphasize the soundness of their relationship as well as their seeming acceptance of civilization. In a photograph of Felix Corbett and his wife, their closeness to each other causes them to fill the space of the image so that they appear almost a monument to civilization, framed by their home (see fig. 4.13).

Other images show civilized identity to be performative. One of Gay's more striking photographs is of a group of Nez Perce girls enacting a tableau vivant. Judith Fryer Davidov writes that at its best, the tableau vivant image relies on a collaboration between artist and model that centers on the remaking of identity, the construction of or trying on of an alternative self (see fig. 4.14).[66] Yet this image is memorable because that trying-on seems so unnatural; the pose the girls hold is an awkward and elaborate fabrication in which collaboration is clearly lacking. Posed before a curtain, six girls enact a scene that requires their bodies to be cloaked in shapeless robes of brilliant white. As they look heavenward, their faces and garments form a pyramid, from the girl lying on the ground to the girl who stands at the top of the group, her white-draped arms

Figure 4.13. E. Jane Gay, *Felix Corbett and Wife*. Idaho State Historical Society (63-221-83a).

outstretched. Ironically, because of the effect of dark-skinned faces against bright white fabric, the beatific face of the girl at the top of the pyramid hovers in darkness. The most arresting face is that of the girl at the foot of the human tower; her expression is much more equivocal. She peers almost sullenly from beneath her lids, her mouth hard and small, her jaw set, and her face and hair unmistakably dark. Her posture takes on not an attitude of submission to whatever higher force it is that keeps them in thrall but an attitude of immobility, of solidity rather than etherealness, of rootedness rather than uplift.

The trying on of another identity that is the foundation of a tableau vivant is made more complex here by the historical fact that performing identity was compelled by the government and by institutions such as schools and churches. Participating in this artistic construction obliges the girls to estrange themselves from their own cultural heritage and to adopt positions that are far from self-affirming. The Nez Perces that Gay encountered and photographed, however, were not necessarily naive in presenting themselves to the Euro-American gaze. Gay reported several incidents in which Nez Perces performed as "savages" for white audiences. In one case, a former student at an eastern school came into

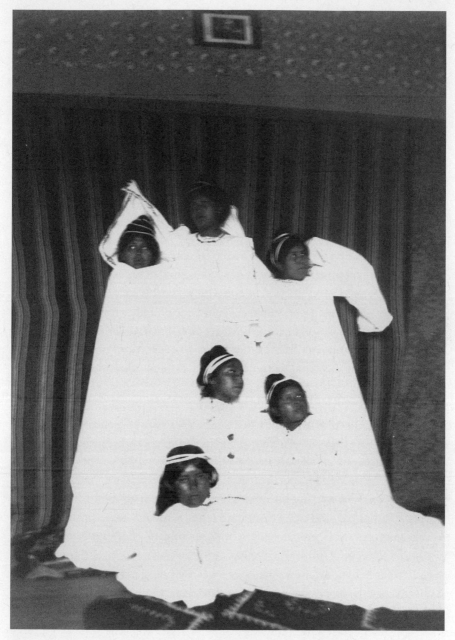

Figure 4.14. E. Jane Gay, *Girls in Tableau*. Idaho State Historical Society (63-221-312a).

camp in a breechcloth in order to shock and dismay guests at the agency who had come to check up on him. Gay asked some Nez Perces why they dressed in and were photographed in blankets on trips to Washington, while on the reservation they wore trousers and hats: "Because the white people expect, and like to see it, they replied, laughing at the fun they saw in the performance."[67] Gay condemns this behavior as self-destructive, but the Nez Perces' control over their representations in these instances implies that they understood that Euro-American society regarded their culture and bodies as spectacle. Like Gay herself, they expressed their resistance through humor and irony and by performing identity. Gay even implicates herself as a facilitator of this performance, including a photograph of Nez Perces in traditional dress — and one in a suit — to illustrate this anecdote. The photograph suggests that all image making is a matter of performance.

Gay's alarm when the Nez Perces asserted native identity may have encouraged her to intervene in what she regarded as pressing matters of civilization versus savagery on the reservation. A solid Presbyterian, Gay felt empowered to intervene in matters regarding morality and the church, and she seemed particularly disturbed by insinuations of uncivilized sexual conduct on the part of a Presbyterian minister. In fact, her focus on accusations of illicit sexuality blinded her to the ways that factionalism on the reservation was a result of the Nez Perces' complex history. She represented Nez Perce resistance as deceptive, childish, and wrongheaded, simplifying what was a multivalent response to intervention in deep-seated political and social rifts among the Nez Perces.

The religious strife they encountered on the reservation in the summer of 1890 was caused by an allegation of adultery on the part of a native preacher, Robert Williams, who had allegedly engaged in inappropriate conduct with his cook. Gay was incensed on more than one account. First, she was both a Presbyterian and a cook and came from "the outer world, where it was not a sin to have a woman cook." Second, her friendship with the McBeths gave her close ties to the Williams family, who were part of the "aristocracy" of Christianized Nez Perces that the McBeths had been accused of creating. Robert's father, Billy, was also Fletcher's most important informant on ethnographic matters. Robert was tried before the presbytery at the instigation of "the shrewdest men of both Lapwai and Kamiah."[68] Gay believed that the trial was a farce and accused the Nez Perces of deception, complaining that "the testimony was all in the vernacular, the interpreter doubtful and the commission mistook the identity of the witnesses. The prosecuting Indians were skilful [sic], some of them being astute enough to blind any set of well meaning men ignorant of the Indian's language and tactics."[69] Gay viewed the discord on her own terms, reinventing a complex political conflict as an epic battle of civilization against barbarism. She read it as an outcome of "the waning power of the old chiefs, who die hard," and saw it pragmatically as "the throes of evolution." Gay read resistance as sneakiness; culture and language, as subversion of justice. Moreover, she insisted that the factionalism was rooted in a dialectic of old-versus-new, when in fact Lawyer, the leader of the other faction, was himself a Presbyterian minister, and his followers left as a protest against the light punishment Robert Williams was given. Gay characterized Lawyer as "dangerous" and "pernicious," primarily because he had the power of tradition behind him: "He stands for the power of the old chiefs as Robert stands for simple right and justice and godliness."[70]

James' Belfry (fig. 4.15) depicts Gay's response to the dispute. After learning of the split between churches, Gay sprang into action. She resolved to put her architectural interests to work and to repair the first church of Kamiah. A gift donated by Mary Copley Thaw, Fletcher's friend and benefactor, enabled Fletcher and Gay to purchase paint and supplies to update the 1874 Greek Revival church into late Victorian Gothic Revival during the summer of 1890.[71] Gay took great pride in constructing a new belfry, setting window glass, and painting the pews. Fletcher and Gay had a number of supporters from the First Church faction, but other Nez Perces watched the process and derided the busy workers. Both the church building itself and the process of construction endowed Gay with new purpose, however. She relished the way both process and product symbolized order, civilization, and godliness. She herself supervised the renovation of the pulpit and described in loving detail the way she had "grained it with high mahogany finish and painted two chairs and a table . . . to match. The 'platform' was carpeted in red to harmonize with the plush cushion and the ten Commandments were nicely framed and hung on the wall." The new belfry, "sharply defined against the sky," signaled a new horizon to Gay. Especially gratifying to her was the way the new church seemed to influence home construction on the reservation, for "several of the little home cabins are to have a beautifying touch when the money is saved up to buy the paint."[72] She believed that she had helped to set in motion a dialectic of moral evolution and regarded the deep rift between factions as the precursor to uplift borne of conflict.[73] Gay resorted to the Photographer's evolutionary rhetoric to explain her intervention, yet her commitment to the project and her photographs of the final structure testify to the Cook's belief that such changes had to be deliberately built. Only when the church had been finished, even to the belfry, did Gay believe that order had been reestablished.

An untitled photograph of a mother with her children shows their identity as a function of their familial ties (see fig. 4.16). The terrified expression of the girl at right, however, reveals a relationship that recenters the viewer's attention on what is taking place outside the family and outside the photograph's frame: the making of an image. The shadow in the lower right corner most likely is Gay's; the figure wears a woman's hat and leans over a box camera. Her shadowy arms jut out to position the camera, and her head tilts down to peer into the box. While Gay looks at the family indirectly, as revealed through the medium of the box, the girl looks at and shrinks from the photographer. The image, with Gay's shadow unwittingly recording her presence, is evidence of the play of representation in the late nineteenth-century contact zone. Attempts by white reformers to transform Native Americans via assimilation policy reveal reformers' desires to see civilization validated in the transformation of the nation's new subjects. Both Gay and the Nez Perces, however, were well aware of the imbalances in power that attended social evolution's rigid divisions, and this knowledge at times comes through in Gay's letters as pointed criticism of the white man's civilization.

During her time on the reservation Gay observed a great deal of injustice directed toward the Nez Perces. In 1892 she witnessed with a sinking heart the arrival of government agents whose duty it was to negotiate for the final sale of "leftover" reservation lands. She wrote that "one can foresee that before many years, under the pressure of the encroaching white man's civilization, all the valley gardens of the Nez Perces will be destroyed by the railroad lines and the Indians driven back from the water courses; and when one considers that all their little agricultural endeavors and their homes are upon these streams where alone gardens can be made, it is not difficult to conceive of the suffering which will follow this sort of opening up of the Reservation."[74] Gay's prophesy simultaneously condemned government seizure of lands and upheld the vision of domesticity that sustained her belief in Euro-American civilization. She feared that the entire attempt to reproduce domestic structures — the home and the garden — among native peoples would be destroyed by the imperial avarice of the government she was raised to revere. In 1893 a tribal council signed a document ceding 542,000 acres of unallotted land for $1.5 million. President Grover Cleveland declared the sale effectual in 1895, and on 18 November the land was rushed by white homesteaders. Days before the projected land rush, the *Lewiston Teller* exulted in the prospects that lay before the waiting set-

Figure 4.15. E. Jane Gay, *James' Belfry*. Idaho State Historical Society. (63-221-90d: *Kamiah Church "Old Church Made New"*)

Figure 4.16. E. Jane Gay, *Nez Perce People*. Idaho State Historical Society (63-221-165d).

tlers and for the town itself, poised to become a "great commercial center." The paper was quick to allay fears that allotment had exempted the best of the land, assuring readers, "It is a mistake to suppose that the cream of the Nez Perce reservation has been secured by the Indians. An Indian loves the association of his childhood. He loves his hut[,] his garden spot, his fishery, his bath pool and his sweathouse." The Nez Perces, the *Teller* reported, had opted to own woodland nooks and shady creeks, but the "broad bench lands" were open to settlement. When the cannon sounded to open the territory to homesteaders, it rang out the "death knell of the great Nez Perce reservation."[75]

Her own, Fletcher's, and the McBeths' inability to stop the tide of the land grab struck Gay with her own powerlessness. By the end of their stay, Gay's faith in the ideology of civilization was shaken by her own status within Fletcher's imperial household, by the injustices of the government, and by Nez Perce resistance, leading her to teeter on the edge of modernist angst. Gay wrote, "There sits Her Majesty, calmly writing, a placidity about her that is aggravating. Has she come so near the heart of the Universe that she can rest content in the stillness of the centre of it all, while I, on the outer edge, am whirled by the endless revolution into confusion of spirit with no power to listen below the noise of the mechanism?"[76] The machinery of social evolution, as a civilizing and professionalizing force to which Fletcher had much greater access than she, constituted a threat to Gay as well as to the Nez Perces. In the battle over souls and lands that was crucial to cultural and geographic assimilation, it was evident that the government would get the land, while the Nez Perces would care for their own souls. And Jane Gay, whose passions conflicted so violently (and perhaps shamefully) with civilized domesticity's heterosexuality and separation of spheres, had to question a kind of progress that left the Nez Perces and herself at the outer edges.

Gay's experiences in the Vale of Kamiah showed her that the march of civilization often conflicted with her own and the Nez Perces' real-life needs and experiences, yet in the late nineteenth century it was difficult for anyone to escape the categories that social evolutionary theory imposed. Gay's life after Idaho suggests that she continued to search for a physical and emotional home; she was not to find it with Fletcher. Gay may have hoped that by working as Fletcher's photographer and partner, she might gain a greater piece of the affection and respect that Fletcher bestowed on her collaborator and son, Francis La Flesche. In a letter to La Flesche that she wrote from Lapwai, Gay boasted of the difficulty of the surveying and allotting work. Referring often to La Flesche's absence and distance, she told him of "our work . . . all the digging and the photographing, all the gathering and keeping." She also reminded him of her affection for Fletcher: "Miss F. is well and more blessed than ever, the dearest little woman on earth, as you know, and you do not mind my knowing it also do you?"[77]

Unable to be Fletcher's professional and intellectual partner as well as her domestic companion back east, however, Gay finally moved out in 1906 after an explosive argument with La Flesche at Alice Fletcher's sickbed. Shortly thereafter she moved to England, where she began a lasting relationship with Caroline Sturge, a British midwife thirty years her junior. Gay and Sturge built a country cottage in Somerset, where they lived until Gay's death in 1919. Gay christened their home "Kamiah."[78] Borrowing a name from the Nez Perce people, Gay intimated that she had finally found the valley of paradise that she had sought and failed to find in Idaho.

The Somerset cottage's name suggests that Kamiah was an idyllic place, but the work Fletcher and Gay did in Idaho was neither easy nor, as Gay's narrative so bluntly reveals, innocent. Problematizing domesticity itself as a construct that divides families and even individuals according to work roles and gendered traits, Gay could not resort to domesticity as a gloss on imperial endeavors. Instead, her photographs and letters expose domestic work and imperial work as equally burdensome, equally deceptive, and equally unable to contain the unruly elements in the nation's family as well as in the more intimate spaces of home.

CHAPTER FIVE

A Model of Its Kind

Anna Dawson Wilde's
Home in the Field

J ane Gay's struggle to envision herself and the Nez Perces as properly domestic reflects broader changes in the way women's understanding of the meaning of domestic work influenced relations between white and Indian women. As the nineteenth century drew to a close, concerted efforts to assimilate Native American women by impressing upon them the virtues of domesticity had placed increasing strain on cracks already present in ideologies of middle-class women's domestic work. The experiences of reformers, field matrons, and government agents belied the rhetoric that coded imperial housekeeping as a benign endeavor and exposed even professional domestic work in service to the government as undervalued and often untenable in western environments. At the same time, however, several decades of schooling and mission work on reservations was effecting indelible change on native women's lives. Education, allotment and home building, and the greater presence of white women and men on reservations created new economic imperatives and social experiences for indigenous women. Whether or not these women adopted Euro-American forms of domesticity, the changes wrought by assimilation policy affected the environments in which they lived and worked.

White women's growing discomfort with the uneasy fit between domestic work and an increasingly industrialized society revised earlier tendencies to look on Indian women as practitioners of a barbarous form of domesticity at best. By the early twentieth century, some white women were reversing the claims of earlier reformers by alleging that native women were *more* domestic than their white sisters, and that this propensity was part of their heritage. Native women seemed to exhibit an attachment to home and home work that white women regarded as a more primitive incarnation of their own more highly evolved and efficient domestic performances. This reinterpretation of native domesticity was a response to several factors that changed the way white and Native American women experienced their domestic work. Education for Indian girls, emerging associations of domestic labor with primitivist nostalgia, and professionalized domestic science all helped to construct Indian domesticity anew. Not only native people but domestic work itself needed to be brought more clearly in line with the systematization and industry associated with civilized society. Domesticity could best be regarded as the mechanism of civilization, reformers reasoned, if it could be quantified and measured. Yet even as they widened the gap between the authoritative domesticity represented by professionals and the less structured domestic labor of Native American women, some reformers began to see a common heritage of domesticity as a way to build bridges between cultures. Thus, white women developed distinctions between their own professionalized domesticity and the domesticity of native women even as they sought to use domesticity to bridge the gap they envisioned. This was a gap that could be mediated by professionals trained to understand both cultures, to appreciate the commonalities between them, and to make native women's domestic labor compatible with present conditions.

An educated Native American woman would seem to be the perfect mediator between cultures. Raised in one culture and schooled in another, she would be ideally positioned to appreciate the shared experience of domestic labor and the need to bring women's work into the modern, industrial present. Arikara Anna Dawson Wilde was a field matron whom white reformers lauded for escaping the bonds of her tribal heritage and for returning to her people to help women to see their domestic roles as newly viable in the present. Dawson Wilde herself claimed the evolutionary narrative teachers and reformers endorsed, framing her own history as progress from an uncivilized past to a professionalized present. Likewise, she embraced domestic work as duties that could be tallied, registering her acceptance of Euro-American systems of order and industry. But while white women may have seen the bridging of cultural differences as part of a professional identity, for a woman whose feet stood less firmly on the side of Euro-American culture the gaps between generations, between races, and between teachers and learners upon which professionalism depended may not have been as easy to span. Dawson Wilde attempted to construct her self and her home as bridges between the primitive past and the civilized present even as she struggled to maintain the expertise and critical distance that professionalism demanded. Her considerable efforts to "make home" on her reservation through her duties as a field matron exposed the constructed quality of the forms of domesticity intrinsic to assimilation; reform-minded observers and Dawson Wilde herself stressed the mechanical and professional aspects of making home. Moreover, opponents on the reservation suggested that what Dawson Wilde was really building was not a home with room for all but a home built on a professional identity that was untenable on the reservation. Her experience and the response of her opponents show that the women's work that professionals imagined as a common thread between women was, in fact, fractured by differences in power and authority. Those who resisted Dawson Wilde deconstructed her home and professional image, exposing them as fortresses meant to uphold Euro-American values in an environment where native women's work was not a relic of the past but a necessary part of the present.

Before and After

Dawson Wilde came from a tribe that had been established on the northern plains for nearly a thousand years. The Arikaras combined women's agriculture with men's hunting, and during the warmer seasons they lived in permanent earth lodge villages organized by matrilineal and matrilocal relationships. Along with their neighbors the Hidatsas and Mandans, the Arikaras suffered from several waves of smallpox brought by European traders during the late 1700s and early 1800s. In 1862 they moved to Like-a-Fishhook Village on the banks of the Missouri River to join the Mandans and Hidatsas. The groups became known as the Three Affiliated Tribes, and in 1870 all three were incorporated into the Fort Berthold Reservation in North Dakota. As people long engaged with whites in trade, they were seen as potential converts. In 1876 missionaries arrived, followed shortly thereafter by a day school. In spite of these early attempts at assimilation and a spate of log home building, the groups maintained their own languages, religions, and medicine.[1]

The reputation of the Three Affiliated Tribes for peacefulness made them an early target for national Indian educators as well. Anna Dawson and her mother arrived in Virginia in November 1878, part of the first group of students recruited to Hampton by Captain Pratt. The first Native Americans brought to Hampton, earlier in 1878, were Pratt's Kiowa, Comanche, Cheyenne, and Arapaho prisoners from Fort Augustine in Florida. Anxious to show that education could subdue even the most aggressive tribes, Hampton founder General Samuel Chapman Armstrong next sought to recruit Sioux children. He hoped to bring girls as well as boys to the school. Like WNIA reformers, he believed that educated women were necessary to help their husbands uphold new values. The forty-nine people in the second group to arrive included thirty-six Sioux recruited from the agencies along the Missouri River and thirteen Mandans, Arikaras, and Hidatsas from Fort Berthold. Among them were nine girls, the first Native American girls at Hampton.[2]

According to longtime Hampton Institute teacher Cora Folsom, two of the Arikaras were "a sad-faced woman knowing nothing of civilization nor the English language" and her "pretty little bright-eyed daughter, *Spahananadaka*, or Wild Rose." These two were Dawson and her mother. Dawson's "mother knew herself to be in consumption and was so anxious to leave her child among civilized friends, that she came all the way to Virginia." When she died a few months later, she left "little Annie . . . with no other home than Hampton."[3] Spahananadaka's teachers must have been delighted by the symbolic resonance of her translated name, which implied wildness with the potential to become the most valuable and cultivated of blooms. After the death of Dawson's mother, the teachers determined that the child had no home in the West to return to. She did not go home in the summer as other students did and remained at Hampton for seven years, until her graduation in 1885. For the teachers at Hampton, Dawson was like an adopted daughter.[4] After graduation, she stayed on as a teacher for several months before going to the Normal School in Framingham, Massachusetts, and later to teach at the Santee Sioux agency school.[5] Folsom noted that the staff's foster child was not only "one of our best teachers" but "the greatest attraction to visitors we had and a girl whose influence among the Indian girls especially was of the greatest value." Folsom's comments came in the context of her criticism of a school policy mandating that Native American and white instructors be separated in the dining hall. She justified Dawson's inclusion in the circle of white teachers by citing her value not just as a teacher but as an "attraction," a valuable exhibit of Hampton's civilizing power.[6]

Exhibiting Hampton students to emphasize the school's success in converting them was nothing new. Dawson, like so many other Native Americans students at Hampton, was first presented to white audiences as a part of a visual narrative about the benefits of Indian education. Part of Armstrong's scheme for gaining support and notoriety for his program was to photograph Indians upon their arrival at Hampton and again months later. In 1884 Hampton's newspaper the *Southern Workman* described the role of photography in the ritual of arrival:

> The first thing after breakfast . . . was to "take their pictures," before any of the primeval dirt and picturesqueness should have given way before the soap and water of civilization. To be sure the boys had cut their hair, but "I

don't call that citizen's dress, do you?" said one bystander rather helplessly, looking at the coats of some which came down to their knees, the Western sombreros, and moccasins sadly the worse for wear. One tall girl was especially effective in a clinging gown of Turkey red, and a red and black shawl worn with real, if somewhat unconventional grace. . . . The various groups were however taken with the usual success of Mr. B and the deep gloom on the faces of the victims was replaced by a very natural smile.[7]

The writer illuminates Hampton's interest in photography's advertising possibilities, calling attention to the importance of dirt and the potential of an "especially effective" girl whose "clinging" gown might suggest an exotic sensuality as well as the possibility of taming that sensuality into more acceptable "grace." Some months later, another photograph would be made of the students, this time in "citizen's dress," their hair neatly combed and cut and their faces cleaned and lightened by their indoor lives. The paired photos would be sold to supporters of the school's mission in order to raise funds.[8]

The photographs scripted the students' past and present with visual symbols of tribal culture and civilization: clothing, hair, and skin color. In their study of the uses of anthropological photography, Melissa Banta and Curtis Hinsley argue that Hampton's before-and-after photographs were deployed as "photographic biography" that "stood in microcosm for the ascent and improvement of the race."[9] Laura Wexler has added that such photographs record the legacy of sentimental fiction as expressed in novels like Caroline Soule's, for they represent native people as objects of domesticity's transformative power and as inheritors of white, middle-class values. Wexler uses the before-and-after photographs of three Hampton girls (see figs. 5.1 and 5.2) as an example, drawing attention to the accoutrements of nineteenth-century middle-class domesticity, including a doll, a book, a checkers game, furniture, and tailored clothing, that function as props in the after photograph. Wexler identifies the props in the after photograph as "codes" for middle-class culture. She argues that the book, checkers game, and doll symbolize Euro-American ways of asserting power through language, geographic imperialism, and sentimental culture.[10] Native American identity is clearly consigned to the past — even through the reminder of the caption — while the props suggest a future contingent on learning to use domesticity and its material expressions as an entry into middle-class life.

That future, however, is also marked by the students' entry into industrial society. Wexler argues that the props show that the "Indian girls are being reconstituted not just as imitation white girls but as white girls of a particu-

Figure 5.1. *On Arrival at Hampton, Va.: Carrie Anderson, 12 yrs., Annie Dawson, 10 yrs., and Sarah Walker, 13 yrs.* Photographer unknown, ca. 1880s. Courtesy President and Fellows of Harvard College Peabody Museum, Harvard University.

lar kind. They are being imprinted with the class and gender construction of the future sentimental reader." Wexler's own words — "reconstituted," "imprinted," and "construction" — indicate that the image may implicitly link the culture of civilization with metaphors of manufacture.[11] In suggesting that the girls' future domesticity will be contingent upon accepting the tools of their trade, the photographs insinuate that the sentiment the students will experience may not be learned through books at all, but through institutions. Their domesticity, in other words, will also be of a particular kind, one that does not necessarily take place in private homes. As Wexler notes, although the students were regarded as future participants in sentimental culture, that culture itself was changing as institutions took over the domesticating process that had formerly been confined to books and home instruction. Already in 1878 the photographs were pointing toward a future in which domesticity could be shifted into contexts more in keeping with efficient, industrial society. The images show the products of civilization — including the girls — as a metonym for its process.[12]

Wexler points out that the girl on the left "looks like she could be consider-

Figure 5.2. *Fourteen Months After*. Photographer unknown, ca. 1880s. Courtesy President and Fellows of Harvard College Peabody Museum, Harvard University.

ing the checkers game with comprehension and some authentic interest in its strategy." In fact, this girl is winning, as evidenced by the pile of checkers she is building. Wexler notes a symbolic facet to this girl's pose that the Hampton photographer could not have known at the time, as this girl later did learn "to play the game and make the system work for herself, when many others failed." The game player is Annie Dawson. Wexler asserts that it is a "remarkable coincidence" that in 1912 the *Southern Workman* reported on the professional success of Anna Dawson Wilde, one of the first Native American Civil Service field matrons.[13] By 1912 Dawson Wilde was part of the system of government institutions that regulated the lives of native people. Yet if we accept Wexler's argument that cultural power lay in the tools of middle-class society, and that sentimental power lay not only in literary texts but in visual culture and education, it is not necessarily coincidence but a consequence of careful self-construction that Dawson Wilde should have become not just domestic but a domestic professional. As in the before-and-after photographs, Dawson Wilde herself transformed Indian womanhood through a strategic acceptance of the domestic tools — home, books, scrub brush, and curtains — that were part of the field matron's trade. Playing the game, by the late nineteenth century, would mean understanding not just the power of domesticity but the greater power of a domesticity that could adapt to the system of production that characterized industrial society.

Part of Dawson Wilde's education must have included an appreciation of the power to display the difference between what reformers saw as primitive and civilized ways — a power she soon learned to seize for herself. A fair held in Boston in 1889 that was arranged by the Jamaica Plain chapter of the WNIA to raise money for the organization's Indian home-building fund featured Walter Battice, Charles Eastman, and Annie Dawson as examples of successful transformations. The fair combined a hodgepodge of racial decor, including Japanese panels and Chinese lanterns, with an "evergreen bower," a wigwam, and "prettily draped tables" covered with objects that the ladies of the association had collected to sell. While the fair's designers created a "romantic atmosphere" for the Boston philanthropists, they balanced the display of the wigwam and "its occupants in Indian dress" with the presence of "two intelligent, gentlemanly young men and the modest, but self-possessed and refined young woman, who are pursuing their studies in Massachusetts, and came to help us prove to our friends that the Indian is worth the trouble we are taking." The women of the Jamaica Plain chapter delighted in the pleasure of their guests as the three Indians chatted with them in English. The WNIA reported that the fair had not only raised $1,450 in funds but had significantly increased awareness of the benefits of assimilation. "It is so true," the article concluded, "that a civilized, Christian Indian is always the strongest plea for his race."[14]

The Boston event repeated the before-and-after sequence of the school photographs: the wigwam and bower summoned up nostalgia for the "romance" of Indian life, while Dawson, Eastman, and Battice embodied civilized values, especially formal education. They were asked to present themselves as products of the work done by educators and by the ladies of the club themselves. Less actors in their own right, the students were placed in the context of other kinds of exhibits meant to persuade potential donors of the "worth" of their cause; they were walking, talking versions of the Hampton photographs.

Yet Dawson's appearance at an 1890 event arranged by Armstrong and held at Colonel John Hay's home in Washington, D.C., suggests that Dawson was beginning to take control of her own self-display. At this event Dawson reversed the before-and-after sequence that Hampton's photographs had used to mark students as products of their education. The *Southern Workman* reported,

> The last speaker of the evening was Annie Dawson, an Arikaree, who has just graduated from the Normal School at Framingham, Mass. She told of the first coming of the Indians to Hampton and then gave a short sketch of her life. She spoke too of what she hoped to do in the future. In conclusion, she read Whittier's poem, Rain-in-the-Face, illustrating the change in feeling among the Indians in regard to education. . . . After the evening's exercises were over, Annie Dawson, who had withdrawn from the scene, re-appeared, dressed in a picturesque Indian costume of white buckskin, handsomely beaded. The style in which the dress was made was graceful and becoming and gave an impression of ease and comfort which is not always given by more fashionable toilettes.[15]

Dawson used her education and understanding of Euro-American cultural values to embrace a version of her cultural past and to unify it with her present self. To be sure, her appearance in white buckskin was calculated to be picturesque rather than threatening, but it also stirred up a sense that Indian women were more free than the middle-class white women who were her audience. It is significant that Dawson changed into native costume after reading Whittier's poem, in which Native Americans are regarded as romantic and aesthetic symbols. By doing so, she enabled her white audience to regard her native identity as part of an American literary and aesthetic history. Dawson legitimated her self-display as a Native American by showing it to be part of a shared intellectual tradition: part of Culture. Though the culture that Dawson ultimately embraced was Euro-American, by indulging a sentimentalized vision of Indian womanhood, she had learned to read and play upon those sympathies and indulge her audience's interest in a past they considered to be both premodern and quintessentially American. She showed herself as capable of being a tourist in her own past, and she demonstrated that her past, moreover, could play upon the sense of freedom that the women in her audience may have coveted themselves. She used her native womanhood to build a bridge between herself and her audience, displaying primitive domesticity with the viewers' understanding that Dawson had tamed and channeled that domesticity through her education in domestic science.

Dawson began to lecture frequently, framing her heritage and education as expertise. Like white women who sought authority as professionals, Dawson was motivated by two desires: the desire to acquire the power of her teachers to exhibit and teach the virtues of civilization, and the desire to lead a life with public value.[16] In a speech at the Friends of the Indians conference at Lake Mohonk in 1898, Dawson explained that it was as a teacher at the Santee Sioux agency — her first visit to the West since her arrival at Hampton in 1878 — that she "received the idea that the homes of the Indians ought to be elevated." Dawson put her epiphany in the context of her homecoming. When she arrived at her old village, she found that the people had come to welcome her back. "It was very pathetic to me as I heard them calling me by my Indian name, for it was many years since I had been with my own people," she told the Lake Mohonk reformers. "As they came to shake hands with me tears fell from their eyes, for they thought I would never come back to the old home. I felt then that my field of work must be among my own people, — that I must devote my life to them."[17]

Dawson's return to her native village generated her desire to work as a field matron. At Fort Berthold, where the people called her by name, Dawson's old identity confronted the civilized self that she had produced and displayed through her years at Hampton. At this moment Dawson felt called to the field, to reproduce the physical and educational structures that had helped to produce her. Dawson's autobiographical account revisits the before-and-after narrative of the Hampton photos, this time inserting the pathos of the moment of encounter between the old life and the new, between Spahananadaka and Anna. But Dawson recalled this incident as not only one of "pathetic" sympathy but one of professional self-making. It was then that she decided to reconstitute her old home as her "field of work." In so doing, Dawson seized Hampton's civilizing practices as the technology of her own work.

Her epiphany prompted Dawson to return east to attend the School of Domestic Science in Boston. According to Folsom, the two years Dawson spent in Boston were ones of intense intellectual work in which the young woman's schedule of "studying, writing, planning and speaking" nearly caused a breakdown.[18] Folsom argues that Dawson's education was not only a rite of passage into the professional world but a rigorous one at that. Dawson was appointed a field matron in 1896, not long after the position became part of the Civil Service and only a year after Indian women were allowed to hold the post.[19] She was probably one of the first indigenous women to receive a Civil Service appointment as a field matron.[20] She returned to Fort Berthold, claimed her allotment, and hired native men to build her a house, where she and her assistant took up residence. Dawson held cooking and sewing classes as well as "mothers' meetings," where she taught the women about hygiene, how to care for the sick, and how to refrain from "bad habits." After two years of service, Dawson concluded that the "homes are being better fitted to receive the returned students, and they are encouraged to keep up civilized ways of living so far as possible. . . . I feel that the time would not be far off when this Indian question would be settled, and the blanket would be transformed into the robe of righteousness."[21] Effecting this transformation, however, would necessitate making her own body and home into exhibits that could, like photographs or museum displays, put indigenous women's domestic practices into a specific context: the past.

Museums, Labor, and Cultural Heritage

Dawson describes her moment of professional self-making in a manner similar to that of Jane Addams, who discovered in an encounter with an elderly immigrant a key connection between past and present in the form of women's labor. A chance meeting with an old woman spinning on her doorstep led Addams to the method she had been seeking to reach out to older immigrant women as well as to evoke in young people a sense of pride in their work. In 1900 the Hull-House Labor Museum was born; it was a space at the settlement house that showcased traditional women's textile crafts as well as metalwork, woodwork, and cooking. Addams combined demonstrations with lectures, photographs, products, and equipment in order to illustrate the industrial history of this labor. Most importantly for Addams, the museum was meant to demonstrate "that culture is an understanding of the long-established occupations and thoughts of men, of the arts with which they have solaced their toil."[22]

For Dawson as for Addams, an encounter with a past she regarded as primitive brought the inspiration for a professional life spent teaching others. Addams noted that the Labor Museum "has revealed the charm of woman's primitive activities," helping young women to understand the pasts their mothers had come from.[23] In the museum the past confronted and informed the present through visitors' appreciation of preindustrial forms of labor. This interest in older forms of labor was part of the burgeoning antimodernist movement, which identified traditional craft production as a remedy for the alienation that seemed to be a result of industrial society.[24] A return to the past, made possible by the museum, was a way to surmount divisions between generations and cultures by showcasing past forms of labor in order to invest present forms with the dignity, aesthetic appeal, and craftsmanship of the past. Addams believed that the museumgoer was uniquely positioned to better understand and appreciate both past endeavors and the potential of the present by witnessing the historical progression of domestic industries.[25] Addams feared that young people failed to appreciate their mothers' roles in their original domestic contexts; women's labor of the past needed a new, updated environment in order to be viable in the present. The museum, the settlement house, and even industry itself, where tasks like sewing and spinning were given new life as wage labor, could reinvigorate domestic labor. Those new environments could be mediated by professionals who could bring to light the connections that both older and younger women failed to see.

In museums like the one at Hull-House, women's preindustrial labor could be characterized as more natural, simpler, and more aesthetically gratifying than factory labor. But others argued that this simplicity was backwardness that was better escaped than revived. With this sensibility, Hampton commemorated Native American traditions, arts, and industries in a museum of its own. Armstrong began collecting Indian artifacts in 1881 as an attempt to teach students to respect their heritage even as they were taught new traditions. One of the most important collectors was none other than Cora Folsom, who gathered artifacts as well as students on her recruiting trips to the West. Folsom eventually curated the museum, which exhibited not only specimens of Indian and African life but also images of conditions at the students' homes in the South and West. In counterpoint to these images of the students' pasts, the museum displayed slides of the industries taught at Hampton and how they might be practiced at home.[26]

Much like the Hull-House Labor Museum, Hampton's museum was aimed at "stimulating race pride," as Cora Folsom phrased it, allowing students to see connections between the past labors of their ancestors and the future industries for which they were being prepared. By encouraging students to look at their pasts with scientific and aesthetic detachment as much as with race pride, the cultural awareness fostered by the museum and Hampton generally was meant to suggest the progress made by blacks and Native Americans toward civilization.[27] Hampton's museum, rather than inviting students to regard their culture as living, urged them to take pride in their ethnicity only insofar as its artifacts recorded racially specific progress toward civilization already attained by Euro-Americans. The museum thus shared some of Charlotte Perkins Gilman's philosophies that both women's work and nonwhites were part of a more primitive past. Gilman propounded the idea that the races should remain distinct and that while primitive, preindustrial forms of labor — including domestic labor — were to be escaped rather than celebrated, some races were more able to escape than others.[28] Likewise, the Hampton museum ultimately upheld racial divisions by suggesting to students that their place was with their own people — that an educated Native American could do the most good by, like Dawson Wilde, returning to work at home.

The Hampton museum suggested that the past was worthy only because it gave students an understanding of their heritage and their place in civilized society. It could stimulate them to recognize that Native Americans (or African Americans) could be productive in the present, and that their industry would contribute to their civilization. The museum did not necessarily celebrate traditional crafts and industries for their own sake but as part of history — a history that was to be overcome. In this narrative, women's traditional work was not a source of significant economic, political, or social gains in the present. While women's industries might, as in the Hull-House Labor Museum, foster a connection to the past, both museums looked at preindustrial work in terms of its practicability in the capitalist present. It was the worker, not necessarily the work itself, who would find a place in industrial society.

In the Plains economy Dawson Wilde came from, women had long played an important productive role, and their work did, in fact, garner recognition and rewards for them. In the Mandan, Hidatsa, and Arikara societies, women's and men's work roles were distinct. While men hunted, women were responsible for providing most of the society's material goods: beans, corn, squash, tanned hides, baskets, beadwork, and lodges.[29] Because kinship was matrilineal and matrilocal, women also maintained family relationships, aided one another in housework, and shared child raising. Various men's and women's societies helped to regulate both social practices and production in the communities. While women working in groups took care of household needs, many women also gained notoriety for specialized skills such as basketmaking and beadwork. These skills afforded them remuneration and entrance into women's craft societies; many were exclusive, as rights in certain skills could be passed between generations.[30] Women seem to have adapted these skills to new conditions, such as trade needs. Among the Hidatsa, for example, women passed on the right to build chimneys in log homes that were erected in the later nineteenth century.[31]

But white observers of the Three Affiliated Tribes' society in the nineteenth century saw only the division of labor between men and women. Using the separate spheres model that governed their own society, they saw women's tasks as household drudgery, made even more valueless by the onset of trade in skins that made the role of men in providing for the material welfare of kin groups more important. Early observers saw Indian women as trapped by their drudgery; later reformers, like the women associated with the WNIA, sought to elevate women's domestic labor to make it more applicable in the present. Emphasizing connections among women, missionaries and field matrons hoped that native women would adapt their traditional domestic roles to the new conditions by learning how to keep house and, eventually, to turn their craft skills to their economic benefit. But in order to effect this change, reformers believed, a link needed to be forged between cultures. The home — specifically the field matron's home — could re-create the museum experience for Native Americans on the reservation. Looking at other cultures objectively would influence women to see their labor in a new light and to adapt their skills to a new kind of domesticity more in keeping with Euro-American values.

For this reason reformers celebrated Dawson Wilde's work as a field matron. WNIA President Amelia Stone Quinton lauded her professionalism, gushing, "I have seen Miss Annie Dawson teaching, and I never saw better teaching, more alert thinking, and better management of pupils."[32] "Miss Dawson's work about her own people has been remarkable," another reformer proclaimed, "and every one who goes there speaks of the beautiful home which she provides as an object lesson."[33] But reformers apprehended her work differently. Dawson Wilde's home, like the Hampton museum, could be regarded as a site that prodded Native Americans to leave past forms of work behind in favor of the industrial present. Or it could, like the Hull-House Labor Museum, help to infuse the architectural, social, and economic present with the integrity and aesthetics of the preindustrial past.

Brilliant Examples

Dawson Wilde contended with both ways of understanding women's work and the labor that Native Americans performed. For some witnesses, Dawson Wilde's work as a field matron was to be apprehended in the context of her race and the racial progress of her people. There was little to be celebrated in forms of labor that did not lead directly to the incorporation of Native Americans into industrial society. Rather than provoking a return to the work of her ancestors, Dawson Wilde's domesticity would stimulate a break from the past, even though racial divisions between whites and Native Americans could not be surmounted. As in the Hampton museum, Native American incorporation — and Dawson Wilde's own incorporation into the world of work — was an industrial process that preserved distinctions between the races, reformulating them as differences between creators and rote copiers, between innovators and laborers.

In 1897, a year after Dawson Wilde's appointment as field matron, Hollis Burke Frissell, who had taken over the leadership of Hampton after Armstrong's death in 1893, reported at the Lake Mohonk Conference on Dawson Wilde's progress and the influences of her home on the reservation. Delighting in the vision of the matron making ice cream for a lawn party at Fort Berthold, Frissell put her work in terms of her earlier transformation: "As I watched each come up and bid the young hostess good-night at the door of her little home, I recalled the picture she had once given me of herself — a little girl stealing watermelon, and offering a part of it with a little prayer to the sun god, with whom she felt obliged to share even her stolen blessings. About as many years of education as a white girl would consider her due, had transformed the heathen child into an efficient, earnest woman; one who has already repaid, in simple service to her people, all the money and time that has been spent upon her."[34] Frissell recounted the assimilation of Dawson Wilde in terms similar to that of the Hampton photographs and the Hampton museum, recalling her transformation as a movement from the primitive, heathen past into the productivity of the present. Dawson Wilde, the product of "about as many years of education as a white girl would consider her due," had become the picture of womanly tenderness and professional efficiency.

Frissell's account of Dawson Wilde's education, however, is hedged by conditions. His language suggests limited amounts, not infinite possibilities. Not only Indian girls but white girls could only expect a certain number of years of schooling — an amount that was due them, ostensibly in exchange for their service to society. Frissell stressed that Dawson Wilde received an amount of education quantified by time and money, thus emphasizing both education and service as quantities that could be tallied. Transformation through education, Frissell suggested, was no miraculous process, but an investment of funds and energy. While he extolled Dawson Wilde's work on the reservation, he also considered it a repayment of Hampton's investment. Regarding transformation as an exchange and investment process, Frissell suggested that Dawson Wilde's access to middle-class identity was also an exchange, and one in which whites held the upper hand. Frissell emphasized her identity as the outcome of investments and implied that the products of her work belonged not only to her but to educators like himself. Indeed, Donal F. Lindsey has argued that sending students back to work on reservations was, in effect, a method of keeping them under government control, thus preserving the "white supremacy and paternalism" that characterized Hampton.[35]

Frissell acknowledged that Dawson Wilde had repaid her debt, but he stressed her role in establishing homes as structures of civilization on the reservation. Her home in the West mediated between premodern and industrial cultures just as Hampton did in the East. Her dwelling, according to Frissell, was a "little log house" with a sod roof and whitewashed interior, "its three rooms tastefully and simply arranged." He asserted that the house was "a model of its kind. . . . Already five houses after the exact pattern of this (mistakes and all), have been completed, and three more are going up now." As Frissell shared a meal with Dawson Wilde one day, "the dining room was suddenly darkened by a big six-foot Indian, who, quite unconscious of the gloom he was casting over our dinner table, stood just outside the one window, taking very exact measurements of its frame and sash. The next day another model cabin was started." The face darkening the doorway, Frissell gloated, had been transformed into that of a burgeoning carpenter.[36]

The anecdote of the Indian in the window confirmed Dawson Wilde's success in reconstituting Hampton's object lessons on the reservation. Frissell located the transformative power of Hampton in the physical frame of Dawson Wilde's own home, particularly in the window frame that channeled vision to productive ends. The image of the Indian "darkening the window" was a common trope in white women's writings about their encounters with natives in the West, generally evoking the threat of Native American entry into the private space of the Euro-American home and endangering the notion of middle-class security.[37] Lori Merish has identified window-gazing in antebellum sentimental novels as a metaphor for the longing to be an "insider" — with the civility, spirituality, subjectivity, and healthy consumerism that such insider status symbolized. She notes that while outsiders were welcomed into the domestic realm, sentimental window-gazing at middle-class interiors also "identified specific, class-based social and material forms as constitutive signs of 'civilized' personhood" — in this case, the home itself.[38] Yet in Frissell's story, the big Indian is linked not to the threat of attack or to a future as a middle-class insider but to his possible strength and performance as a skilled laborer. Because the Indian does not simply long to be inside the domestic scene but desires to make his own home, he turns an otherwise private, domestic scene into a scene of industrial reproduction. In Frissell's account, the window does not frame a cozy interior; it frames, instead, the process of constructing a home and becoming a productive laborer. Ironically, the Indian threatens the notion of middle-class domestic security by implying that home is a mere good to be attained, allying home more with production than privacy. He can be an insider only through his labor, limiting his access to middle-class status. The Indian's looking exposes not only his own labor as a home builder but Dawson Wilde's as well, as his work reproduces her home's construction, "mistakes and all." Dawson Wilde's home is less the locus of sentimental feeling, a refuge from labor, than a stimulant for rural laborers like the big Indian. His looming savagery, Frissell suggests, will be consigned to the past as he channels his strength and size into productive activity.

That Frissell interpreted Dawson Wilde's home as a stimulant to reproduction as well as civilization is implicit in his description of home building as a process akin to factory production. Her home was a pattern to be reproduced exactly, mistakes and all. Frissell described the five new homes not as unique creations but as models built from a model that was in itself imperfect. Frissell believed that in viewing Dawson Wilde's house, the big Indian was induced to create, through his labor, the structure that would enable his own transformation. Frissell interpreted native people's home construction as an imitation of white culture and a commitment to labor in which they built models (and flawed ones at that) rather than fabricating more complex spaces that integrated their cultural practices into their home building. As in the Hampton museum, Frissell framed his image of Dawson Wilde and her home with a narrative of productive labor and reproduction of institutionalized racial hierarchies. He thought of her home and the culture it symbolized as the outcome of a historical progression, and he maintained that both homes and civilized culture could be reproduced by Native Americans who were willing to participate in a specific set of actions. These actions, he believed, could never be more than mechanical mimicry of a Euro-American structure, and moreover, it was a technique of copying so automatic that all the homes were faulty. Like the indigenous people she worked for, Dawson Wilde was first and foremost a reproducer of civilized structures. Her native identity as well as the racial identity of her Native American clients suggested that their domesticity, though it be oriented toward industry rather than a return to the primitive past, was distinctly different from the more authentic domestic productions of their white teachers and supervisors.

Folsom admitted of her colleague that "Frissell did not like Indians and they did not like him. . . . He was a poor storyteller."[39] Though Folsom, as the organizer of the Hampton museum, no doubt shared some of Frissell's views, she told a slightly different story about Dawson Wilde's home, directing her interpretation at middle-class white readers. For Folsom as for Addams, womanhood, domestic work, and the home were the common denominators among women of different races. Dawson Wilde's home and domestic work were part of a professional identity that could help to translate the past into a workable present.

Folsom's comment on Frissell's storytelling abilities makes it worthwhile to compare her story of Dawson Wilde's childhood watermelon escapade with his. She wrote that "a little story illustrates in a measure the life the child had come from. One hot day she and two other little girls, coming back from a bath in the river, were sorely tempted by some watermelons growing near their path. They could not resist, and picking one they sat down to enjoy their stolen feast. The child remembers so well, she says, how each little brown face was devoutly raised as with upstretched hands the choicest bit of the melon was offered to the sun god."[40] Folsom told the story of Dawson Wilde's past as a quaint episode that could be attributed to any child. She incorporated racially specific details — the girls' brown faces and sun worship — into an episode that resembled a girls' tea party or picnic. In Folsom's story, the "life the child had come from" linked her native culture, what reformers regarded as the childhood of the race, to girlhood in general. In the same way that Addams's Hull-House Labor Museum connected preindustrial labor to a comprehensive, historical sense of women's industries, Folsom's article framed the life of Dawson Wilde in terms of her evolution as a working woman more so than her progression from tribal culture to civilized life.

Like Frissell, Folsom stressed the power of Dawson Wilde's home, but Folsom also emphasized the field matron's education, expertise, and hard work. Folsom described Dawson Wilde's homemaking as the practiced work of a professional whose endeavors showed the virtues of progress, who created goods essential to those she served, and whose expertise distanced her from the household labor of nonprofessional women. Folsom's biography of Dawson Wilde in an article in the *Congregationalist and Christian World* combined a photograph of Dawson Wilde in native dress with two photographs of her cottage on the Fort Berthold reservation. "Miss Dawson's Log Cabin" shows the exterior of a small house with one outbuilding. "Interior of Log Cabin" shows the inside of Dawson Wilde's home, ornamented with pictures and furnished with books, pictures, a sewing machine, and a writing desk. The photograph of Dawson Wilde is above and between the photographs of her home; along with the head-ing on the page, "The Home and Its Outlook," the images of home frame Dawson Wilde's body. Even as Dawson Wilde appears in buckskin, the images of her home suggest that she also has to be regarded as the producer of these domestic spaces. Juxtaposing Dawson Wilde's clearly Indian body with her home and its interior showed that Dawson Wilde's Native American womanhood existed simultaneously with domestic womanhood — the kind of domestic womanhood that, properly inscribed in a home through material artifacts, could carry the historical weight of civilized culture. Dawson Wilde's body seems to function here, as in the Hull-House museum, as a connection to the past that stresses domesticity as a phenomenon shared across cultures and generations. The images accompanying the article display a native woman's body in a new context, that of the scientifically modern and well-appointed home.

Dawson Wilde's home was a museum in miniature where educational and moral lessons could be reproduced for visitors who had no access to such institutions. Dawson Wilde's allotment cottage stood as "an example of inexpensive, tasteful comfort that soon found many admirers and not a few imitators."[41] The shelves on her parlor wall are filled with books, reinforcing her status as an educated woman and symbolizing literacy and access to Euro-American culture and knowledge. Photographs and a painting gesture toward cultivation and good taste and underscore Dawson Wilde's career choice. After all, she was more than just a domestic woman; she was a woman who had been educated in the emerging field of domestic science. Because of her scientific training, readers of the *Congregationalist and Christian World* would have recognized that her home was a sort of laboratory as well as a home. It was to be a model for the people of Fort Berthold to recognize the differences between their lives and the practices that Dawson Wilde exemplified in her housekeeping. Part of Dawson Wilde's emerging professionalism, then, was her ability to interpret Euro-American values and work to her people as well as to interpret reservation life to reformers and supporters in the East, all through the medium of her home. White readers would have seen Dawson Wilde dressed in buckskin as evidence of past domesticity, but they also would have seen her home as evidence of a professionalism that distanced her work from the domestic labor of other Indian women.

Though Folsom presented Dawson Wilde as a link between cultures, her professional career rather than her return to preindustrial work established the connection. While Folsom suggested that Dawson Wilde's professionalism was a sort of domesticity writ large, it was a certain kind of domesticity that she encouraged, one that was in keeping with the ideals that Folsom espoused in the Hampton museum exhibits. Indeed, Folsom lamented that too many native girls embraced inherited forms of domesticity rather than constructing newer, more prominent roles for themselves. "If there is anything in inheritance," Folsom wrote,

> There is every reason to expect the Indian woman to take life seriously. She does. Even as a child she is eminently domestic, with that strongly developed protective instinct that shows itself most with children, and which leads her, earlier than her white sister to find her happiness in the home or in a school among the younger children. Occasionally a bright girl flashes meteor-like across the eastern sky, is written up, photographed and flattered until her little head is a bit turned and then as suddenly and quite as fortunately — disappears. Sought out, she will be found in some quiet little home, glad after the first agony is over, to have exchanged the pedestal for the cook stove and the adulation of sentimental friends for the safer joys of a prosaic husband. Thus the "prominent Indian woman" is nipped in the bud and we have no very brilliant examples of what she might be.[42]

Folsom declares that as girls retreated into the very homes that reformers had endorsed as a tool of advancement, their potential to exemplify progress was lost. Indian domesticity snuffed the spark of brilliant possibility.

Race links Dawson Wilde and her people, but in creating her home as an exhibit, she needed to cultivate the detachment from traditional culture that the museum also encouraged. For a Native American woman like Dawson Wilde, her work as a field matron was the ultimate in professionalism. Her home symbolized her commitment to Euro-American notions of progress among her own people, whose social practices both justified her work of uplift and provided an example of an alternative way of life that threatened the very values she espoused.[43] The photographs show her home to be free of "Indianness," but in reality it was located far from centers of Euro-American culture. The professional work description for field matrons demanded that they be "immersed" in native culture yet at the same time exhibit "professional autonomy."[44] Yet it was a great challenge for a Native American woman to be so professional as to protect the purity of Euro-American culture even among her own people.

Accounting Housework

As a professional woman, a domestic expert, and a Native American, Dawson Wilde was caught between contending understandings of the connection between preindustrial forms of labor, women's work, and racial heritage. Clearly, her choice to become a field matron was conditioned by her belief that her people were in need of civilizing as well as a sense that she could do the most good by choosing professional service over unpaid domestic labor. At the same time, she cultivated a sense of herself as a bridge between cultures, a woman who could slip easily between her cultural past and her professional future and who believed that an understanding of cultural heritage was essential to productive work in the present. On one hand, she seemed to celebrate her heritage, as Addams suggested. But Dawson Wilde may have succumbed to beliefs in the lesser status of indigenous women's domestic labor in her attempts to distance herself from her people in order to cultivate a professional self.

Field matrons, no matter what their ethnic heritage, faced a difficult task in professionalizing their homemaking work. In her history of the field matron corps, Lisa Emmerich shows that attempts by Commissioner of Indian Affairs Thomas J. Morgan to secure appropriations for field matron positions entailed "elevat[ing] domestic duties and care of the family to the status that 'real' professions like smithing, carpentry, and farming enjoyed." Because government officials considered field matrons' work to be mere housekeeping, the program had to present its workers as housekeeping "technicians."[45] While white women had long made a practice of keeping household accounts and recording income from their domestic work in their journals, submitting these accounts to the government separated this work from that of lay housekeepers and justified the salaries field matrons received.

Dawson Wilde was expected not only to model the virtues of domesticity and domestic labor to Native Americans on the reservation but to record her work and to report on the people's progress by clearly enumerating her observations and duties. Field matrons' monthly, quarterly, and yearly reports recorded daily work and summed up changes over time for the Office of Indian Affairs (OIA). For these reports, field matrons were required to specify the number of days occupied visiting homes, the number of families visited, how many of those families were being visited for the first time and how many had been visited before, the number of people in each family, how many were living in houses and how many in teepees or "other Indian habitations," and the number of women educated in matters such as child care and hygiene. The reports also documented improvements made to field matrons' homes and elaborated on the homes' adornments. Dawson Wilde, in accordance with descriptions of field matrons' duties, believed that a good part of her work was to keep her home and person in order. She wrote to explain why she had spent much of one month at home working on her house, submitting that "example and object lessons are worth equally as much to the people as the daily precepts."[46]

In November 1901, Dawson Wilde spent twenty-two days visiting and met with forty-two families. One hundred four callers came to her home, including men, women, and children who came to read, look at pictures, do "fancy work," and sew. She reported that nearly everyone participated in the Thanksgiving Day celebration she arranged, including Protestants, Catholics, and "Dance People," or those who adhered to native religions.[47] Dawson Wilde also requested items to improve her home and her working conditions. In the spring of 1900 she wrote to the Commissioner of Indian Affairs to request a team, harness, wagon, sheeting, bed linens, steel kitchen range, and camp outfit for overnight visiting.[48] Finally, the reports included Dawson Wilde's daily interactions with the people, as she invited men, women, and children into her home for prayer meetings and sewing circles, to read and look at pictures, and to be instructed in animal husbandry. In the summer of 1901 Dawson Wilde offered prizes to "two women, who would work most diligently, in keeping clean and orderly houses" for a year. The prizes were bestowed upon the most industrious at the Fourth of July celebration.[49]

The reports emphasized Dawson Wilde's skills in domestic science and in the art of homemaking. The statistics in her monthly reports quantify the process of civilization as a series of tasks that could be described and counted. By counting the number of families visited and "number of women actually instructed," Dawson Wilde was translating her domestic activities into work that justified itself through enumeration of the services she provided. Her monthly reports were a way of exhibiting assimilation work as a series of tasks accomplished; they were a way of claiming that work as the basis of a professional identity. The connection between producing a professional self and exhibiting labor is particularly conspicuous here, because Dawson Wilde's authority stemmed from her position as a model; her work was to encourage others to produce themselves after her example and by copying her home, her methods, and her way of life.

In her reports, Dawson Wilde tried to quantify her influence by enumerating individuals who had changed. She did not, however, account for those individuals' reasons for their actions. For example, Dawson Wilde counted the number of women to whom she had given work in a particular time period and how many men had placed money in the bank.[50] She described at length the transformation of one woman, "one of the oldest of returned students," who had held out forcefully for years against whitewashing her home. "She and her children were the least attractive in appearance," Dawson Wilde attested, claiming that the woman "purposely would wear a most uncleanly gown to church, 'to see if it would kill Miss Dawson, (my maiden name), to see her in such a dirty dress!'" As a former student, the woman certainly knew the standards of appearance and hygiene the field matron was meant to encourage; her resistance ridiculed those standards by suggesting that Dawson Wilde was so steeped in domestic order that to see it flaunted would "kill" her. Yet in 1910 Dawson Wilde reported with relief that the woman had become more tidy, had interpreted for her, and had helped with the housework in Dawson Wilde's home. To signify the change in the woman's attitude, Dawson Wilde "gladly transferred her name on the list with those who are of a genuine comfort to me."[51] But what appeared in Dawson Wilde's reports as yet another tale of transformation elided the woman's motivations behind her conversion. In fact, many native women selectively embraced facets of Euro-American culture in order to strategically provide for themselves and their families. What seemed to be capitulation could often be a response to a husband's economic difficulties, a play for political power or social respect, or an adaptation of a traditional role to new circumstances.[52] But presenting herself as a professional, Dawson Wilde needed to construct both indigenous and Euro-American cultures as much more rigid formations than they were — as ideologies rather than sets of practices that could be selectively accepted or rejected.

Accordingly, Dawson Wilde counted her adopted children as part of her "mission" on the reservation. When her former assistant and sister-in-law, Mary Howard, died in 1910, Dawson Wilde took over the care of Howard's three children. In adopting them as her own, Dawson Wilde explained in a report that "I have considered them as part of my work for this people. Tho many times they go without close attention, I try to make them as object lessons to the women." She indicated that the children helped her show the women of the tribe by example what she had tried to explain in her many talks. The children served as examples at "every important religious festive day or on national holidays," when they "learned and recited simple pieces appropriate to the occasion." While it was not uncommon, in her native culture, to take responsibility for relatives' children, Dawson Wilde felt compelled to justify to her superiors the "extra care and responsibility" she had taken on by adopting these children by showing how they, too, could be made part of her work. By stressing the children's usefulness as "object lessons" in her report, Dawson Wilde translated what may have been a social obligation into a professional duty.[53]

In all ways, from home life to family life, Dawson Wilde attempted to represent herself as a professional. To accomplish this, she needed to suggest that other forms of domesticity, including women's seasonal agricultural work, were not legitimate. In the interstices of her reports lie suggestions that her work involved more than the systematic betterment of homes and that much of her work involved negotiation between the cultural ideals symbolized by her home and the context of reservation space, where domestic work had functions not necessarily mediated by capitalistic or governmental imperatives. In September 1901 Dawson Wilde wrote that harvest season had dispersed the people: children and women stayed home to help with the harvest, and her women's group, the Kings Daughters, was "so scattered that it has not been possible to gather them together."[54] Her reports, in stressing the work that she did, also made explicit the problems with women's housekeeping at Fort Berthold, alleging that dirt floors, the size of families and condition of children, and the decoration of homes were not up to standard. Distinguishing her homemaking from mere housekeeping, she also distinguished her professional work from indigenous women's domestic labor. Domestic work not systematized by the context of an industrial economy was, Dawson Wilde's reports concede, less civilized.

Because Dawson Wilde was keenly aware of the people's financial straits, however, the economic troubles of the Three Affiliated Tribes come through in her reports. She suggested that her battles were against not only the people's resistance to her admonishments but their inabilities to model themselves after her due to their financial problems. Men could not put money in the bank when they did not have it; men could not cultivate land in years of drought. Dawson Wilde argued that her standards were difficult to uphold in homes with "mud plastered walls, with dirt roofs and dirt floors" that were not "inducive to the highest ideals and standards of home." She advised the commissioner that "Mr. Hannah's Bill," likely the treaty ratified in June 1910 that opened reservation lands to non-Indians, include a provision that would allow a "plain, two roomed frame building to each head of a family" in exchange for the lands the tribes were ceding. Such homes, she claimed, could stimulate women to better habits of life.[55]

In spite of such concessions to the troubles that plagued the reservation, many the result of government intervention, Dawson Wilde consistently presented a professional self to the OIA in her field matron reports.[56] Dawson Wilde's commitment to quantifying her duties and constructing herself as a technician, even in raising her adopted children, underscored that the value of field matrons' domestic work had to be proven continually. While it was difficult to show the economic value of this work, particularly in the depressed environment of the reservation, Dawson Wilde attempted to reveal this value by quantifying persons and duties. Dawson Wilde counted cultural negotiations among her people as tasks performed, presenting herself as impeccably professional to her employers.

Every Day I Walked by Mrs Wilde's House

Ironically, Dawson Wilde's attempt to professionalize herself by making her home into a bulwark of civilized domestic values may have made her a less effective field matron. Lisa Emmerich notes that Dawson Wilde was one of the only Indian field matrons to "directly challenge the authority and power of traditional healers" on the reservation; no doubt, then, reservation inhabitants responded to her challenges by accusations of health violations and even land fraud.[57] More than defying traditional medicine, however, Dawson Wilde also, it seems, came into conflict with traditional forms of women's work. In October 1905 Commissioner of Indian Affairs Francis Leupp received a letter via Fort Berthold agency superintendent Amzi Thomas from Mrs. Ella Ripley, a Mandan woman from the reservation, charging Dawson Wilde and her fellow field matron, Adeline Beauchamp, with neglect of duty and asking that she be removed from the position. Ripley's complaint was prompted by the deaths of Mamie Elder and Esther Crows Ghost, both of whom succumbed to tuberculosis. Ripley submitted that the field matrons had "failed to visit or help" the women. Ripley organized a petition for the matrons' removal, affirming, "We, undersigners Mandan Grosventre, and Arikara of Fort Berthold N.D. reservation, desire to abolish the positions of field matrons, as they have not been much use to us all these years, And the money put away for the benefit of the sick." The petition contained more than 150 signatures. Ripley added that many people were away from the reservation at the time and that more were afraid to sign their names to the document, but "stick to it that the field matrons have not been any good to them." Ripley supported her complaint by claiming that "Mr. Red Bear[,] Mr. Ghost Crows or Knows Ghost[,] Mr. Little[,] and Mr. Boy Chief request to be the first ones to be call up on to give testimonies about Mrs. Wilde" and that "Mrs. Huntly[,] Mr. Yellow Bird[, and] Mrs. Howling Wolf (Jr.) are fraid to go on the list, but said they will tell an inspector when he comes about the field matron Mrs. Wilde."[58]

Like Dawson Wilde, Ella Ripley knew the power of quantification. Just as Dawson Wilde produced lists of names of accommodating and resistant individuals, Ripley produced a document listing the names of those who condemned the field matron. She provided the names of individuals whose names did not appear on the list but whose opinions she claimed to know. In her letter, Ripley exhibited a keen understanding of the duties of field matrons and shrewdly formulated charges that undermined the professional and exhibitionary power upon which Dawson Wilde relied. Ella Ripley had attended the Carlisle School and had worked for Dawson Wilde several years earlier, which accounts for her literacy and for her knowledge of the matrons' responsibilities.[59] But unlike Dawson Wilde, who entered a service career as a professional, Ripley followed the path of most Indian school graduates who returned to their reservations to marry, farm, keep house, or find work as a domestic servant — a "hired girl."[60] Her charges were informed both by her belief that the field matron's duties were those of service and by her concern for the people of the reservation, whom she felt were being ignored.

Through her petition, Ripley submitted that professional expertise was not necessary to function as a mediator between cultures and that the day-to-day domestic chores necessary to sustain life on the reservation also constituted a valid kind of knowledge. Ripley's letter and the names of the petitioners suggest that at least some people saw Dawson Wilde's mission as the accumulation of cultural power through the display of her home and body rather than an attempt to rectify the real problems on the reservation. While Frissell, Folsom, and Dawson Wilde herself saw the field matron as a model of industry, professionalism, and cultured womanhood, some of the people of the Affiliated Tribes considered her home and work as part of the creation of what Mary Sylwester has called the "hostile domestic geography" of the civilizing mission — domestic architecture that not only excluded native people from the home but also symbolically excluded them from the nation.[61] In Ripley's view, Dawson Wilde had built a house dedicated to the service of the people of her tribe, but the house stood as an empty display to people who badly needed medicine, land, and economic justice. The home's focus on expertise and industrial, scientific housekeeping failed to fully account for other kinds of cultural knowledge that were just as appropriate to conditions on the reservation.

Ripley's charges exposed the ways Dawson Wilde's professionalized, systematized version of domesticity discounted the unpaid, undervalued work of indigenous women. Ripley suggested that far from being primitive, women's work of visiting, preparing food, and caring for the sick met pressing needs. Beauchamp's and Dawson's visits were merely cursory, she maintained, reporting that "Mrs. Wilde knows how to get out of anything." The visits that the field matrons so assiduously enumerated are reformulated in the letter as only that — tasks to be counted on reports. Ripley knew the field matrons' responsibilities to report their duties and disdained the superficiality of that work. Ripley related that Dawson Wilde stopped briefly at houses to ask "if they had any eggs to sell, or [at]another house gave them news paper for their shelves or cubbards. . . . When she come to make report, she would counted these house among the houses visited, making appear that she had done some work."

Dawson Wilde thoughtlessly spoiled bread in teaching women "who would have to wait a long time for the next issue" of flour rations. Ripley contended that Dawson Wilde's assistant, Mrs. Howard, did not even know how to make corn bread herself. In Ripley's perspective, Dawson Wilde and Beauchamp did not, in any real sense, enter the lives and homes of the people. Rather, Ripley argued that their presence and influence were fleeting and insignificant and that they did not show sensitivity to the physical and economic conditions on the reservation.[62]

Dawson Wilde's cursory visits and gifts of shelf paper contrast sharply with Ripley's description of other women's work on the reservation, which also included visiting, cooking, and caring for the sick. Ripley not only recounted her work with an insistence on its value, but she placed her work in the context of familial relations to in-laws, fourth cousins, aunts, and uncles. Describing her own contributions of eggs, bread, milk, and health care to families on the reservation, Ripley highlighted tribal and familial relations as a support network and stressed Dawson Wilde's indifference to them. Dawson Wilde's house emerged in the letter as a symbol of her apathy to this alternative system. Ripley wrote that "in June, Miss Mamie Elder a promising young lady, went to bed with sickness, she was only one mile from Mrs Wilde's house. Miss Elder had no father or mother, but her uncle came to me every day for raise bread and milk and fresh eggs, she was a fourth cousin of mine, every day I walked by Mrs Wilde's house to go to see Miss Elder, always having something prepared for her to eat."[63] Ripley also related her visits to Mrs. George Wash, a widow with three children, who was immobilized by illness and was covered with "maggoty sores" from shoulder to thigh. Ripley claimed that the field matrons stopped in on the ailing woman only to say "how do you do," and that the other women's work in caring for Mrs. Wash did not "soften the hearts of the field matrons." While Dawson Wilde was anxious to account for her status as a home technician by counting rolls of shelf paper distributed, Ripley argued, she distanced herself from illness and isolation on the reservation. Ripley and her sister-in-law were left with the job of cleaning Mrs. Wash's dirty body and the sores that were filled with blood, discharge, and maggots.[64]

Ripley's letter shows that by rejecting some forms of domestic work, matrons could drive a wedge between themselves and the women on the reservation, for they seemed to separate their professional work from the unpaid domestic labors of native women. As professionals, female moral reformers in general and field matrons in particular challenged the model of "True Womanhood" that they were meant to inculcate in others. Margaret D. Jacobs asserts that field matrons "transmitted their desire for independence and their rebellion against social norms" to native women rather than the piety, purity, and submission associated with mid-nineteenth-century domesticity.[65] Jacobs points to the empowering aspects of this rejection for both indigenous and white women, but for the women of Fort Berthold, this rejection may also have been alienating. Ripley attested that Beauchamp had built a house three miles from the Indians' village, out "among the high hills." Beauchamp had told Ripley that "she was going there where the Indian can not get to her and eat her up" but that "she will have an Indian with her, no matter where she goes for she married an Indian and is supporting him. . . . Good example to set for these Indians by these two field matrons, is to support their husbands."[66] Ripley argued that field matrons' marriages were strategic moves that created power blocs; Ripley likened their marriages to political faction-building. In Beauchamp's marriage particularly, Ripley saw a double standard: Beauchamp ostensibly wanted to create a divide between herself and the people by building her house at a remove from their homes, but she was willing to marry an Indian man and support him. Both her removal and her marriage may have seemed, to Ripley, like ways to assert cultural and economic power over the people. The location of Beauchamp's house, at once obscured in the hills and elevated, may have seemed like a deliberate move in which Beauchamp would be able to view the people of Fort Berthold without their seeing her. Both in their marriages and in their support of their Indian husbands, the two field matrons contradicted the model of female domesticity and male industry that they preached. In the process, they seemed to reject the kin systems and household chore sharing that had long constituted traditional women's power networks.

Just as Ripley stressed Beauchamp's removal from the village, she argued that Dawson Wilde's house was not an object lesson but an exclusive place constructed by Native American labor but not open for their use. While the house was built by and for the Indians, it was available only to a privileged few. "The house that she is living in the Indian men [built]," Ripley insisted; the men had also dug a well in front of the house, at the cost of one man's life. Dawson Wilde had procured shingles for the house "for the benefit of the sick" and had also requested a range from the government, for the women "who will come to this house to cook, iron, bake, and heat water for washing on this range." Ripley expressed her interest in these appliances by repeating the refrain, "The Department granted such a good thing for the Indians." She submitted, however, that the women never saw the range and it stood in Dawson Wilde's shed. "The only Indians who have the benefit of all things done on this house, are Mr. and Mrs. Wilde, Mr. and Mrs. Howard, and the Howards['] children," as well as two men who worked for Dawson Wilde, Mr. Wells and Mr. Badger.[67]

Ripley clearly felt that the house did not belong just to Dawson Wilde, but that by virtue of its status as an object lesson and by the government's investment in its furnishings the home belonged to the native people as well. Dawson Wilde's failure to open her home to them constituted a grievous failure: a withholding of communal property and services.

Ripley further charged that Dawson Wilde had invited a man for dinner for the purpose of bribing him. This charge of bribery characterized Dawson Wilde as flaunting her connections with the white women and men of the reform movement. The man who had been invited to dinner claimed that Dawson Wilde told him she was only interested in helping the Arikara people, not Mandans, and that she had many friends in Washington who were backing her. Ripley justified her own letter and the appeal it contained by pointing out that Dawson Wilde had petitioned to have the minister removed from the agency and to have the post office taken from him; she had also petitioned to have day school teachers removed. Dawson Wilde, Ripley wrote, "brags that she has power in Washington, she says 'with a snap of my finger, I can put any employee out.'" Yet Ripley claimed that same power for herself and the petitioners, stating that Dawson Wilde "hates to see any body pass a pettion [sic], she wants to do the passing and we want to pass it once."[68]

Dawson Wilde's home, according to Ripley, was not a welcoming place but a fortress she used to consolidate her power and prestige, and one that correspondingly devalued women's work that was so crucial to survival on the reservation. Ripley intimated that if Dawson Wilde had participated more fully in the life of the reservation, her help would have been welcome, but in making her home a citadel, she cut herself off from the spaces that, on early twentieth-century reservations, were crucial sites for keeping culture — and people — alive. Ripley's suggestion that native women's work could harmonize with the professional aims and architecture of the field matron's cottage does resemble Addams's ideas; the settlement house for working women fostered a supportive community among women that paid homage to older forms of domestic labor. Yet for Ripley and her kinswomen, such networks and structures were neither new developments created by professional women nor vestiges of an older, less complex culture. The networks that helped sustain women on the reservation did not grow out of middle-class women's reform movements and were not artifacts of a less developed culture. The very systems that reformers sought to eradicate, Ripley's letters suggest, were adapting to new conditions and doing the work that the field matron and her home could not.

The petitioners implied that Dawson Wilde and her cottage ultimately helped to bolster a new form of professionalized Euro-American domesticity by reinforcing the image of Indian labor and lifestyle as primitive. While white readers of the *Congregationalist and Christian World* may have seen Dawson Wilde's home as useful because it seemed to connect native heritage to white culture through the common denominator of domesticity, Mandan, Arikara, and Grosventre readers of Dawson Wilde's house may not have perceived those messages in the same way. Ripley, at least, understood that the house was for Native American people, but she felt that it should not be just viewed but used by them. The home did not welcome all people into the community of viewers who could, as reformers Folsom and Frissell did, see the home as a product of their own work and worldview. Ripley wanted the home to be opened as space for the people to work and to create, but she protested that the technologies with which Dawson Wilde had been furnished could only constitute Dawson Wilde herself as a professional and did nothing to help people to support themselves. And in constituting herself as a professional, Dawson Wilde reinforced the devaluation of domestic work; in Ripley's words, "All this time the field matrons never came into our house to make our burden light."[69]

Fort Berthold Indian Agent Amzi Thomas advised the OIA that Ripley was "likely to prove her case if given the opportunity," but it may not have been given. Dawson Wilde did have friends closely connected to government.[70] As Wexler notes, the *Southern Workman* mentioned Dawson Wilde in March 1912 as a "leader" among the Indians. What the journal did not mention is that Dawson Wilde had been relieved of her position at Fort Berthold the previous year. In 1910 the new Commissioner of Indian Affairs, Robert G. Valentine, appointed Indian school inspector Elsie Newton to compile a report on field matrons' work.[71] Newton visited the Fort Berthold reservation, and in 1911 she sent a report to the commissioner recommending that Dawson Wilde's position be abolished. Newton described Dawson Wilde as "one of the best educated Indian women I have ever met" who in "her dress, her family life and her home . . . appears to keep up well, those standards of living she acquired in the east. Whether a field matron or not, her manner of living should be an example to the community." Newton noted that "latterly Mrs. Wilde's influence among her people has not been what it was during the first years of her work." She suggested that Dawson Wilde was "naturally" more interested in her family than in her work as a matron. Newton cited Dawson Wilde for failing to act in a detached and professional manner.[72] Perhaps the notion that Indian women were inherently more domestic, less capable of surviving in the professional realm, had caught up with Dawson Wilde at last. In December 1911, Dawson Wilde's position was abolished.[73]

Clearly, Dawson Wilde's attempt to provide object lessons on the reservation put her directly in the center of intertribal politics and contests over the meaning of home and women's work.[74] Ella Ripley's incisive criticisms of Anna Dawson Wilde reveal the essential flaw in the professional domesticity that Dawson Wilde and others so assiduously constructed: power, authority, and the benefits of cultural visibility came only in being the creator of the object lesson, not in learning the lesson. Anna Dawson Wilde's home could not reflect the lessons of the museums without a population of willing learners whose domestic traditions needed to be devalued, simplified, made primitive, and even erased in order to support the new vision of Euro-American domesticity that professional women espoused. Moreover, Ripley's reaction to Dawson Wilde's house and work suggests that even those Native American women who embraced some forms of Euro-American domesticity and looked eagerly upon opportunities to learn new skills need to be reevaluated. As Patricia Albers has noted, "We know so much about the material conditions of labor but understand so little about the experience of performing labor and even less about the languages and cultural constructs within which its agency gets expressed."[75] Resistance, in other words, might lie as much in the ways indigenous women interpreted their work and the work of reformers as in the work that they did. In a reservation climate already changed by years of assimilation policy that valorized the domestic, Ripley's familiarity with the home as an object lesson enabled her to imagine the ways home spaces might be used to empower rather than exclude native women and their work. Ripley acknowledged her position as the object lesson's viewer without embracing the passive acceptance and historical gap between primitive and professional forms of domesticity that the lesson's ideology required. Along with her co-petitioners, she deconstructed Dawson Wilde's model home, exposing it as an object lesson that excluded rather than invited Native Americans to participate in its organization. Ella Ripley's reaction is a powerful testament to the ways nonprofessional native women seized their own opportunities to function as bridges between two conflicting forms of domesticity.

CHAPTER SIX

Border Designs

Domestic Production and
Cultural Survival

nna Dawson Wilde's experience on the reservation shows the difficulty of maintaining strict divisions between professional housekeeping and less routinized forms of domesticity — those shaped by kinship ties rather than bureaucratic responsibilities. What may have been a deeply personal conflict for Dawson Wilde was, by the first decade of the twentieth century, present in widely held beliefs that linked domestic labor with the idea of Native American primitivity. Increasing secularization and systematization of the home and marketplace prompted Euro-Americans to seek new repositories for the values that had formerly been preserved in domesticity: morality, authenticity, purity, and altruistic labor. Native American arts and crafts, which seemed to hearken back to a premodern past, served that very purpose.[1] The idea that home and market existed in separate spheres extended into a newly racialized context, as Native American artisanal labor — typified by the figure of the Indian woman artisan — came to signify the kind of pure values that white women's work at home had long symbolized.[2] The antimodernism that blossomed in early twentieth-century art and literature relied on notions of spatial difference, in which reservations, like homes, could be regarded as repositories of authenticity separate from economic life. Euro-Americans downplayed the economic contributions of native labor to focus, instead, on the way Indians' crafts preserved cultural values — the very strategy that writers and lawmakers had used to distinguish domestic work from wage labor.

At the turn of the twentieth century, Native American domestic arts were in the midst of a crucial shift. Government assimilation efforts, combined with the commercial intents of philanthropic organizations like the WNIA, service workers such as field matrons, and independent entrepreneurs, encouraged native people to produce baskets, beadwork, blankets, and pottery not just for domestic use but for sale to white consumers.[3] Janet Catherine Berlo has called the years between 1875 and 1925 the "great era of collecting," in which scientists, patrons of the arts, casual collectors, and tourists scrambled for Indian artifacts.[4] Systematic efforts at deculturation and geographic dispossession were accompanied by interest in native women's crafts, as middle-class Victorians purchased needlework curios, ceramics, and blankets to decorate their parlors and gain access to the free and natural life that Native Americans had come to symbolize. Their crafts were regarded with nostalgia and placed within the sentimental economy of the middle-class home, where their alleged authenticity could evoke the images of community, maternalism, and pastoralism that, for whites, were associated with prehistory.[5]

Most investigations into the early twentieth-century celebration of the primitive focus on Euro-American appropriation of Native American craft and culture. Yet Native American artists, writers, and intellectuals participated in this discussion as well, as new studies are beginning to reveal. Perhaps most notable, members of the Society of American Indians, founded in 1911, engaged crucial questions about Native Americans' class status and cultural contributions, and several of its leaders have garnered significant critical attention from historians and literary critics.[6] Zitkala-Sa, in particular, is regarded in literary history as a transitional figure, because she was one of the first Native American women writers to publish in a popular journal. Critics have read her stories as regionalist texts, as co-optations of nineteenth-century genres such as sentimentalism, travel writing, and ethnography, and as pointed indictments of the economic and political agendas of Euro-American moral authority.[7] Yet Angel DeCora (Hinook-Mahiwi-Kilinaka), a Winnebago (Ho-Chunk) artist and teacher, wrote and illustrated two stories for *Harper's New Monthly Magazine* in 1899, one year before Zitkala-Sa's autobiographical tales appeared in the *Atlantic Monthly*. DeCora's drawings illustrate an edition of Zitkala-Sa's collection *Old Indian Legends* that was published in 1901; these illustrations are among the first published by a Native American woman in a book. DeCora seemed less openly critical of Euro-American culture than Zitkala-Sa, who published her critique of assimilation, "Why I Am a Pagan," in the *Atlantic Monthly* in 1902. DeCora's work, however, was affected deeply by turn-of-the-century battles over the meaning of culture as it pertained to artists, women, and Indians as workers. The racialized and gendered meanings of labor as well as judgments about the relative value of domestic and industrial production were at stake in these battles.

Angel DeCora emerged onto the national literary and artistic scene in the midst of the turn to the premodern that celebrated arts and crafts, ideally made by unknown women carrying on ancient traditions in far-off places, to take aim at the division between "primitive" domestic and "modern" economic values. DeCora counted among her friends and acquaintances such prominent artists as Cecilia Beaux and Alice Barbour Stevens and ethnologists Natalie Curtis Burlin and Francis La Flesche. In 1902 DeCora became one of a few women elected to the American Academy of Design.[8] She was hailed by her contemporaries as one of the leading Native American women of her time, sharing prominence with other early twentieth-century Native American professionals such as Zitkala-Sa and physicians Charles Eastman and Carlos Montezuma. In her artistic work and public writings, Angel DeCora attempted to define a new sense of Indian identity based on older forms of domestic production even as she struggled to distinguish native craft from white women's devalued domestic labor. It was to be an identity that would neither reject nor be contained by the literary, scientific, architectural, and economic structures that had supported Euro-American domesticity. Instead, her theories emphasized the borders, where indigenous ways of knowing and seeing encountered Euro-American ways to produce something entirely new. Like white feminists who crusaded for the economic value of domestic labor in the mid-nineteenth century, DeCora saw the work produced by Indian artisans as economically valuable. In the aftermath of cultural and geographic losses, Indian culture and its values did not exist in some mystical premodern space but, in fact, needed to be produced through skilled work. But also like earlier Euro-American feminists, DeCora infused domestic production with new cultural imperatives. Native American crafts should be legitimated not just as commodities that supported white consumers' needs or a therapeutic recovery of premodern values but as an avenue to a specifically Native American identity.[9] Appropriating the tools that whites had long used to define the economic, gendered, and racial separations crucial to white, middle-class domesticity — literary texts, ethnographic science, displays, and the home itself — DeCora embraced work as a tool for creating Indian identity while redefining domestic production as having both cultural and economic value.

A Very Promising Career

DeCora was the daughter of Winnebagos who, as the Prophet Wabokieshiek's descendants, had been pushed west into Nebraska and settled on a reservation near the Omahas. Her maternal grandfather was French Canadian, and DeCora's mother received some education in a convent as a girl; but as DeCora recalled in her ironic fashion, "When she married my father she gave up all her foreign training and made a good, industrious Indian wife." DeCora's education at home was disrupted by the arrival of an emissary from the Hampton Institute: "A very promising career must have been laid out for me by my grandparents, but a strange white man interrupted it."[10] Twelve-year-old DeCora had recently enrolled in the reservation school when the strange man asked her if she wanted to ride on a train. She and six other children, excited by the opportunity, decided to try the excursion. The next day they were "piled into a wagon" and driven to a train station. "We did not get the promised ride," DeCora remembered, for the children were left on the train for three days and nights until they arrived at Hampton. DeCora's parents found out about the deception too late to prevent their daughter's departure.[11]

When DeCora arrived at Hampton in 1883, teachers translated her real name, Hinook-Mahiwi-Kilinaka, into the English approximation of its meaning: Angel. DeCora stayed at Hampton for a little over three years, until her allotted time for government-funded schooling was up. In 1887 she went back to the reservation. She recalled in her autobiography that when she returned, her mother told her "that for months she wept and mourned" after her daughter's abrupt departure. DeCora's father and grandfather had died, and with them their stories, lessons, and the "old ways" of life. DeCora lost not only the environment that had fostered her education but the familial and cultural ties that had supported her as a child. DeCora's teacher Cora M. Folsom elaborated on her predicament: "A representative from Hampton found her living with her grandmother and very unhappily situated. Old and new customs were at that time strongly conflicting currents, and a young girl had hardly more weight than a leaf between them. It was not easy to get her out from the stronger of these two currents, but it was accomplished and she was brought back to Hampton."[12]

Back at school, DeCora was an active member of the Lend-A-Hand Club, a group that raised money for supplies and gifts on reservations. DeCora served as its secretary in 1889 and as the editor of its monthly newsletter, *Talks and Thoughts*, in 1890. The Lend-A-Hand Club raised funds by selling the newsletter and by making and selling craft items at fairs run by "friends of the Indian." Most likely these were the "table covers, bureau covers, splashers, tidies, [and] mats" produced in the girls' fancy-work class — a class open only to those girls who diligently spoke English all week.[13] The girls at Hampton participated in the economic exchanges of the trinket trade, relying on the patronage of white, eastern women to raise money for work on reservations in the West. DeCora's early experience with fancy work may have introduced her to the appeal that Indian arts and crafts held for white consumers, yet in later life

DeCora derided the floral designs and beadwork that Hampton encouraged, saying it relied too much on white people's tastes.

DeCora's Hampton instructors originally believed that her talent lay in piano playing, and they supported her education in music at the Burnham Classical School for Girls in Northampton, Massachusetts. It was not long, however, before DeCora left Miss Burnham's school and enrolled in the art department at Smith College, where she paid her tuition by working as a custodian at the college art gallery. DeCora studied under Dwight Tryon, an artist whose delicate, tonalist works were meant to evoke moods and thus were associated with high art. Art historian Sarah McAnulty notes that while Tryon taught at Smith for nearly forty years, he believed that art instruction for women would produce a better, more tasteful society — not necessarily women artists. At Smith, DeCora won a number of prizes; upon graduation she was honored for her work on two color studies and a nocturne, and she was praised for her abilities in drawing from casts and models.[14] She went on to study at Philadelphia's Drexel Institute, where she worked with the prolific illustrator Howard Pyle. He started the "Practical Illustration" course at Drexel, a class that rapidly gained popularity and national attention, and by 1896, the year DeCora started at Drexel, the class had developed into a school of illustration. In 1898 Pyle began a special summer course for exceptional students at his home in Chadds Ford, Pennsylvania. DeCora was one of these and, thus, was in the company of students such as Maxfield Parrish, N. C. Wyeth, and Jessie Wilcox Smith. Unlike Tryon, Pyle was dedicated to commercial art and was more interested in pleasing audiences in order to sell his realistic illustrations than in cultivating moral sentiments. His work consisted mainly of masculine subjects such as buccaneers, knights, and cowboys, and he did not elide the functionalism of his work, referring to his studio as his "workshop."[15]

Given the distinct differences between Tryon's and Pyle's methods, it is not surprising that DeCora was torn between two definitions of art at the turn of the century: art as a reflection of nature, a work of pure genius in service of higher ideals, or art as commodity that thus pointed to the work involved in its own production. She recalled, "I used to hear a great deal of discussion among the students, and instructors as well, on the sentiments of 'Commercial' art and 'Art for art's sake.' I was swayed back and forth by conflicting views."[16] Historian Sarah Burns has shown how complex this discussion was at the turn of the century, and that attempts to define the role of the artist in the modern world encompassed "thorny issues of materialism and idealism, aestheticism and morality, surface and depth, health and degeneration, manliness and effeminacy."[17] The phrase "art for art's sake" implied art that evoked pure ideas and stressed the originality of the artist; on the other hand, high art faced accusations of crass commercialism, effeminacy, degeneracy, and lack of personality. While commercial artists could be regarded as vigorous personalities and businessmen whose work elevated the masses, they were stigmatized by the reproducibility of their art and by the belief that popular art was sentimental, unuseful, domestic, and feminized.[18]

As a woman and as a Native American in an era when artists such as Wyeth, Pyle, and Frederick Remington, who celebrated heroic Anglo-Saxon masculinity, were prominent personalities, DeCora must have wondered how her identity might best compliment her artistry. Much as Caroline Soule had struggled to legitimate herself as an author some forty years earlier, DeCora strove to establish herself as a serious artist. But for DeCora, working at the turn of the century, the stakes involved in artistic production were different. Like sentimental literature, commercial illustration was increasingly associated with domesticity, feminine idleness, and crass consumption. Yet growing antimodernist sentiments contributed to a new interest in native women's domestic crafts as an antidote to those overcivilized values. Moreover, DeCora did not necessarily want to disassociate herself from the marketplace; she was interested in economic survival for herself and her people. DeCora's art education opened opportunities for her that led her to ponder the very distinctions that supported white, middle-class identity: distinctions between marketplace and sentiments, between masculine and feminine roles, and between civilized and uncivilized societies. In her own work and life, these differences were not so clear-cut. Perhaps recognizing that the meanings of Indian women's domestic work and of the cultural work performed by Euro-American art and literature were in flux, DeCora took her first step into the bastion of middle-class values that Soule and other domestic writers had staked out by the middle of the nineteenth century: literature.

Coming inside the Text

Like Soule, DeCora turned to the Midwest and Native American subjects to find fodder for her work — she turned toward home. Sponsored by Pyle, who himself embraced premodernity as part of the trajectory toward progress, DeCora traveled to Fort Berthold, North Dakota, during the summer of 1897.[19] She stayed with former schoolmate Anna Dawson, who recently had been appointed as a field matron there. While Dawson visited homes, DeCora sketched and photographed the people in order to collect models and sources for her art.

Her friend and teacher Cora Folsom noted that DeCora was successful in getting the people there to pose for her, and they allowed her to make portraits of some of the "old chiefs" that were "of great value as well as beauty."[20] DeCora also took photographs while on the reservation; these were not all of "great chiefs" but may have been primarily of women and children. DeCora was compiling an archive of faces and forms to use in her illustrations.

DeCora returned to native culture and to the environments that produced Indian art as an attempt to claim a professional identity as much as to reclaim her native identity.[21] But as a professional artist, DeCora chose to disassociate herself from earlier painters, such as George Catlin, who made Indian portraits their stock-in-trade. The Smithsonian Institution wished to commission more portraits from her, but DeCora turned away from the museum and its impulse to preserve presumably dying cultures. She looked instead to domestic subjects and popular illustration.[22] DeCora's collection of photographs and sketches provided her with the materials to produce the two stories and six illustrations that were published in *Harper's New Monthly Magazine* in 1899. One of the oldest and most established literary magazines in the United States, *Harper's* subscriptions exceeded 100,000 and included primarily middle- and upper-class readers. *Harper's* was a powerful forum for establishing notoriety for writers and artists.

Like Zitkala-Sa, DeCora turned to literary regionalism and conventions that celebrated domestic landscapes and cultural preservation. Indeed, integrating native arts into the home's material culture through commercial sales occurred concurrently with antimodernist lionization of the so-called primitive within literary culture. Charles Lummis's magazine *Land of Sunshine*, started in 1895, regarded the landscapes, lifestyles, and folklore of the Southwest and its native people as repositories of the tradition, pastoralism, and authenticity that modern industrial culture lacked. Mary Austin's collection of tales in *Land of Little Rain*, published in 1903, celebrated Native American women and their domestic arts in stories such as "The Basket Maker." In this story, Austin reverently described the Paiute artist Seyavi, who "made baskets for love and sold them for money." Seyavi's works were at once "wonders of technical precision" and evidence that "the weaver and the warp lived next to the earth and were saturated with the same elements."[23] In this literature, domesticity could be lauded as a return to core values, as part of the craft ideal in which women's work was essential, virtuous, and industrious and the marketplace came second to love.[24]

DeCora's stories "The Sick Child," published in February 1899, and "Gray Wolf's Daughter," published in November that year, are both tales in the regionalist genre that was widely printed in popular magazines like *Harper's*. The stories take place in Native American settings that, for many white readers, evoked traditionalism and purity of belief; both are rich in descriptions of ritual and feature women and domestic scenes. "The Sick Child" is written from the perspective of a young girl charged with making an offering to the spirits in order to cure her baby sister. The girl struggles through the snow with the memory of the medicine woman's imperative of laying the offering of tobacco and red feathers directly on the earth. Unable to find bare ground, the girl eventually pours the offering into the small opening in the snow made by a reed waving in the wind. She reasons that the "reed must be rooted in the ground, and the hole must follow the stem to the earth." At home, a medicine man gravely tells the family that their baby is lost, but he gives her medicine and performs a dance to ease the child's suffering. The next morning, the girl awakens to find her mother working on a small white garment, tears streaming down her face. The child has died, and the girl, touching her sister, "realized what death meant. Remorse again seized me, but I was silent."[25] In this story, death is accompanied by rituals — religious, medicinal, and domestic — and loss is balanced by the preservation of identity through these performances.

The second story, "Gray Wolf's Daughter," presents rituals as important even to one who has decided to begin a "new life" by gaining knowledge of "the white man's ways." Gray Wolf's daughter, with her parents' blessing, has already decided to go to boarding school. The night before her departure, however, she dons "a great pile of beads . . . silver ear-rings that jingled with every movement of her head," silver rings on her fingers, and bracelets on her arms. So ornamented, she joins the other girls of the village at the vapor bath purification ceremony and dances with them around the fire. The next day, the girl "took all her beautiful things from the basket and told her mother to give them to her sister-in-law. . . . She put on her plainest dress, one little silver ring on her finger, and that was all." The story thus records the physical removal of the accoutrements of native culture from the girl's body, a removal detailed in the illustration that appears above the story's title. The story does not end, however, by validating the white man's ways but with an equivocal nod to the girl's own choice. Her plea to her father that he visit often is paralleled by her father's sadness at parting from "the joy and life of their home," but Gray Wolf recognizes that "she had always had her own way." The title thus becomes an ironic comment, in that Gray Wolf's daughter is no longer his, nor is she entirely of "the white man," who is Gray Wolf's opposite. She is fiercely her own.[26]

Both stories seem to reinforce what Richard Brodhead has defined as one of the primary functions of the regionalist genre: preserving premodern cultures for the leisured enjoyment of middle-class literary "travelers."[27] While regionalist fiction might celebrate women's domestic work and rituals, like the Hampton museum it places that work firmly in some other time and place to be visited only by tourists. D. K. Meisenheimer argues that "the regionalist impulse to preserve and curate what Progress supplants" is a combination of "proto-ethnography and elegy" that, much like the catalogs and museums of earlier ethnographers, simultaneously celebrates and condemns to extinction the cultures it explores. Yet Meisenheimer goes on to argue that for an indigenous writer like Zitkala-Sa, such "self-curation" was an impossibility. He suggests that rather than giving herself up for a ghost, Zitkala-Sa represented "the cultural-natural aspects of her native region embodied in her own person as an inherently movable quality."[28] Instead of representing her culture as dead, Zitkala-Sa depicted it as very much alive within her own body as it moves from East to West and back again within her texts.

DeCora's *Harper's* stories and illustrations suggest another way of looking at the cultural embodiment that Meisenheimer has identified. Meisenheimer reads this embodiment as a function of textuality and the formal qualities of metaphor and imagery. DeCora's stories lack the sophisticated use of genre conventions and literary allusion that are central to Zitkala-Sa's work; DeCora was a visual artist and not a fiction writer. Rather than exposing culture as embodied in language and tropes whose appropriation signals mobility, DeCora's stories and illustrations suggest that culture can be embodied in work — not only, as in Soule's novel, in the domestic rituals described in the literature but in the work of the artist herself. In the stories, Native American culture comes alive in intermediate places: between death and life, between home and away, and most important, in the interplay between the work of the artist and the literary marketplace.

DeCora's publications combine simple stories with vivid illustrations, and her version of culture occurs where indigenous designs become part of the visual iconography of the text itself. The illustration of Gray Wolf's daughter, for example, shows the girl in the act of removing her beads — stripping herself of her native culture (see fig. 6.1). Yet in reproducing this moment through her artistic work, DeCora brings indigenous designs into the literary marketplace dominated by middle-class magazines such as *Harper's*. The illustration's photographic quality places the girl's pensive expression within a dazzling display of traditional Plains women's work. It is this work that represents the Indian identity of Gray Wolf's daughter. The figures on the hide in the background, the girl's beaded dress and belt, and even the line of her arms fuse artistic styles. DeCora incorporated native design work smoothly into techniques of figure-

Figure 6.1. Angel DeCora, Gray Wolf's daughter removing her beads. Illustration from DeCora [Hinook-Mahiwi-Kilinaka], "Gray Wolf's Daughter."

drawing and detached observation that characterized her training in illustration. Because this illustration is more detailed than the others, it is possible that DeCora wrote her story around the image; the text might merely be an illustration for the design work DeCora wished to showcase. In the story's final illustration, the landscape of the prairies is literally fading away, even as Gray Wolf's daughter leaves her village behind (see fig. 6.2). But if we read the image another way, the picture begins to take shape only where the image meets the text. The story and the image both intimate that Gray Wolf's daughter's identity takes shape not through stagnation but through movement to new places. In the same way, DeCora's identity as an artist began to take shape as she moved native designs into the mainstream literary media. She removed her beads, as it were, only to place them in the pages of *Harper's*.

Unlike Caroline Soule's Indians in *The Pet of the Settlement*, DeCora's characters suggest that moving into literary texts need not mean relinquishing native identity. DeCora preserves that identity, in part, by putting her work on display. While Soule erased signs of labor and native histories in order to affirm the ideology of influence that was the province of middle-class white women, DeCora's identity is embodied here through signs that overtly point to her work as a Native American artist. In the drawing of Gray Wolf's daughter leaving the village, the fading edge of the landscape makes DeCora's work obvious. Though realistic, the scene has clearly been created through the artist's effort; the borders are not tidy but unfinished and ambiguous, revealing the role of the artist in giving form to the scene. In this same image, DeCora inscribes her name just where the ragged bottom of the landscape meets the page. In fact,

Figure 6.2. Angel DeCora, Gray Wolf's daughter leaving her village. Illustration from DeCora [Hinook-Mahiwi-Kilinaka], "Gray Wolf's Daughter."

DeCora wrote her name twice: both her Ho-Chunk name and her initials, "A. de C.," mark the edge of the disappearing landscape.[29] In the illustration of Gray Wolf's daughter removing her beads, DeCora's Ho-Chunk name appears in the upper right corner, above the girl's bent head, while "A. de C." appears opposite, in the lower right corner. Including both her Ho-Chunk and English names, DeCora points to her identity as a Native American and insists on the presence of that identity as producer of the image that readers are consuming. In both drawings, however, the words that form her name become part of the drawing's design. Translating her name into the simplest of elements, "Hinook-Mahiwi-Kilinaka" becomes "A. de C.," a name so close to "ABC" that it seems to indicate language itself. In making her identity into part of the design, DeCora blurred the divisions between language as Euro-American cultural property and symbol-making as the individual's authorial and artistic work. She suggests that the mobility of her work, which projects traditional design into new textual spaces, makes way for an identity that takes shape just where English text and indigenous design meet.

Crafting Culture

DeCora's two publications combine ethnographic detail with an insistence that culture must be deliberately made, through ritual, work, and artistry, and is therefore constantly in flux. For the preceding fifty years, art and ethnology had collaborated to freeze native cultures in premodern time and space. But as her career burgeoned, DeCora strove to wrest Indian cultures from the ethnographic past and into the present by emphasizing that Native American cultures were embodied not just in artifacts but in practices that were made manifest in work — primarily women's work. Calling on the language of ethnographic science and definitions of labor as a quality that belonged to the body, she suggested that native crafts constituted a crucial link between cultural preservation and economic survival.

In 1899, the year that her stories were published, DeCora began studying life drawing at the Cowles Art School with Joseph DeCamp. After DeCamp left the school the following year, DeCora moved on to the Museum of Fine Arts in Boston, where she studied with Frank Benson and Edmund C. Tarbell. These impressionist artists were all part of "The Ten" American artists who resigned from the Society of American Artists in 1898 to disassociate themselves from commercialism and to uphold "art for art's sake."[30] DeCora worked from her own studio in Boston between 1899 and 1903; in 1903 she moved to New York City and opened a studio there.[31] She worked steadily as an illustrator for publishers Small and Maynard Company and Ginn and Company in Boston, and she produced illustrations, landscapes, and portraits in New York.[32] In addition to illustrating Francis La Flesche's autobiographical tale *The Middle Five* in 1900, DeCora created illustrations for Mary Catherine Judd's *Wigwam Stories Told by North American Indians* (1906), Zitkala-Sa's *Old Indian Legends* (1901), Natalie Curtis Burlin's *The Indian's Book* (1907), and Elaine Goodale Eastman's novel *Yellow Star: A Story of East and West* (1911). Between 1899 and 1901 DeCora produced a number of items for the Indian Bureau Office in Washington, D.C., including a charcoal sketch titled "Young Indian Warrior" (which was lost in the mail) and the designs for a wooden settle and mantle and a set of andirons that were made by Carlisle students and displayed at the Pan-American exposition in Buffalo in 1901. She showed some of her paintings at that exposition, including the frontispiece from *The Middle Five*. Her work, including a painting of a Mandan lodge, was also on display at the St. Louis World's Fair in 1904.[33]

The different media and subjects DeCora used during this time suggest that she was torn between Euro-American and Native American artistic traditions and was searching for a middle ground. The art she made between 1900 and 1907 somewhat erratically fused those two traditions. For example, the drawing and furniture she designed for the Indian Office combine Native American and Euro-American designs. She decorated the settle, mantle, and andirons that were all foreign elements in Native American cultures with "designs simple and some what Indian in character."[34] In a similar translation of Indian forms and figures into Euro-American representation, an illustration for *Old Indian Tales* uses Euro-American stylistic traditions to portray the trickster figure Iktomi — a moment that McAnulty identifies as "one of the first times an Indian artist tried to translate legendary or supernatural figures, such as the Trickster, into a non-Indian visual format."[35]

This fusion of Indian and Euro-American art forms suggests that DeCora was increasingly influenced by native artists working outside European artistic traditions and in locations outside metropolitan centers such as Boston and New York. DeCora's work borrows from the multitudes of indigenous artists who were producing craftwork for sale to tourists from the Southwest to the Canadian borderlands. Her designs use the motifs that Native Americans had been producing for more than a century and incorporating into souvenirs and other items for exchange with whites. The growing popularity of Indian design on blankets, ceramics, and basketry probably influenced DeCora's movement toward design as a way to integrate native culture and its productions into the national culture.[36]

In what may have been her most significant shift toward design, DeCora created pages bearing the names of each of the tribes that Natalie Curtis included in *The Indian's Book* (1907), a capacious collection of Indian songs, stories, traditional drawings, and ethnographic photographs. Curtis, the niece of erstwhile *Harper's Weekly* editor George William Curtis and a former teacher at Carlisle, claimed that she found her inspiration in Alice Fletcher, one of the first ethnologists to study Indian songs and music.[37] Unlike Fletcher, however, who represented Native American musical styles and traditions as scientific data, Curtis stressed indigenous music as an art form, and her publication of *The Indian's Book* heralded the entry of Native American poetry into Western literary aesthetics.[38] It also marked an entry of the new anthropology of cultural relativism into the aesthetic arena through its combination of native artistic styles with traditional ethnographic practices of collecting information and ordering images. Curtis also was influenced by anthropologist Franz Boas, whose publications and museum work helped to popularize his theory of cultural relativism, a concept that opposed Victorian ideas of temporal progress through stages of civilization. For example, Boas's 1897 treatise, "The Decorative Art of the Indians of the North Pacific Coast," examined native craft in terms of iconography and representation rather than ordering crafts in terms of the evolution of "technic forms."[39] Boas and his students, including Edward Sapir, Alfred Kroeber, and Margaret Mead, argued that cultures should be understood as varying according to geographic differences that gave rise to distinct cultures. Boas's brand of fieldwork, rather than stressing the salvage of artifacts from dying cultures, instead investigated different groups on their own terms and within the environments that produced them.[40] Any given culture's material artifacts were an outgrowth of specific local circumstances rather than a sign of a culture's degree of development, and crafts signaled adaptation and innovation rather than stagnation. Boas's ideas caused enthusiasts like Curtis to see Indian culture as art rather than artifact.

Curtis herself suggested that her book helped DeCora emerge as a designer. She reported that while DeCora got her start in illustration, "she later looked down upon these early efforts, for her greatest work lay in decorative design." Curtis was already acquainted with DeCora when she asked her to design a title page for the section on the Winnebago tribe. Curtis recalled, "When she brought me the finished page, it bore, in addition to the design, the legend, 'Lake Indians — Winnebago,' in letters so beautiful and of such startling originality that my publishers declared: 'We can't have the page looking like this and the others labeled with prosaic printing!'" The lettering was brought to the publisher's designer to copy, but the designer declared that he could not possibly produce such designs. He exclaimed, "Whoever did that lettering is a genius!"[41] DeCora's artistic genius lay in defamiliarizing, for Euro-American readers, something as recognizable as language itself. DeCora designed different lettering for each of the tribes Curtis had studied, using motifs from the drawings the letters accompanied and shapes culled from the design styles of each tribal group (see fig. 6.3). Each page was a collaboration, in which DeCora worked from the drawings made by native artists. "The letters were not conceived as *letters*; the Indian girl had looked on them as so many different shapes and as structural ideas for decorative forms," Curtis wrote, "and the forms were Indian."[42] Captions for the title pages explain the meanings of the symbols that are repeated in the drawings and the lettering.

The enthusiastic response of Curtis and her editors to DeCora's designs suggests the novelty of DeCora's adaptation of indigenous forms and figures to Euro-American styles within print culture. Specifically, she was redesigning the forms and figures that make up the English language. Curtis's acute observation that DeCora had rendered English letters not as letters but as "shapes and structures" that could be adapted to native designs implies that DeCora saw native arts as a powerful way to infuse, and perhaps even to undermine, Euro-American forms of representation with indigenous ones. The English language had long been a way for Europeans and Americans to exert power over indigenous people through legal and scientific narratives, yet DeCora's designs deconstruct the figures of that language, making it look foreign to Euro-American readers. The letters work against the ethnographic impulse to order artifacts through descriptions and categories printed in English by rendering those descriptions themselves as elements of design. DeCora complicates lit-

Figure 6.3. Angel DeCora, Kwakiutl title page. 1907. Illustration from Curtis, *Indian's Book*.

eracy by implying that reading these words and border patterns involves more than apprehending familiar visual codes; the observer must recognize the connections between the border designs and the language signs. Without both, the captions insist, the message cannot be read.

DeCora's appropriation of the printed word and, perhaps more important, the words that organize ethnographic study of North American tribes, marked a crossroads between scientific and artistic production, between Native American ways of designing the world and Euro-American ways of ordering it. DeCora remade lettering into an iconography that symbolized not just language itself but Native American forms of production as embodied in indigenous designs. Inserting Indian designs into English texts and thereby calling into question the hegemony of language as a tool of history- and culture-making, DeCora hoped to legitimate native craft work as viable cultural, aesthetic, and economic practice. Indeed, economic survival, as much as cultural preservation, was part of DeCora's agenda. DeCora admitted that she drifted away from landscapes, figures, and other artistic forms that might be considered fine art because, for one, she found design to be a more "lucrative" opportunity. DeCora was no doubt aware that more and more, Indian design was growing in popularity among middle-class whites and providing work for people living on reservations. She regarded this exchange as both an economic and a cultural opportunity, a chance to bring the "crafts and industries . . . that the mechanically minded American considers of the smallest value" to "all the world."[43] But she was also motivated to bring both cultural pride and economic opportunity to people who were suffering from the lack of both.

DeCora called on the ethic of the arts and crafts movement in order to formulate ideas of culture as practice, suggesting that work could express and reinvigorate cultural ideals. Proponents of the arts and crafts ideal, like the women of the WNIA, touted the civilizing function of production. Others, like Jane Addams, celebrated Native American arts and crafts as a return to the primitive, believing such work to be uncorrupted by relations of production. Just as sentimental culture had denied economic value to women's productive labor, the new value placed on production in what were seen as economic hinterlands denied the history of relations between Indians and whites and the fact that for decades (sometimes centuries) indigenous people had been engaged with the marketplace through labor and trade. The new values placed on Indian arts as a result of antimodernism altered the stakes for indigenous producers, as home craft evolved into cottage industry.[44] Praise for the primitive celebrated the authentic productions of native artists while eliding the real economic relations that governed their production — emphasizing love over money, and connection to nature over labor.[45] The growing market for native arts and crafts, according to Ruth Phillips and Christopher Steiner, "signal[ed] the entry of colonized people into industrial-age consumerism" through cottage industries that used factorylike systems of production.[46]

DeCora, however, was formulating a craft ideal that would find a middle ground between total cultural assimilation and traditional, localized, and often exploitative domestic craft production. If culture could be carried within the body, it could become a property of that body and had the potential to be reproduced through an individual's work. DeCora specifically connected cultural embodiment with the products of independent work in her descriptions of Indian women's craft. In a biography of DeCora, Curtis quoted DeCora's theory of art and work, drawing from one of DeCora's speeches:

> The Indian woman from prehistoric times has been an artist. The work of her hand, the product of her thought, has been enshrined in the white man's museums throughout the world. Each basket, each pottery urn shaped by the Indian woman is an individual art expression created by its maker. The imagination that prompts the symmetry and beauty of pattern, and the dexterity that gives the skill of perfect workmanship — these are inherent in every Indian. The only difference between me and the women on the reservations is that I have chosen to apply my native Indian gift in the white man's world. We are a race of designers, and I look for the day when our art may be as generally recognized as that of the Japanese, and when America will be proud to have her Indians make beautiful things for all the world.[47]

Clearly, DeCora subscribed to theories that saw native women's domestic work as inherent in tribal memory. Yet women's work was neither thoughtless nor a product of tradition only. DeCora prominently employed a Lockean definition to describe Indian women's traditional artistry. Significantly, she included not only the "work of her hand" but also "the product of her thought" in native women's work, calling not only on Locke's definition of labor as a physical property of the body but on the idea of intellectual labor. DeCora's work ethic and educational theories stressed independent work in the liberal tradition rather than the rule-bound educational tactics of industrial schools that prepared Native American students for lives of routinized wage labor. In direct opposition to the disciplinary tenets integral to Indian industrial schools, DeCora declared in a 1907 speech to the National Education Association that "I have taken care to leave my pupils' creative faculty absolutely independent and to let each student draw from his own mind, true to his own thought, and as much as possible, true to his tribal method of symbolic design." She went on to say,

> No two Indian drawings are alike and every one is original work. Each artist has his own style. What is more, the best designs were made by my artist pupils away from my supervision. They came to me for material to take to their rooms and some of the designs for rugs that you have seen were made in the students' play hour, away from the influence of others — alone with their inspiration, as an artist should work. It may interest you to know that my pupils never use practice paper. With steady and unhesitating hand and mind, they put down permanently the lines and color combinations that you see in their designs.[48]

Hands and minds were at work in the art of her pupils.

Doing away with the highly structured spaces and regimented activities that reformers praised as part of Indian schools' "homelike" environments, DeCora cultivated an image of the Indian student as a self-directed worker, retreating into private spaces to find inspiration in his or her own mind. Like the entrepreneurs who elided economic relations of production in favor of a vision of authenticity, DeCora located artistic genius in properties of native blood as well as in independent work. Yet she also acknowledged that these artists were produced at Carlisle as well as in the so-called premodern hinterlands. This dual interpretation of artistry fused an understanding of labor's relationship to the market with a belief in the centrality of work to cultural embodiment, in which creations embodied both the physical efforts and the thought of their makers. Like midcentury middle-class women who called on women's perceived innate moral goodness to justify the value of their housework, DeCora drew on perceptions of Indians' innate artistic talents to separate native women's domestic artistry from routinized labor. Likewise, she argued that Indians' work did have market value and was not limited to domestic use on reservations. The baskets and pottery urns once used at home and later enshrined in museums would be free to circulate in not only a national but a global marketplace. And along with them, indigenous cultures would enter and thrive in places beyond the reservation. DeCora believed that her innate proclivity for artistry allied her with other Native American women. But her choice to make native arts visible and valuable by practicing them in the white man's world reveals her belief that work could fuse long-standing divisions between periphery and center, racial destiny and individual genius, home and marketplace, domestic labor and wage work, and "the work of the hand" and the "product of thought."

The Building at the Gateway

In 1906 the Carlisle School marked its own border by erecting the Leupp Indian Art Studio near its new gateway (see fig. 6.4). School officials described the building, named after Francis E. Leupp, who had been appointed Commissioner of Indian Affairs by President Theodore Roosevelt in 1905, as "a magnificent monument to the industrial training to be obtained here by the Indian youth who seeks to better his condition and to make of himself a self-supporting, universally respected craftsman." To those who worked at and supported Carlisle, the building's battlement style — which bore strong resemblance to the western forts used to quell Indian uprisings — represented not continental conquest but native labor. Carlisle's paper, the *Arrow*, elaborated on the structure's significance: "To the stranger it appears to be a well-built, beautifully arranged, well laid out edifice, but to the Indian and to the friend of the Indian it means more. It means that *there* is a perfect, finished product of Indian handicraft."[49]

The Leupp building was designed by Carlisle graduate and Cheyenne George Balenti and built by students. It housed a classroom for crafts such as ceramics and weaving, a photography studio, and an exhibition space for the art produced on campus.[50] Francis E. Leupp was influenced by new views of native arts and crafts that emphasized ethnographic primitivism; he believed that Native American art forms were worth cultivating in Indian students. When Leupp assumed office, Captain Pratt, who had been the driving force behind Carlisle's mission to "kill the Indian and save the man" since the school began in 1880, was removed from his position. While Pratt's policy of instant assimilation was indeed problematic, the Leupp administration's seeming embrace of native cultures had its own inherent devaluation of those traditions. Rather than attempting to increase the visibility and cultural worth of native workers, the government suggested that the inability of natives to compete with whites as equals in the marketplace relegated them to the status of laborers in devalued industries. For Leupp, Indian arts and crafts were not necessarily a tool of integration but a way to set Native Americans apart as a separate class. The government and school emphasized the transformation of Indian culture into commodity and Indian students into laborers.

As part of Leupp's plan to promote native arts and crafts at Carlisle, he asked DeCora to accept the position of Indian arts instructor, a move McAnulty describes as a "token response by the government to the reformers' demands."[51] The government approved DeCora's appointment in December 1905, and her degree from Smith's art department was deemed adequate evidence of her

Figure 6.4. Leupp Indian Art Studio, from the *Arrow*, 1907. Reproduced by Cumberland County Historical Society, Carlisle, Pa.

qualifications for a civil service position.[52] DeCora was initially reluctant to give up her career in New York City, but in early 1906 she went to Carlisle. Shortly after DeCora's arrival, Carlisle drew up plans for an art studio, and in early 1907 Carlisle opened the new building.

During the nine years that Angel DeCora taught at Carlisle, she presented her classroom as a space where young people who had been displaced from their tribal cultures would remake themselves not in the image of white people but in their own image, through art. For DeCora, and perhaps for her students as well, the Leupp building was a hybrid space. She emphasized cultural practice, for as a teacher, she encouraged students to rediscover their culture, to take pride in it, and to regard their domestic cultures as sources that could transform them into independent workers rather than dependent laborers. DeCora attempted to build an empowering space for Native American work within American culture by advocating its inclusion in architectures of institutional control that had been used to displace Native Americans and their cultures in the nineteenth century — in particular, the displays common to museum and marketplace.

Jacqueline Fear-Segal has pointed out the significance of the new art building's position just inside and to the left of the new entrance to the Carlisle grounds, a significance that was not lost on early twentieth-century commentators. In an examination of Carlisle's "spatial record," Fear-Segal shows that for the first twenty-five years of its existence, Carlisle was not organized for pupils to gain access to the outside world. All students entered the grounds through the guardhouse, and Pratt carefully controlled who and what was seen from both inside and outside the tall white fence that surrounded the campus. In 1905, however, Carlisle constructed a new entrance gate on the opposite side of campus from the guardhouse.[53] The new art building stood directly inside this new gate. Carlisle's newspaper regarded both gate and building as viewer-oriented and reported that "its position at the entrance to the beautiful grounds adds greatly to the general appearance of the school property, and creates favorable first impressions."[54] Unlike WNIA cottages, the Leupp art building was a public place, and its location capitalized on the growing popularity of viewing Indians as premodern craftspeople. Indeed, the Leupp Indian Art Studio was no model home, but it was advertised as a space of production and exhibition. The studio's position at the entrance to the campus made it the first place that visitors would encounter, and the studio was also designed as a salesroom and exhibition hall. Its interior, hung with pictures and draped with "exotic" blankets, resembled popular images of artists' studios, only with an order that would facilitate sales as well as "enchantment."[55] The art room that DeCora oversaw was twenty-four by thirty-two feet and held a collection of paintings, drawings, leather work, beadwork, and basketry that students had made. The floor was covered with colorful blankets in the Navajo style, and cases held student photography developed in the state-of-the-art studio also housed in the building. Those images were made into souvenir postcards that represented Carlisle students working and showcased "views of the grounds and buildings" that prepared the students for industrial occupations. Articles printed in the *Red Man* and the *Indian Craftsman* (the *Arrow*'s name between 1908 and 1910) lauded the primitive appeal of native arts and crafts but looked to the arts as a way for girls, in particular, to spend time at home in a practical way.[56]

DeCora's emphasis on design and its application to modern goods helped Carlisle students to produce a multitude of utilitarian items marked by Indian designs. Her students made belts, slippers, chains, and purses; they decorated furniture and wagons; and they designed "interior decorations for walls, ceilings, and panels." Art students created simple designs inspired by traditional arts, and these were reproduced and applied to many products made by students practicing the various industries that Carlisle taught, so that indigenous designs found their way onto domestic goods ranging from wall borders to book covers.[57] But the studio also sold crafts produced on reservations for direct sale to customers. Advertisements in the *Indian Craftsman* publicized Carlisle's sales of the "Handicraft of the American Indian." These ads capitalized on the fact that "people who are interested in the Indian usually have a liking for his Arts and Crafts — desire something which has been made by these people." Carlisle suggested that in a market where authenticity was valuable, its studio could vouch for the genuineness of its commodities. Carlisle played into the desire for authentic art, telling potential consumers that "if you wish Genuine Indian Handicraft, [Carlisle] is where You Absolutely Know you are going to get what you bargain for." Carlisle boasted "a fine line of Pueblo Pottery, Baskets, Bead Work, Navaho Art Squares, Looms, and other things made by Indian Men and Women." Carlisle capitalized on its institutional notoriety to assure consumers that all the products were made by Indians and proceeds would be used to help Indians become even more efficient laborers.[58]

Carlisle promoted sales of Indian goods as a way to raise funds for individuals on reservations and to cultivate public interest in Indian crafts. For example, the *Arrow*'s article on the studio's opening described the Navajo rugs that decorated the floor as enough to "make the heart of the connoisseur beat faster." In 1907 the *Arrow* reported that Fred Harvey's southwestern Indian craft business was experiencing a shortage in Navajo blankets. Limiting the definition of work to blanket production, the article noted that the Navajos were having a prosperous agricultural season, and "Indians with full grain bins . . . are not inclined to work." The article also pointed to the high incidence of fraud in blanket sales, in which blankets were produced in eastern factories and shipped west to be sold as genuine. Carlisle, in contrast, vouched for the authenticity of its blankets, insisting that every "blanket exhibited at the Studio is exactly what is claimed for it. A record is kept of the time, place, and weaver of every blanket and prospective purchasers may rest assured of the absolute genuineness of every one of them." The article reported that a school representative, in the course of a routine visit to the Chilocco Indian School, had picked up a number of blankets made by Navajo weavers, and these were for sale to "responsible persons" for prices between $10 and $100.[59]

The building thus supported Commissioner Leupp's understanding of Indian arts and crafts as valuable because they represented premodernity. This view legitimated control of indigenous products and labor by government authorities and entrepreneurs. Popular acceptance of Indian arts represented a widespread belief in the status of Indians as economic outsiders who, by virtue of their culture, were unable to compete as equals with whites in the marketplace. Carlisle itself denied the commercial aspects of its sales and argued that exhibiting and marketing crafts was an act of benevolence rather than an enterprise. It emphasized the authenticity and primitive production techniques of its wares and the genuine Indianness of the producers. Rather than celebrating the economic successes of Navajo farmers enjoying a good season, Carlisle despaired that economic success would make the farmers lazy and prevent them from producing the "authentic" crafts that consumers craved.[60] As salesroom, the studio encouraged white consumers to regard Native Americans as exotic and primitive, but it showed that those qualities could be harnessed to productive ends by making natives into laborers.

But unlike the businesses of many white entrepreneurs who specialized in Indian craft sales, the Leupp building symbolized a potential fusion between indigenous culture and modern economic life, encompassing in its physical space the cultural exchanges that were a reality for all Native Americans. The art building, in fact, was not financed by the government but had been funded by the profits of the Carlisle football team, whose excellence at the sport made it extremely popular and profitable. The *New York Tribune* described the building as a "mute reproach to the legislators who would have withdrawn the appropriation from the Carlisle Indian School."[61] Just as the famous Carlisle football team played against and defeated competitors from elite colleges and universities, the students at Carlisle aimed to compete with whites in the marketplace, using new as well as traditional technologies.[62]

DeCora levied criticisms at the educational system that had produced her and declared her resistance to assimilation, arguing that "in the United States, the method of educating the Indian in the past was to attempt to transform him into a brown Caucasian within the space of five years or a little more. The Indian educators made every effort to convince the Indian, that any custom or habit that was not particular to the white man, showed savagery and degradation."[63] The trouble with Indian education, she asserted, was that it did not teach students to blend the two ways of life successfully, and it produced people who wholeheartedly imbibed the assimilationist agenda and rejected indigenous cultures, or people who returned to their reservations but were unable to feel at home there. DeCora positioned her work at the intersection between white and Native American cultures, framing her instruction as a gateway to help regulate what traditions indigenous people might keep and what, in her opinion, should be discarded. DeCora regarded the Leupp art building as a crucial site of production that was between the domestic space of the reservation and the industrialism of modern white middle-class culture.

One of DeCora's first acts as the new instructor of Indian art was to order a number of publications: the twentieth through twenty-third volumes of the publications of the Bureau of Ethnology, the "Third Annual Report on Prehistoric Textile Fabrics," illustrated catalogs of the pictographs and pottery of the Pueblos, and studies of "form and ornament in ceramic art," Navajo sand painting, the Ojibwa medicine society, the symbols of the Mayan year, and Omaha dwellings, furniture, and implements. She also ordered the U.S. National Museum and Smithsonian reports on pottery, primal shaping arts, shell ornaments, and flint remains and the report on the exhibits at the Pan-American Exposition.[64] Those texts figured prominently in DeCora's attempts to recuperate Native American cultures via the representative technologies that had produced them for a white public in the past — scientific knowledge and museum display. DeCora taught all her students the design styles of all tribes, making various design characteristics available to Indian students for whom such designs were not part of their traditions. Tribal specificity was less important than the practice of creating these designs together, which DeCora hoped would "impress upon the minds of my pupils that they were Indians, possessing native abilities that had never been recognized in the curriculum of the Government schools."[65]

When DeCora gave a speech titled "An Effort to Encourage Indian Art" at the International Congress of Americanists in Quebec in 1906, she suggested ways that her teaching relied on ethnographic studies: "I endeavored to recall to my pupils' minds, the days of the old life and to send them back in imagination to the time when their grand mothers, and their fathers and mothers produced the native art-work. But . . . I found that I had to manufacture my Indians. I advised my pupils to try in every possible way to learn something of the Indian lore of the past, and the best that I could do, for these Indians who were transplanted from all contact with their own people, was to refer them to the Reports of the Bureau of Ethnology." One example DeCora used was that of a Carlisle student who could not respond to her questions about his tribal culture. Because he did know that he was a native Alaskan, DeCora brought him "a booklet by Dr. Boaz [sic] on the Northwestern Indians and began turning the pages. When I came upon some reproductions of the Haida decorations and blankets, he exclaimed with joy, 'That's my tribe!'" The student immediately told DeCora "something of the family organization of his tribe" and proceeded to make "a very beautiful and interesting border design, using the killer-whale as the theme."[66] Her discussion of the Haida artist undermines the idea the idea that native craft was primitive, authentic, and rooted in nature and memory. The knowledge of his tribal identity loosened the boy's tongue as he told DeCora that he "belonged to the 'black fish' family and also to the beaver," yet his art did not come out of some ancient memory but out of an encounter with an ethnographic text.[67] In reclaiming history, the boy moved outside it, for tribal Haidas never designed book covers.

DeCora's speech to the assembly appeals to representations of Indians as repositories of premodern artistic sensibilities (the "native art-works" of the mothers, fathers, and grandmothers); moreover, she suggests that these sensibilities are located in the property of blood as a racial trait. Yet as much as she celebrated what she saw as a native instinct for artistic production, DeCora recognized that her students' sensibilities needed to be, at least in part, "manufactured." She claimed that while artistry might be inherent in Indian blood, efforts to reunite native children with their culture — to remake Indians and to reclaim a cultural identity — took work. Identity was both natural and made, and re-creating culture for Native Americans, even through traditional domestic production, would take the effort of teachers like herself.

This new cultural work, however, would differ dramatically from the cultural work that earlier writers, scientists, and reformers had engaged in as part of their efforts to preserve and co-opt Native American history, culture, and labor. Her work would demand new forms and spaces for production. In her speech DeCora blasted salvage anthropology's focus on collecting artifacts from cultures that early ethnologists believed were quickly vanishing, contrasting her classroom to the exhibitionary space of the museum. She asserted that while "a great deal has been said and written on the art-industries of the [Indian] race and much of their art products have been gathered into museums . . . nothing has ever been done to encourage or further their progress." Developing Indian arts, she argued, was impossible in the stagnant spaces of museums that froze materials in primitive time. Museums' anachronistic spaces for the display of native arts, DeCora suggested, corresponded to the loss of the physical spaces that had fostered indigenous arts previously: "All the invironments [sic] and motives that inspire the art of a race just at this particular stage of development, have been taken from them." DeCora presented Euro-American culture as acquisitive but argued that taking land and collecting native arts and culture into museum rooms and ethnological reports did not necessarily leave the Indian's mind and body as a vessel emptied to receive Euro-American, middle-class culture. She directly addressed the Euro-American tradition of understanding the Indian, as artists such as Catlin and Soule had, as blank or palimpsest waiting for new inscription. "Go to him if you think it worth while, and get his story," she challenged the assembled professionals. "After he has given you what you want, don't think that what he gave out has left a vacancy in his spiritual nature for you to fill in with your own ideas."[68]

DeCora linked salvage anthropology with attempts to take away native culture through assimilation. She connected the anthropologist who "gets the story" of native people with efforts to assimilate them by "filling them" with the ideas and ideals of white culture. She asserted the continuing strength of native traditions by arguing that salvage anthropology had not stripped indigenous people of their cultures; they were not, in fact, empty vessels, but living examples of alternative ways of life. Likewise, domestic articles such as baskets and pottery urns that her students made were not empty vessels to be filled with Euro-American meanings, but they were indicative of Native American cultural survival — survival that had to be, in part, economic.

Designs on Domestic Work

DeCora did not believe that the work of Indians needed to be rooted in a particular kind of space, such as the Indian home or reservation, any more than it was frozen in time. Believing that art was authentic when it reinforced the identity of its maker, DeCora had no qualms about adapting native designs to new forms and exporting them to new places. DeCora visited various western tribes, "with the view to getting an insight into the Indian woman's life and her natural tendencies in domestic life: not with the purpose of giving her instruction in the improved methods of domestic science, but to find out other kinds of work she does in which she employs her nature designs." For DeCora, domesticity was not a specific form of housekeeping but any kind of work that women did to support home life. Careful, therefore, to distinguish herself from a field matron, DeCora nonetheless was interested in extending new ideas to native women by suggesting that traditional design practices might be applied in new places. "If I see other ways in which she can apply . . . the same design, I suggest the idea to her," DeCora explained. "It had never occurred to her that their beautiful designs could be used on anything else than pottery."[69]

DeCora argued that indigenous designs should be applied to items for sale to whites and that such sales were a way for women to help support their families. But economic survival need not mean selling out to the white-dominated marketplace; it need not mean losing cultural identity, as earlier white women had also feared in their crusades for remuneration for domestic labor. DeCora's plan was to "create designs according to these old established methods and apply them to the products of the workshops of the school."[70] Curtis wrote of DeCora's reaction to the state of artistic production at Carlisle upon her arrival:

Angel's heart must have sunk . . . when as a newcomer at Carlisle she surveyed the work of her predecessors. For our widespread tuition of Indians has been based on the principle that the Indian must copy the white man. The Art Department at Carlisle had been engaged in teaching Indian children, whose own mothers were masters of decorative design, to paint pansies on plush pillows and forget-me-nots on picture frames. It was not the fault of Carlisle that the standard of art in an American school should resemble the counter of a department store; it was the fault of our whole civilization.[71]

Curtis's indictment of the department store ethos included methods of assimilating Indian children. By training them to produce knickknacks for sale in department stores, the school was transforming potential artists into dependent laborers. Curtis appealed not just to the language of authenticity, however (referring to the talent as heritage), but to the class-based rhetoric of the arts and crafts movement. Yet what DeCora witnessed at Carlisle when she arrived was itself a product of the arts and crafts movement, which was also aimed at promoting morality and civilized values among racial others. As Eileen Boris notes of the arts and crafts movement in the United States, "Few saw any inconsistency between art's ability to instill moral values and its role in shaping labor" through unequal relations of production.[72]

Like the Iowa feminists, DeCora wished to avoid the stigma associated with rote labor even as she advocated incorporating native work and workers into the economy. She derided lessons that were only meant to produce "brown Caucasians," and she noted that assimilationists' squelching of native traditions "would have discouraged me too if I had been successfully CIVILIZED."[73] Refusing this mode of education, DeCora taught students to blend native traditions with American commercial culture by applying traditional designs rather than pansies and forget-me-nots to useful commodities such as tools, home furnishings, and rugs. "With just a little further work along these lines," she declared, "I feel that we shall be ready to adapt our Indian talents to the daily needs and uses of modern life. . . . The young Indian is now mastering all the industrial trades, and . . . there is no reason why the Indian workman should not leave his own artistic mark on what he produces." DeCora prompted her students to produce "genuine, legitimate Indian work," discouraging "any floral designs such as are seen on Ojibway beadwork." She argued that true "Indian art seldom made any use of the details of plant forms, but typified nature in its broader aspects, using also animal forms and symbols of human life."[74]

While she discouraged the use of hybrid designs in art and advocated a return to designs that symbolized native belief patterns, DeCora did not oppose applying traditional designs to novel objects. DeCora encouraged using such designs on modern domestic furnishings such as wall friezes, embroidery patterns, and rugs. DeCora promoted innovations in which students would fuse traditional designs with new forms. For example, in New York City during the summer of 1906 DeCora took a class in Asian weaving. In asking for this summer detail, DeCora acknowledged that her request seemed at odds with her duty to teach Native American arts and crafts; however, she argued that the study of Asian weaving could only add to the students' skill. In 1909 the Carlisle School advertised not only authentic Navajo rugs but the entirely new — and hybrid — "Indian rug" produced by DeCora's students.[75] Purity and authenticity were clearly less important to DeCora than creating a market for Indian designs in the Euro-American home.

At the conference of Americanists, DeCora excoriated the destructive past by referring to older practices of art instruction for Native Americans and to the display of their art. Most Indian art exhibitions, she argued, were as carefully manipulated as displays of Indian artifacts in museums. They represented a similar seizure of power by Euro-American authorities, this time over the work of Indian artists and over their individual expression as well. She stated,

At an Educational Conference last summer, I saw an exhibit of Indian school work. . . . The art work was the usual insipid spray of flower or budding twig done in a slap-dash style, and some geometrical designs apparently made under the strict directions of a teacher. The only trace of Indian in the exhibition were some of the signatures denoting clannish names. The art show was a farce, and as I stood there looking at the work, I could not help but call to mind the Indian woman, untaught and unhampered by white man's ideas of art, making beautiful and intricate designs [on] the pouches and belts she makes of beads.[76]

DeCora's criticism of the art display is also a denunciation of power relations embedded within the production of that art and within aesthetic principles themselves. She stresses the students' lack of freedom as they are made to produce banal and shoddy work. Significantly, the designs she derides are symbolic of the pretenses and orderly aims of middle-class domesticity. The students' work consisted of both the "insipid" sentimental flower and the rigid geometrical designs that were the teacher's expression rather than the artist's. The floral designs DeCora consistently scorned were a potent sign of domesticity's assimilating agenda. The petals that students embroidered on containers, cozies, and hangings were supposed to stimulate moral sentiments in their producers, but they were also made to be sold to middle-class whites who would decorate their parlors with art that was at once exotic and familiar, a gesture toward the premodern, natural past and an affirmation of the culture of commerce and consumption.[77]

DeCora elaborated on the connection between school-produced Indian art and domesticity by comparing the work at this particular exhibit with white women's work. "The white designer sits within four walls embroidering on velvet or cloth her little spray of flower or a single leaf," DeCora scornfully declared. Yet the Indian woman is no petty domestic producer but an "artist" who sits in the open, "drawing her inspiration from the broad espects [sic] of Nature. Her zig-zag line indicates the hills in the distance, and the blue and white back ground so usual in the Indian color scheme denotes the sky. . . . She makes her strong color contrasts under the glare of the sun, whose brilliancy makes even her bright tones seem softened into tints."[78] DeCora condemned the middle-class home, which reformers regarded as one of the best examples to stimulate progress among native peoples, as an unproductive, confining space. Moreover, she stressed that while the white woman's embroidery was a weak cultural design, as evidenced by the confined spaces where women did this work, creating crafts brought Native American women into the wider world.

DeCora shrewdly called on evaluations long part of U.S. culture when she made middle-class women's household production the symbol for production that was neither part of the aesthetic tradition of high art nor of value in the larger marketplace. She belittled the white woman's needlework, investing embroidery's "little spray of flowers" with connotations of confinement and stressing the worker's place "within four walls." DeCora compared middle-class women's restriction within household space to the freedom of Native American women, whose work was not dainty or insignificant but robust, colorful, and more reflective of the power and grandeur of nature. Native women's work bore more resemblance to the work that the middle class valued: that of (usually male) landscape artists. DeCora, always drawn to landscape art herself, called on aesthetic principles that her North American audience would recognize and connect to descriptions of high art — especially the emerging principles of modernist art and its bold use of colors and forms.

Middle-class white women, contained within the home and confined to producing trifles, became a symbol for all of white culture when DeCora condemned the banality of middle-class culture in general. If Indian women's bold productions did not find places in the bourgeois parlor, she suggested, it was because homeowners were too weak to appreciate them. If the native woman's work were placed "in a gloomy museum or within the darkened walls of the white man's home . . . what was meant to be seen in the sunlight now looks glaring and bold. It shocks the sensitive whiteman, whose perception has grown softened and perverted thro' artificial living."[79] DeCora feminized Euro-American domesticity, which was, like the "insipid" needlework that hung on parlor walls, a perversion of natural forms produced by those who had lost contact with nature. DeCora then suggested that Indian students were at risk for a similar weakening and feminization, a similar loss of natural environments not as a consequence of industrialization and artificial living but of imperialism. DeCora asserted that losses precipitated by geographical conquest could be partially remedied by Native Americans' cultural and economic conquest of aesthetic principles.

Balenti's battlement design for the Leupp Indian Art Studio suggests a struggle to conquer the most powerful space of middle-class selfhood: the home. DeCora relocated the geographic warfare of the nineteenth century, situating battles between white and Native American cultures in the realm of domestic production. Here, she argued, native cultures would surely dominate the contained, feminized, valueless art symbolized by floral needlework. DeCora's argument about aesthetics located the battleground in two places. First, it could be found within the individual Indian, where "racial pride" would come to dominate infusions of white blood and white institutions.[80] Like her Hampton instructors, DeCora wished to foster race pride, but she believed that Indian race pride would change white institutions and not the other way around. Second, the contest took place in the middle-class home. Even as DeCora belittled the parlor as a place of containment and highly directed domestic labor, she recognized that she and her young artists needed especially to capture these grounds in order to survive economically. The middle-class white woman was a consumer as well as a domestic producer, and her tastes needed to be conquered so that Indian artists might not just execute their designs but produce them for buyers eager to display this work in their homes. DeCora joined writers like Soule, feminists who crusaded for new legal definitions of the homestead, WNIA reformers, field matrons, and reservation women in seeking the authority to define the meaning of home and the work performed in it.

Angel DeCora desired for her students a share in American culture and industry through native artistic practices. In celebrating the Native American woman artist as cultural producer, she advocated a more vigorous and valuable kind of domestic production than what she saw as the artificial productions of white women, symbolized by the middle-class home. She envisioned meanings far in excess of the product itself, and she believed that native identities could be constructed outside the reservation and outside the laboring mentality that many reformers assigned to them. But in negotiating for space in American sites of cultural production such as literary magazines, museums, and the home, DeCora was nonetheless bound by standards of value that separated the cultural work of professionals and artists from the labor of producers, domestic labor from economic production, and white workers from indigenous ones. Like white feminists before her, Angel DeCora failed to fully fuse evaluations of the cultural worth of domestic productions with affirmation of their economic worth. Indigenous artists' work was quickly absorbed into the domestic economy as a way to deny the alienating effects of industrialization and to reconnect the middle class with the seemingly separate sphere of premodern cultures. Celebrating Native American artistry as cultural work quickly dissolved into evaluations of authenticity that denied the economic value of the effort that went into production.

DeCora's tenure at Carlisle did not last long. When Cato Sells was appointed Commissioner of Indian Affairs in 1914, the Carlisle School became even more focused on producing Native American wage laborers. Sells was not, as Leupp had been, interested in Indian art as an educational tool. During World War I, Carlisle became a satellite factory for the Ford Motor Company; in 1917 it closed its doors for good. DeCora left Carlisle in 1915, frustrated with the refusal of politicians and school officials to see Native American art as more than a quaint nod to past cultures or to see their crafts as more than training for wage labor on assembly lines or as domestic servants. DeCora died in 1919, a victim of influenza.[81]

Angel DeCora's death came at the end of an era for both women and indigenous people. DeCora did not live to see government policymakers announce the end of the allotment campaign that had begun in earnest some forty years earlier. The Meriam Report of 1928 concluded that the attempt to force indigenous people into the U.S. body politic through the homestead requirement was a failure. Rather than improving the living conditions of reservation inhabitants, allotment wreaked havoc. Deaths from tuberculosis and infant mortality far outstripped the national average, illiteracy and poverty plagued reservation residents, and millions of allotted acres had been lost to settlers and speculators. Eventually, under the leadership of Commissioner of Indian Affairs John Collier, the controversial Indian Reorganization Act of 1934 repealed allotment laws; returned surplus lands to tribes; encouraged indigenous art, religion, and rituals; fostered wage work opportunities on reservations; and established tribal sovereignty. The allotment era was at an end, though assimilation efforts would continue. The demise of the domestic imperative that allotment represented can be read as a victory for indigenous people, who were finally granted citizenship — including voting privileges — by act of Congress in 1924.

DeCora died just before women citizens were granted suffrage in 1920, a change that ostensibly marked women's entry into full citizenship. Yet women's attempts to claim status for domestic work was a failure in the face of this considerable victory for women's rights. The Nineteenth Amendment passed without incorporating the concerns of feminists who had fought for recognition not only of women's political voices but of the value of their housework. Voting rights paved the way for women's advancement in politics and in public workplaces but turned feminists' attention away from domestic labor. Like the nineteenth-century feminists who crusaded for the cultural and economic value of household labor, DeCora tried and failed to integrate economic power into the government's plan for citizenship. Just as the cultural value of women's domestic work seemed to preserve what appeared to be lost as a result of the growing economic and political value of female public work, the cultural potency of images of Indian artisans as reservoirs of premodernity overwhelmed other possible perceptions of Indians as workers participating in the economic present.

When Curtis published her tribute to DeCora, "An American Indian Artist," a year after DeCora's death, she wrote that DeCora "passes to-day without public recognition." Curtis astutely noted that DeCora's anonymity stemmed from the consistent undervaluation of the arts she had chosen to celebrate: her "native art expression, even when practically applied to crafts and industries, had failed to find space in the American's 'mechanical mind.'"[82] DeCora's investment in indigenous domestic culture compromised her promotion of industrial production, while the relegation of native crafts to the status of domestic commodities compromised her hope of investing them with cultural values that would support not just Euro-American culture's vision of itself but indigenous identity as well. In attempting to fuse domestic production with cultural practice, however, DeCora had tried to bind domestic identity and industrial production together and to put this forth as part of a new Native American identity, one in which work at home and within the marketplace produced not only value but a sense of Native American community invested in a shared set of practices. Those practices were a product neither wholly of a localized native culture nor of Euro-American science, capitalism, and domesticity; they were realized at the borders, where different cultures met one another, exchanged ideas, and remade themselves.

The Map and the Territory

Why look to women's work to understand Native American assimilation? Why look to relationships between white and indigenous women to better understand the history of women's work? Those who participated in the Native American assimilation process also helped to define what it meant to do women's work and the role that household labor would play in distinguishing "savage" from "civilized" households. The rhetoric and imagery that helped Euro-Americans recognize domesticity as a barometer of civilization played a role in shaping the kinds of images, structures, and even forms of labor that they would impress upon indigenous people. Looking carefully at the changing forms of work through which white women asserted their domestic mission to the Indians, as well as outlining the ways that native women responded by characterizing their own work, gives a fuller sense of the social and material situations that shaped women's work in an imperial era. While the novels, photographs, and instruction that helped white women — and many Native American women — create a frame of reference for what it meant to do domestic work, not all work experiences fit neatly within that frame. Gender dynamics within the household, homes that blurred the line between household labor and market-oriented work, and the political, cultural, and economic environments that shaped women's work in western contact zones more often challenged than confirmed tidy notions about the value of women's work.

Patricia Albers, an anthropologist who studies Native American political economies, distinguishes between the "map" and the "territory" of work experience. The map, she argues, is "a body of ideas people share and engage when they conduct their work." The map differs from the territory, which "encompasses the social and material worlds that labor engages. . . . The territory often contains features not easily read or even registered by a preexisting and culturally-constituted map, and indeed, the two may even stand in contradiction to each other."[1] By the mid-nineteenth century, Native American and Euro-American cultures had developed normative ideas about certain kinds of work and workers — for example, how work was distributed according to gender, age, or status. These normative ideas took form in "maps" that American studies scholars locate in literature, art, and displays that they designate as sites of cultural work. Such maps include Caroline Soule's western settlement novel, Alice Fletcher's plat maps, and Anna Dawson Wilde's cottage. The territory where work unfolds, however, concerns people, materials, and economic resources. Glimpses of the territory come through in Iowa women's letters to the *Woman's Standard*, in field matrons' laments, in Jane Gay's photographs, and in Angel DeCora's classroom. Understanding work, Albers argues, means being able to read both the map and the territory, recognizing the differences between the two ways of seeing as well as how they influenced each other. We cannot regard labor simply as the action that issues from ideology, nor can we see it as distinct from the social relations and ideas that determine its value. To do so, Albers warns, is to fall back on past distinctions between home and market, male and female, and capitalist and indigenous forms of production.[2] Those distinctions determined whether and in what contexts certain kinds of work would be valued — as women's and Native Americans' work, for example, might be assessed in terms of cultural preservation rather than economics. To uphold such categories is to retreat into a kind of nostalgia about work that favors a well-marked map over the trickier terrain of the territory.

Ideological maps that located domestic work, however, established the terms women used to speak to one another about their work. Certainly the maps created by domestic novelists like Caroline Soule, feminists like those who wrote for the *Woman's Standard*, scientists like Alice Fletcher, and reform organizations like the WNIA were essential for women's belief in the value of household labor. Seeing housework as part of a civilizing process assisted women in assembling mutually held meanings regarding domestic work. Those meanings helped them integrate domesticity into expansionist politics, challenge existing laws, and develop professional identities and coalitions. Literary, legal, and scientific discussions about the value of women's work in the expansionist West built a definition of domesticity as integral to white, middle-class identity by appealing to a set of common terms.

First, they suggested that domesticity was natural to women. Caroline Soule used her prairie setting to propose that the fruits of women's work were, like the prairie itself, outpourings of their feminine natures. The prairie's abundance was matched by the abundance of maternal love that allowed westering women to incorporate adoptive children, both native and white, into their homes. Later feminists in Iowa, though they rejected the idea that women's work was simply a labor of love, did accept the idea that household labor fell naturally to women. Even as they fought the law's tendency to conflate women's housework with a subordinate economic status, they turned to new theories of social evolution to argue that women's household labor should be recognized because it was crucial to the development of the race from savagery to civilization. White women, they argued, had first developed domesticity and made it crucial to the moral health of the race; they used the natural development of gender roles as justification for their labor's economic value and their inclusion in the middle rather than the laboring class. Reformers who applied evolutionary theory to Native American assimilation firmly believed that developing women's domesticity was part of this progression and that white women were, by virtue of historical development, more suited than men to transmit domestic values to indigenous women. Yet they also believed that domesticity could be artificially induced — that women's work, in fact, consisted of the very act of effecting civilization.

Second, women who discussed the value of domestic work in the West helped to develop it into a way of defining white and Native American racial traits. Conflating domestic work and civilization, they created a scale that made household labor into not just a set of tasks but a ladder of progress. In Soule's novel, the Indian characters' transformations legitimate white women's work; as Indians adopt Euro-American ways and make their homes in Euro-American cottages, white women become more secure in their own middle-class identity as transmitters of culture. The ascendancy of white women is measured through movement away from the "savage" conditions of the prairie as well as their ability to help Indian characters do the same. Iowa feminists took the idea of racial difference further, using the idea of Native American women's subordinate status to create a gauge by which their own status could be measured. Certain kinds of domestic labor could be associated with different levels of achievement on an evolutionary scale. For women who found too many similarities between their own plight and that of the working class, the rhetoric of evolution promised a more fruitful language in which to speak about household work. The WNIA helped to take this ladder, which measured progress and women's household work step for step, to the public by embedding it in images and architecture. Seizing on the idea of the model home simultaneously being developed by urban reformers, the WNIA made the racial differences between white and Native American women visible through images — both photographic and textual — of women's homes and housework.

Finally, these nineteenth-century mapmakers shared the idea that domesticity — and who would be domestic — could be controlled and determined by deliberate action. Soule, the Iowa feminists, and the WNIA each attempted, in their own ways, to draw new maps of the sites and contours of women's work. Soule suggested the special role that women's natural domesticity could play in a prairie state inhabited by Indians whose histories and properties would need to be absorbed in order to complete the middle-class mission of expansion and Christianization. To do so, she implied, would entail women's authorial work as well as their domestic labor. Iowa feminist writers attempted to give new value to women's housework by situating it within economic and evolutionary contexts. They exposed the economic as well as cultural value of their work in order to define themselves as analogous to laborers in the marketplace and to women in other cultures, but they used their race to position themselves within the middle class. The WNIA and its cohort of mission workers and field matrons attempted to redraw the map of Native American assimilation by marking it with homes spread across the West. Assimilation, they argued, was a domesticating process that could only succeed if located in the battleground of the reservation cottage. In so doing, white women carved out new spaces for domestic work within the professional class.

It is here, though, that the dissonance between the map and the territory becomes most apparent. For as each of these groups drew on common terms in order to define the features of the map and who belonged on it, their own efforts become apparent. White, middle-class identity became not a natural feature of the landscape but a product of the mapmakers' own work. Authorial work, household labor, exhibitionary display, and professional ambition went into drawing the maps that appeared to be a true depiction of the landscape. In making their maps, these women conceded — sometimes overtly, sometimes covertly — that some features of the territory had been redrawn or erased in favor of neater demarcations that separated Euro-American from indigenous forms of domestic work.

As Jane Gay recognized in the 1890s, carefully constructed maps could never contain all the elements that made up the much rougher and more unpredictable territory of women's lives and work. Gay, Anna Dawson Wilde, Ella Ripley, and Angel DeCora were all able map readers, and to some degree they understood and shared the notions that domesticity was part of women's nature, that it was a marker of racial difference, and that who and what counted as domestic was under women's control. They used these ideas to assert their own claims to power by emphasizing the value of their work. Gay believed that the Nez Perces needed to be domesticated in order to survive, and she used her work as a cook and photographer to make analogies between domestic labor and assimilation work. Dawson Wilde used the ladder of civilization to construct her identity as a civilized woman and to chart her way to a professional career, reporting her charges' progress toward civilization as well. Ripley understood that Dawson Wilde's role was to manipulate the reservation environment, and she used the matron's failures to challenge her authority. DeCora adapted the metaphor of naturalness to define Native American artistry, but by bringing her work to the white, middle-class public, she suggested that Native Americans could also control the terms under which they and their work would be integrated into Euro-American homes.

Less subtly than Soule or the Indian reformers, these women revealed the territories where domestic work took place in the West, and in doing so, they exposed the artifice, unstable categories, and unpredictability that character-ized domesticity. Gay's account undercut the sexual divisions crucial to civiliza-tion by revealing the work necessary not only to effect civilization but to enact traditional gender roles within her two-woman household. She saw the gender and racial categories on which civilization depended as a matter of performance and manipulation. Her photographs expose more than a narrative of allotment, as they suggest that there was little that was natural about the domesticity that she and Fletcher were bringing to the Nez Perces. Not nature, but plat maps, chainmen, survey instruments, and Fletcher's own considerable acts of will were behind change on the reservation. For Gay, domesticity was neither natural nor a stable category for understanding women's domestic work, as Fletcher's work and her own, both domestic in a sense, afforded them very different kinds of power. Like other artists and reformers, Gay attempted to exert control over the civilization process in ways that other women had also tried, dabbling in writ-ing, photography, architecture, and even science. But her attempts generally returned her to the disturbing conclusion that orderly ideals conflicted with radical contingency, and that her representations reflected her sense of irony and insecurity much more than they captured Nez Perce identity.

Dawson Wilde's story implies that the making of a domestic woman was not necessarily natural but a process of self-creation through image making. In the face of emerging antimodernist ideas that described Indian women as natural, primitive, and domestic, Dawson Wilde cultivated an image of herself and her work as modern, systematic, and deliberately made. Ripley capitalized on this story of self-making to suggest that the field matron and her home were dedicated not to the hard work of survival on the reservation but to superficial scene creation. Juxtaposing Dawson Wilde's work against the realities of the reservation, Ripley argued that the domestic object lesson was of little substance unless it was to be a useful site for Indian women's work. She argued that the differences between teachers and learners on which Dawson Wilde's author-ity rested were based on flimsy and even dangerous distinctions between life-sustaining housework and professional domesticity. Ripley exposed the pillars of civilized identity — home architecture, order, and domesticity — reformers used to support the dubious categories of savagery and civilization as no more substantive than the paper on which Dawson Wilde recorded her acts.

More so than Gay, Dawson Wilde, or Ripley, Angel DeCora entered the realm of cultural production. Like Soule, she established herself on literary terrain in order to claim new meaning for domestic work. She criticized some of the ways through which whites had established authority over indigenous people, including writing, science, and domestic ideology. She suggested that the categories of difference on which they rested were not natural but created in books, museum displays, and the marketplace. She boldly made her work visible in literary and commercial contexts, submitting that Native Americans were both true artisans and viable workers in the economy. Arguing that native people were capable of supporting themselves in the modern marketplace, she undermined the idea that Indians were vessels of premodernity. The idea of Indian primitivism, she argued, was more a product of schools and museums than a reflection of truth. DeCora responded by seizing some of those spaces of cultural production, such as books, exposition display, Indian industrial schoolrooms, and the commercial realm, for herself and her students. Like the Iowa feminists before her, she attempted to link the map with the territory, arguing that Native American domestic craft could bear the weight of culture and of economic legitimacy.

How did these women change the way we understand domestic work? In some ways, very little. We continue to correlate cultural ideas about women's work with the actual experience of that work. In the twenty-first century as in the nineteenth, we continue to imagine domestic work in monolithic terms, thinking that if we can paint a picture of what home and housework ought to be, we can understand the work it takes to turn image into reality. In policy and popular culture, we continue to believe that the images we hold of domestic work convey the truth of experience, whether we believe that household work is truly a labor of love that needs no compensation or that commercial images of home are simply outpourings of cultural or personal expression rather than the outcome of efforts — mediated by class status — on the part of their makers.

In other ways, though, each of the individuals and groups this book explores can shape the way we understand domestic work today. My focus on contact zones that brought white and Native American women together emphasizes that ideas about domestic work did not simply appear but were purposefully forged. Domesticity did not always veil divides between men and women, laborers and professionals, and whites and Native Americans. Instead, these differences were refined through discussions of domestic work, as those discussions engaged ideas rooted in economic values, social evolution, and exhibitionary display. Rather than shunting these ideas to the side as extraneous to domesticity, both white and indigenous women made them central to their attempts to define the meaning of domestic work, for themselves and for others. Far from regarding domesticity as a safe haven, the women I have studied here dared — consciously or unconsciously — to expose the work involved in making home. From them we can learn that the home still functions as a contact zone where some groups attempt to establish control over what kinds of women's work can be regarded as legitimate, what kinds of women will do different kinds of work, and what social or economic value will be assigned to that work. And from them we can learn that those categories are not natural but the result of ongoing efforts to define gender, race, and the social value of women's work.

NOTES

. . . .

Abbreviations

BIA   Record Group 75, Bureau of Indian Affairs, National Archives
CIA   Commissioner of Indian Affairs
LMC   Lake Mohonk Conference of Friends of the Indian
LR   Letters Received
PS   *The Pet of the Settlement*

Introduction

1. Gay, *Choup-nit-ki*, 14, 129, 216.
2. Ibid., 14.
3. The term "cultural work" is from Tompkins, *Sensational Designs*. Other studies of the cultural work of domestic fiction in the United States include Douglas, *Feminization of American Culture*; Carby, *Reconstructing Womanhood*; Samuels, *Culture of Sentiment*; Brown, *Domestic Individualism*; Brodhead, *Cultures of Letters*; and Merish, *Sentimental Materialism*. Works that discuss the imperial dimensions of domesticity include Pratt, *Imperial Eyes*; Sánchez-Eppler, "Raising Empires Like Children"; McClintock, *Imperial Leather*; Romero, *Home Fronts*; Wexler, *Tender Violence*; and Kaplan, *Anarchy of Empire*.
4. See, for example, Smith, *American Archives*; Jacobson, *Barbarian Virtues*; Reynolds and Hunter, *National Imaginaries, American Identities*; Wexler, *Tender Violence*; Kaplan, *Anarchy of Empire*.
5. For works that discuss domesticity in interrogating gender, race, or sexuality in the American West, see esp. Riley, *Women and Indians on the Frontier*; Tucker, *Prophetic Sisterhood*; Deutsch, *No Separate Refuge*; Pascoe, *Relations of Rescue*; Georgi-Findlay, *Frontiers of Women's Writing*; Sherer Mathes, *Helen Hunt Jackson*; Yohn, *Contest of Faiths*; Jacobs, *Engendered Encounters*; and Hurtado, *Sex, Gender, and Culture in California*.
6. Pratt introduces the term "contact zone" in *Imperial Eyes*. Those who use the idea of the contact zone to explore the complexities of imperial encounter include Said, *Culture and Imperialism*; Bhabha, *Location of Culture*; Stoler, *Race and the Education of Desire*; McClintock, *Imperial Leather*; Kaplan, *Anarchy of Empire*.
7. New western historians also draw on the contact zone concept, revising the idea of the progressive frontier in favor of processes of conflict and adaptation. See esp. Limerick, *Legacy of Conquest*.
8. A number of essays in Lippard's *Partial Recall* foreground this dimension of photographs of Native Americans.

9. See esp. Kelley, *Private Woman, Public Stage*; Tonkovich, *Domesticity with a Difference;* and Boydston, *Home and Work*.

10. For more on women's work, see, among others, Kessler-Harris, *Out to Work* and *Woman's Wage*; Strasser, *Never Done*; Dudden, *Serving Women*; Jensen, *Loosening the Bonds*; Sterling, *We Are Your Sisters*; Hayden, *Grand Domestic Revolution*; Boris, *Art and Labor*; Stansell, *City of Women*; Jones, *Labor of Love*; Matthews, *"Just a Housewife"*; Boydston, *Home and Work*; Folbre, "Unproductive Housewife"; Roediger, *Wages of Whiteness*; Ardener, *Women and Space*; Hanson and Pratt, *Gender, Work, and Space*; Siegel, "Home as Work"; Stanley, *From Bondage to Contract*; Silbaugh, "Turning Labor into Love."

11. Bromell, *By the Sweat of the Brow*, 4–6.

12. See esp. essays in Albers and Medicine, *Hidden Half*; Shoemaker, *Negotiators of Change*; and Littlefield and Knack, *Native Americans and Wage Labor*. Analyses of labor in Indian industrial schools include Trennert, "Educating Indian Girls" and *Phoenix Indian School*; Lomawaima, *They Called It Prairie Light*; Adams, *Education for Extinction*; Lindsey, *Indians at Hampton Institute*; and Engs, *Educating the Disfranchised and Disinherited*.

13. Arendt, *Human Condition*, 136. I depart from Arendt's distinction slightly as I use the terms "work" to indicate when the women regarded their activity as self-owned and "labor" to indicate when it was owned or managed by others. Whenever possible, I have tried to retain their own terminology.

14. Some of the best scholarship in this area looks at Native American art production as both labor and cultural work. See esp. Brody, *Indian Painters and White Patrons*; Berlo, *Early Years of Native American Art History*; Phillips, *Trading Identities*; and Phillips and Steiner, *Unpacking Culture*.

15. See Drinnon, *Facing West*; Pearce, *Savagism and Civilization*; Hinsley, *Smithsonian and the American Indian*; Dippie, *Vanishing American*; Carr, *Inventing the American Primitive*; Namias, *White Captives*; and Deloria, *Playing Indian*. Recent works that include attention to Native American perspectives include Dilworth, *Imagining Indians*; Jacobs, *Engendered Encounters*; Lippard, *Partial Recall*; Bataille, *Native American Representations*; Bernardin, Graulich, MacFarlane, and Tonkovich, *Trading Gazes*; and Deloria, *Indians in Unexpected Places*.

16. Siegel, "Valuing Housework"; Silbaugh, "Turning Labor into Love." Other important works that discuss erasures of economic value in legal interpretations of married women's work and property rights include Rabkin, *Fathers to Daughters*; Salmon, *Women and the Law of Property*; Basch, *In the Eyes of the Law*; Warbasse, *Changing Legal Rights of Married Women*; Shammas, "Re-Assessing the Married Women's Property Acts"; Siegel, "Home as Work"; and Stanley, *From Bondage to Contract*.

17. Boydston, *Home and Work*, 158.

18. Ibid., 116.

19. Ibid., 149.

20. Bromell, *By the Sweat of the Brow*, 143.

21. Annette Kolodny discusses women's role in cultivating sites of civilization in the West in *Land before Her*. More recently, Lori Merish's discussion of Caroline Kirkland's *A New Home: Who'll Follow?* stresses Kirkland's positioning of the "middle class mate-

rial landscape" as a method of civilizing unruly classes in the West; see Merish, *Sentimental Materialism*, 100.

22. For a similar argument, see Wiebe, *Search for Order*, 134 – 36.

23. Hayden, *Grand Domestic Revolution*, 3.

24. Beecher and Stowe, *American Woman's Home*. See also Boydston, Kelley, and Margolis, *Limits of Sisterhood*.

25. Gilman, *Women and Economics*. On Gilman and home architecture, see Allen, *Building Domestic Liberty*.

26. Sawaya, *Modern Women, Modern Work*, 2 – 18.

27. On domestic science and professionalization, see Fitzpatrick, *Endless Crusade*.

28. Bennett, *Birth of the Museum*, 83.

29. Ibid., 59 – 88.

30. See Hayden, *Grand Domestic Revolution*; Wright, *Building the Dream* and *Moralism and the Model Home*; Grier, *Culture and Comfort*; and Merish, *Sentimental Materialism*.

31. See esp. Lears, *No Place of Grace*, and Dilworth, *Imagining Indians*.

32. See Phillips and Steiner, *Unpacking Culture*; Berlo, *Early Years of Native American Art History*.

33. For a reading of Gay's metaphor of cropping, see Tonkovich, " 'Lost in the General Wreckage,' " 50 – 51.

34. Bernardin, Graulich, MacFarlane, and Tonkovich suggest that cropping this self-portrait in circular form was an act of refusal to participate in "Cartesian" ways of seeing; see *Trading Gazes*, 23.

Chapter One

1. On Tenskwatawa's role in resistance movements, see Hertzberg, *Search for an American Indian Identity*, 54 – 56, and Dowd, *Spirited Resistance*, esp. 124 – 32, 135 – 46.

2. Catlin, *Letters and Notes*, 118.

3. Ibid., 184.

4. Soule, *PS*, iii.

5. See, for example, Eliza Farnham's *Life in Prairie Land* (1846); E. D. E. N. Southworth's *India: The Pearl of Pearl River* (1856); Susan Maria Cummins's *Mabel Vaughn* (1857); and M. Emilia Rockwell's *A Home in the West, or Emigration and Its Consequences* (serialized in 1858). In addition to these longer works, a host of poems published in the popular press lauded the frontier wife.

6. Soule, *PS*, 47 – 48.

7. Ibid., iii – iv.

8. Ibid., 241 – 45.

9. Smith, *Virgin Land*, 250.

10. Kolodny, *Land before Her*, 171.

11. Ibid., 194; Soule, *PS*, 201.

12. Bromell, *By the Sweat of the Brow*, 31. The erasure of women's physical labor in sentimental novels and other forms of literature has been noted by a number of critics. See esp. Brown, *Domestic Individualism*; Brodhead, *Cultures of Letters*; and Bromell, *By the Sweat of the Brow*.

13. Kolodny, *Land before Her*, 194.

14. Boydston, *Home and Work*, 147.

15. Soule, *PS*, 236.

16. Biographical information is from Seaburg, "Caroline Soule."

17. For these writers' engagements with abolitionism and Indian removal, see Maddox, *Removals*, 95–111, and Kerber, "Abolitionist Perception of the Indian," 273–74.

18. Maddox, *Removals*, 130.

19. For biographical information on Soule, see Kolodny, *Land before Her*, 266–67 nn. 25, 28; and Seaburg, "Caroline Soule." Soule was the corresponding and eventually the assistant editor of the *Ladies' Repository* during her stay in Iowa and went on to be the first president of the Women's Centenary Aid Association in 1871. Sklar discusses Beecher's initiative for education in the West in *Catharine Beecher*, 113–15.

20. Soule, *PS*, 237.

21. Riley, *Frontierswomen*, 33.

22. Soule, *PS*, iii, 17.

23. Ibid., 14–15.

24. Ibid., 28.

25. Ibid., 97, 17, 236.

26. For the history of the Sauk and Fox and Black Hawk's War, see Black Hawk, *Life of Black Hawk*; Hagan, *Sac and Fox Indians*; and Nichols, *Black Hawk and the Warrior's Path*.

27. Quoted in Hagan, *Sac and Fox Indians*, 213.

28. Black Hawk, *Life of Black Hawk*, 43.

29. Ibid., 106.

30. Historians who make this distinction include Parkman in *Conspiracy of Pontiac*, Catlin in *Letters and Notes*, and Hagan in *Sac and Fox Indians*.

31. Bernardin, Graulich, MacFarlane, and Tonkovich, *Trading Gazes*, 6.

32. Nichols, *Black Hawk and the Warrior's Path*, 148; Black Hawk, *Life of Black Hawk*, 170–71.

33. Bernardin, Graulich, MacFarlane, and Tonkovich, *Trading Gazes*, 13.

34. Soule, *PS*, 50–51.

35. Ibid., 86.

36. Catlin, *Letters and Notes*, 184.

37. Soule, *PS*, 194–95.

38. Ibid., 85–86, 196–98.

39. Ibid., 248.

40. Here Soule seems to have bungled her geography, since in 1860 the Sauk, Fox, and Ioway reservations were situated at the northern border of Kansas, just south of Nebraska.

41. Dowd disputes this distinction between the political and spiritual roles of nineteenth-century Native American leaders; see *Spirited Resistance*, xiv–xv.

42. Sánchez-Eppler, "Raising Empires Like Children," 401.

43. Wexler, *Tender Violence*, 53.

44. Ibid., 6.

45. Soule, *PS*, 147–150.

46. Ibid., 172.

47. Ibid., 176–77.

48. Ibid., 197.

49. Ibid., 249.

50. Ibid., 177.

51. On early Native American educational practices, see Szasz, *Indian Education*.

52. Soule, *PS*, iii.

53. Hill, *World Their Household*, 11–13.

54. Beecher and Stowe, *American Woman's Home*, 457.

55. Ibid., 458.

56. Ibid.

57. On Beecher's changing understanding of women's work roles, see esp. Sklar, *Catharine Beecher*, 166–67, and Boydston, Kelley, and Margolis, *Limits of Sisterhood*.

58. Beecher and Stowe, *American Woman's Home*, 17–25.

59. Soule, *PS*, 247–48.

60. Hagan, *Sac and Fox Indians*, 339–40.

61. Brown, "Hawthorne, Inheritance, and Women's Property," 110, 108, 116.

62. Soule, *PS*, 246.

63. Ibid., 86.

64. Ibid., 198.

65. Ibid., 199, 248, 171.

66. Ibid., 200.

67. Child, "Appeal for the Indians," 225.

Chapter Two

1. Roediger, *Wages of Whiteness*, 13.

2. Reva Siegel briefly considers Abigail Scott Duniway's support of joint property statutes in Oregon, suggesting that western women, who were less apt to work for wages than eastern women, did not completely share the desires of eastern feminists for women to gain equality through work outside the home; see Siegel, "Home as Work," 1156, 1163. Louise Michele Newman also discusses Alice Fletcher's understanding of domestic work in racial terms through her work with Native American assimilation; see Newman, *White Women's Rights*, 116–31.

3. Noun, *Strong-Minded Women*, 3.

4. Ibid., 138.

5. Ibid., 203.

6. Ibid., 265–68.

7. *Woman's Standard*, Dec. 1886, 1.

8. *Revision of 1873*, §2205, §2211.

9. Stanton, Anthony, and Gage, *History of Woman Suffrage*, 636.

10. Stanley, *From Bondage to Contract*, 199.

11. "Unpaid Laborer."

12. Dysart, "White Slaves."

13. On the term "white slavery," see Roediger, *Wages of Whiteness*, 65–92.

14. C. T. C., "Women's Wages."

15. "They Never Strike."

16. "Wife Is a Chattel."

17. Donley, "God Made Woman for Man to Take Care of."

18. Read, "Equal Rights in Property" (Sept. 1886).

19. Siegel, "Home as Work," 1126.

20. Ibid., 1128–29.

21. Quoted in ibid., 1126.

22. Weeks, "Partnership."

23. Read started her journalistic career in Indiana, publishing a suffrage newspaper called the *Mayflower* during the Civil War. A supporter of the AWSA, Read lived in Iowa until 1897, when she moved to Arkansas. See Noun, *Strong-Minded Women*, 272.

24. Read, "Equal Rights in Property" (Sept. 1886).

25. Stanley, *From Bondage to Contract*, 191.

26. Read, "Equal Rights in Property" (Nov. 1886).

27. Stanley, *From Bondage to Contract*, 192.

28. See Siegel's summary of this change in "Home as Work," 1189.

29. On Gilman's cooperative housekeeping theories, see esp. Allen, *Building Domestic Liberty*, and Hayden, *Grand Domestic Revolution*, 183–205.

30. On Duniway and western feminist periodicals, see Siegel, "Home as Work," 1156, 1163–66.

31. Ibid., 1166–67.

32. "Miserable Wife."

33. Quoted in Siegel, "Home as Work," 1157.

34. See Stanley's excellent discussion of housework and the wage economy in *From Bondage to Contract*.

35. "Eight-Hour Wife."

36. See Stanley's discussion of time and the wage contract in *From Bondage to Contract*, 90–94.

37. "Harry Brown's Lesson."

38. See Merish, *Sentimental Materialism*, esp. chap. 1, "Embodying Gender: Sentimental Materialism in the New Republic," 29–87.

39. Shawn Michelle Smith argues against an interpretation of female consumption that foregrounds women's loss of agency and suggests that "in circulation and display we might see women claiming self-authorship and self-ownership" (*American Archives*, 97).

40. Weinstein, *Literature of Labor and the Labors of Literature*, 35.

41. See Smith's discussion of interiority and artistic work in *American Archives*, 67.

42. On the popularity of civilization discourse, see esp. Wiebe, *Search for Order*.

43. "Is Woman a Unit or a Fraction?" (emphasis in original).

44. For ways evolutionary theories applied to gender roles, see esp. Bederman, *Manliness and Civilization*; Newman, *White Women's Rights*; and Allen, "Feminism, Social Science, and the Meanings of Modernity."

45. Brumberg, "Zenanas and Girlless Villages," 348, 355.

46. Gilman, *Women and Economics*. For a similar argument, see Newman, *White Women's Rights*, 134.

47. J. E. J., "All the Rights She Wants."

48. "Against Indian Women."

49. *Woman's Standard*, Sept. 1886, 7.

50. "Women of Alaska." For an analysis of how white women's outrage at crimes committed by men against women in the West helped to bolster women's moral authority in that region, see Pascoe, *Relations of Rescue*.

51. For an analysis of racialized discourse in white women's campaigns for suffrage, see Newman, *White Women's Rights*.

52. "Indians Can Vote."

53. "Homestead Law and Women."

54. "Woman and Her Political Peers."

55. Newman, *White Women's Rights*, 66.

56. "Pagan Origin of Women's Subjection."

57. Chapman, "Prayers towards Woman's Enfranchisement an Evolution."

58. "Unjust Laws."

59. H. F. C., "Property Rights of Married Women" and "Man's 'Rights' in Women's Property," 3.

60. Campbell, "Appeal to the Intelligent Men of Iowa."

61. H. F. C., "Property Rights of Married Women" and "Shall Our Country Remain Free?"

62. "Indian Problem Solved."

63. *Woman's Standard*, Jan. 1887, 1.

64. Mallory, "Home of Injustice."

Chapter Three

1. LMC, *Proceedings* (1887), 55.

2. On model homes and interiors more generally, see Wright, *Moralism and the Model Home*, and Grier, *Culture and Comfort*. For a discussion of model homes for Native Americans at Hampton, see Buffalohead and Fairbanks Molin, "'Nucleus of Civilization.'"

3. Bennett suggests that the ways nineteenth-century exhibitions ordered bodies to illustrate progress assumed a white, male body; see *Birth of the Museum*, 189.

4. See esp. Smith-Rosenberg, "Beauty, the Beast, and the Militant Woman" and "The Cross and the Pedestal," in *Disorderly Conduct*; Douglas, *Feminization of American Culture*; Epstein, *Politics of Domesticity*; Flexner, *Century of Struggle*.

5. For the history of the WNIA, see Wanken, "'Woman's Sphere' and Indian Reform." Valerie Sherer Mathes also discusses the WNIA in *Helen Hunt Jackson*.

6. Editorial (Feb. 1889).

7. Quinton, "In Care of the Indian."

8. "Sufferings of Alaska Women"; Eina, "Mission Indians"; *Southern Workman*.

9. Quinton, "Address."

10. See Muncy, *Creating a Female Dominion*.

11. Downing, *Architecture of Country Houses*, 25.

12. See Wright, *Moralism and the Model Home* and *Building the Dream*; Grier, *Cul-*

ture and Comfort; Merish, *Sentimental Materialism*, esp. chap. 2, "Gender, Domesticity, and Consumption in the 1830s"; Leavitt, *From Catharine Beecher to Martha Stewart*.

13. Szasz, *Indian Education*, 218–19.

14. Morgan, *Ancient Society*, 309, 6.

15. Ibid., 5.

16. Hoxie, *Final Promise*, 20. Also see Trachtenberg's discussion of Morgan's influence on the Dawes Act, in *Incorporation of America*, 34–37. For a fascinating account of Morgan's interest in experimenting with Indian identity through "Indian fraternities," see Deloria, *Playing Indian*.

17. On Fletcher and the Omahas, see Kidd Green, *Iron Eye's Family*; Mark, *Stranger in Her Native Land*, 64–79, 88–101; and Boughter, *Betraying the Omaha Nation*.

18. Fletcher, "Winnebagos."

19. Fletcher, "Allotting Lands."

20. Beecher, *Treatise on Domestic Economy*, 156–57.

21. On women reformers' critiques of patriarchy, see Pascoe, *Relations of Rescue*, 34–37.

22. LMC, *Proceedings* (1886), 45.

23. From a letter from Rosalie La Flesche Farley to Alice Fletcher, quoted in Kidd Green, *Iron Eye's Family*, 101–2.

24. Stabler, "Scholarship Letters."

25. "Home Building."

26. Editorial (Oct. 1888), 2.

27. Twenty-three couples were involved in the model home experiment at Hampton while it operated from 1882 to 1885. They included Sioux, Omaha, Winnebago, and Oneida married pairs. See Buffalohead and Fairbanks Molin, "'Nucleus of Civilization,'" 71.

28. Lindsey, *Indians at Hampton Institute*, 198.

29. "Indian School."

30. J. R., "Our Indian House Warming"; LMC, *Proceedings* (1884), 28.

31. Merish, *Sentimental Materialism*, 104–5.

32. "Indian School."

33. LMC, *Proceedings* (1884), 28.

34. Kinney, "Helping Indians to Help Themselves."

35. Gould, "Report of the Home Building and Loan Committee."

36. On Fletcher's exhibit in New Orleans, see Mark, *Stranger in Her Native Land*, 109–14.

37. WNIA, *Annual Report* (1885), 10.

38. WNIA, *Annual Report* (1888), 11.

39. Garrett, "Observer on the Reservation."

40. WNIA, *Annual Report* (1888), 11.

41. LMC, *Proceedings* (1887), 35.

42. LMC, *Proceedings* (1893), 29.

43. See Jackson, *Century of Dishonor*.

44. LMC, *Proceedings* (1900), 106.

45. See Laura Rigal's discussion of the nest as metaphor for familial and national production, in *American Manufactory*, 149–50.

46. LMC, *Proceedings* (1885), 46, 34.

47. Adams, *Education for Extinction*, 114.

48. The extensive scholarship on Native American boarding schools discusses the ways the schools shaped students' work habits and indoctrinated students in the rhetoric of social evolution that honored Euro-Americans as the most "civilized." See, for example, Trennert, "Educating Indian Girls" and *Phoenix Indian School*; Coleman, *American Indian Children at School*; Adams, *Education for Extinction*; Lindsey, *Indians at Hampton Institute*; Littlefield, "Indian Education and the World of Work"; and Engs, *Educating the Disfranchised and Disinherited*. For ways schools influenced students to conform to gender norms, see Mihesuah, *Cultivating the Rosebuds*, and Lomawaima, *They Called It Prairie Light*.

49. "Indian Mothers and Indian Girls," 3.

50. "Indian Emancipation Day," 33.

51. Barb Landis notes that in the serial version, the protagonist was named Mollie, but the name was later changed after Carlisle instructors were enamored by one current Pueblo pupil's name. The real Stiya passed away in 1900, some years after she returned home to Arizona. See Landis, "Carlisle Indian School References to the Publication, Stiya."

52. Marianna Burgess taught at the Carlisle School for twenty-five years, during which time she served as the business manager of the printing department and oversaw the printing and editing of the school papers. She left Carlisle to become the director of a business in Chicago. See "Miss Burgess Resigns."

53. Silko introduction. Amy Goodburn's analysis of *Stiya* suggests that the text and images performed different functions for different kinds of reading publics. The contrasts between pueblo and "civilized" life that the photographs display, she reasons, create "an aura of authenticity and participate in the larger photographic rhetoric utilized by government boarding schools to persuade government agencies and private patrons that boarding schools were 'civilizing' Native Americans" (Goodburn, "Literary Practices at the Genoa Industrial School," 40).

54. Burgess, *Stiya*, 86.

55. Ibid., 48–49.

56. Ibid., 110–11, 114.

57. Alice Littlefield argues that what schools achieved through their routines was "not so much assimilation as proletarianization — the formation of subjectivities and dispositions appropriate to workers in the surrounding capitalist economy" ("Indian Education and the World of Work," 102).

58. Bennett, *Birth of the Museum*, 81.

59. The idea that images on walls could stimulate Native Americans' progress was a common one, and these pictures had their own hierarchies of taste. For example, one white visitor to a western reservation wrote, "The houses contained many evidences of contact with civilized life, among which were pictures which generally [adorned] the walls. I would suggest to the field matrons the elevation of the character of these pictures from the cigarette-box and *Police Gazette* type to that of Prang's chromos, as a step toward higher things" (Garrett, "Observer on the Reservation," 48).

60. The model for the photograph was Carlisle student Lucy Tsisnah, a Chiricahua Apache who was among the prisoners from Fort Marion who came to Carlisle in 1878.

She was married to Burdette Tsisnah. See Landis, "Serialization of What Became the Book, Stiya."

61. Burgess, *Stiya*, 114.

62. This seasonal residence in houses was common. Among the Moquis, for example, one white worker wrote that "the Indians all have homes on the mesa and prefer to live there, and sometimes only stay in their 'American houses' a few days at a time, and with difficulty are prevented from carrying the furniture to their homes on the mesa" ("Other Peeps into the Work").

63. LMC, *Proceedings* (1895), 80.

64. For more on the effects of these laws on Native American women, see Janiewski, "Learning to Live 'Just Like White Folks,'" 175.

65. Dippie, *Vanishing American*, 179.

66. Boughter, *Betraying the Omaha Nation*, 140.

67. Wanken, "'Woman's Sphere' and Indian Reform," 177 – 80.

68. Kidd Green, *Iron Eye's Family*, 97 – 121; Boughter, *Betraying the Omaha Nation*, 134 – 66; Buffalohead and Fairbanks Molin, "'Nucleus of Civilization,'" 85.

69. Buffalohead and Fairbanks Molin, "'Nucleus of Civilization,'" 85; Kidd Green, *Iron Eye's Family*, 172.

70. Kinney, "Indian Home-Building." For more on Susan La Flesche and her work for the Omahas, see Pascoe, *Relations of Rescue*, and Tong, *Susan LaFlesche Picotte, M.D.*

71. La Flesche, "Home-Life of the Indian" (emphasis in original).

72. Tompkin, "Another Letter."

73. For an overview of the field matron program and its endorsement of domestic ideals, see Bannan, "'True Womanhood' on the Reservation."

74. "Field Matrons."

75. Emmerich, "'To respect and love,'" 35 – 36.

76. Dewey, "Field Matrons for Indians."

77. On women's professionalization, see esp. Wiebe, *Search for Order*, 123, 156 – 99; Fitzpatrick, *Endless Crusade*; Muncy, *Creating a Female Dominion*; and Matthews, *"Just a Housewife,"* 145 – 71.

78. Hayden, *Grand Domestic Revolution*, 3.

79. Wright, *Moralism and the Model Home*, 170. In the early twentieth century, domestic scientist Ellen Swallow Richards invented the term "euthenics" to denote the science of ordering the environment in order to control behavior and effect social change.

80. Sterling includes some reports on housing in *We Are Your Sisters*, 318 – 26. For information on model homes and race, see Wright, *Building the Dream*, 129.

81. Leavitt, *From Catharine Beecher to Martha Stewart*, 80.

82. Boris, *Art and Labor*, 78.

83. See Robyn Muncy on the "emerging female professional ethos" of late nineteenth-century reformers in *Creating a Female Dominion*, 20 – 21.

84. On women professionals' participation in bureaucratic commissions during the Progressive Era, see Muncy, *Creating a Female Dominion*.

85. Dodge, "Woman's Work in Indian Homes," 9.

86. Howard, "Grace Mission" and "Indian Civilization Work."

87. French, "Institute Paper of Miss French."

88. "Interesting Letter."

89. "Domestic Training vs. Book Learning."

90. "From the Letter of a Worker."

91. WNIA, *Annual Report* (1898), 32.

92. See Boris, *Art and Labor*, esp. "Women's Culture, Women's Crafts," 99–121, and "Women's Culture as Art and Philanthropy: The Revival of the Textile Arts," 122–38.

93. For more on exhibits in the Woman's Building, see Elliot, *Art and Handicraft in the Woman's Building*.

94. Schneider, "Women's Work."

95. Jacobs, *Engendered Encounters*, 160.

96. LMC, *Proceedings* (1894), 23–24.

97. Ibid., 24.

98. "News and Notes."

99. WNIA, *Annual Report* (1902), 24; WNIA, "Miss Sybil Carter's Address," *Annual Report* (1903), 22; LMC, *Proceedings* (1903), 65.

100. LMC, *Proceedings* (1903), 64.

101. Boris, *Art and Labor*, 135–38.

102. Wheelock, "Woman's Work in the World."

103. Jacobs, *Engendered Encounters*, 39.

104. On these work patterns, see Littlefield and Knack, "Native American Labor," 37, 51.

105. For women's work outside capitalism, see Albers, "Sioux Women in Transition," 175–234.

106. Howard, "Grace Mission."

107. Prins, "Tribal Network and Migrant Labor," 46.

108. WNIA, "Two Ways to Help the Indian," *Annual Report* (1900), 18.

109. For reasons for Native Americans' position in the labor market, see Albers, "From Legend to Land to Labor," 261, and Moore, "Cheyenne Work," 131–33.

Chapter Four

1. A version of *Choup-nit-ki* edited by Joan Mark and Frederick Hoxie and titled *With the Nez Perces* has been published by the University of Nebraska Press. A draft of *Choup-nit-ki*, as well as the negatives of almost all of Gay's photographs, are in the E. Jane Gay Collection at the Idaho State Historical Society. Most of the negatives remained in the attic of the missionary cottage at Lapwai until 1946. The collection includes 450 glass-plate and nitrate-base film negatives. See Dawson, *Jane Gay Photograph Collection Catalog*. The two hand-bound volumes made by E. Jane Gay and her niece Emma Gay, which contain 191 photographs, are located in the manuscript collections at the Schlesinger Library. All quotes in this chapter are from the manuscript of *Choup-nit-ki* held by the Schlesinger Library. Where possible, I have used the titles Gay gave the photographs in *Choup-nit-ki*. Photographs not included in *Choup-nit-ki* are designated by the Idaho State Historical Society's titles.

2. Laura Wexler has examined what she calls the "innocent eye" in late nineteenth- and early twentieth-century photography, a gaze that denies race and class divisions to

portray imperialism as a natural and largely domestic enterprise. See Wexler, *Tender Violence*, 6–7.

3. See Merish on the tendency, by the nineteenth century, of chairs to represent "sociability rather than status" (*Sentimental Materialism*, 92).

4. McClintock, *Imperial Leather*, 32.

5. Gay, *Choup-nit-ki*, 333–34. Tonkovich argues that the focus on material reality rather than idealism is implicit in many of Gay's images; see "'Lost in the General Wreckage,'" 35.

6. "Nez Perce Reservation to be Allotted at Once."

7. "Opening of the Nez Perce Reservation in the Near Future." A letter from Commissioner of Indian Affairs Thomas Jefferson Morgan to the Indian agent at Umatilla Agency, Pendleton, Oregon, indicates that some residents did not want a woman and an "outsider" to allot lands, calling Fletcher a "Carpet Bagger" (Morgan to Moorhouse, 26 Nov. 1889, Fletcher Correspondence, Fletcher Papers, Idaho State Historical Society).

8. Fletcher Diary and Fletcher Correspondence, folder 2, Fletcher Papers, National Anthropological Archives; Gay, *Choup-nit-ki*, 99. For biographical information on Fletcher and Gay, see Mark, *Stranger in Her Native Land*.

9. *Improper Bostonians*, 64–66. For an account of the romantic nature of female domestic partnerships in the nineteenth century, see Smith-Rosenberg, "The Female World of Love and Ritual," in *Disorderly Conduct*. See also Rupp, *Desired Past*, and Vicinus, "'They Wonder to Which Sex I Belong.'"

10. Lutz, *Emma Willard*, 31–32.

11. For Fletcher's reasons for entering the emerging field of ethnography, see Mark, *Stranger in Her Native Land*.

12. Gay, *Choup-nit-ki*, 65–66 (emphasis in original).

13. On nineteenth-century intersections between race and sexuality, see Somerville, "Scientific Racism and the Invention of the Homosexual Body," and Diggs, "Romantic Friends or a 'Different Race of Creatures'?"

14. For various analyses of homosociality, homosexuality, and sexuality in the nineteenth century, see Smith-Rosenberg, "The Female World of Love and Ritual," in *Disorderly Conduct*; Vicinus, "'They Wonder to Which Sex I Belong,'" 483; Newman, *White Women's Rights*, 22–55; Moore, "'Something More Tender Still Than Friendship'"; Bederman, *Manliness and Civilization*, 1–44.

15. On Gay's reasons for taking up photography, see Mark, *Stranger in Her Native Land*, 185.

16. Gay, *Choup-nit-ki*, 44.

17. Ibid., 70–75.

18. It would be difficult to pin down the meaning of this passage, but it is fair to say that Jane Gay had a tumultuous relationship with the other member of their household in Washington, D.C.: Fletcher's research partner and adopted son, Omaha Francis La Flesche. See Mark, *Stranger in Her Native Land*, 146–53.

19. Shepard, *Man in the Landscape*, 235.

20. Mark, *Stranger in Her Native Land*, 167, 185.

21. Tonkovich, "'Lost in the General Wreckage,'" 46–47.

22. For more on women's use of the hand-held camera, see Davidov, *Women's Camera Work*, 80–81.

23. Gay, *Choup-nit-ki*, 47.

24. Ibid., 113, 314, 196.

25. Ibid., 293.

26. Ibid., 119.

27. Ibid., 214, 377.

28. Ibid., 58.

29. Ibid., 308.

30. See the cogent reading of the image of the Photographer in the introduction to *Trading Gazes*. The writers suggest the way that this image reverses the "usual structures of empire and institutional power" by thwarting the viewer's attempt to fully see or comprehend. See Bernardin, Graulich, MacFarlane, and Tonkovich, *Trading Gazes*, 23.

31. Herrmann, "Imitations of Marriage," 612.

32. Gay, *Choup-nit-ki*, 1.

33. Ibid., 9.

34. Ibid., 29–30.

35. Ibid., 14.

36. Ibid., 122.

37. Allen Slickpoo and Deward Walker assert, "There is little doubt that the missionaries helped to bring about . . . settlement, and that the missionary activities supported the expansionist policies of the United States government" (*Noon-Nee-Me-Poo*, 71).

38. Gay, *Choup-nit-ki*, 123.

39. Ibid., 313.

40. Pratt, *Imperial Eyes*, 201–8.

41. Tonkovich, "'Lost in the General Wreckage,'" 51.

42. Gay, *Choup-nit-ki*, 170.

43. Tonkovich, "'Lost in the General Wreckage,'" 54.

44. Tonkovich also notes that the image is "off-plumb" and that the streaks may be due to Gay's trouble in developing the image; see ibid.

45. Gay, *Choup-nit-ki*, 408.

46. Ibid., 409.

47. Tonkovich has called attention to Gay's inclusion of workers in some of her other photographs; see "'Lost in the General Wreckage,'" 53.

48. Gay's images also expose the difficulty in imposing Euro-American definitions of family on Indians in her photographs of Nez Perce groupings; see ibid., 59.

49. Fletcher did ask Billy Williams, an elderly Nez Perce, to make her a map of the area based on his knowledge of Nez Perce culture before white contact. Like much American Indian knowledge, however, Billy's map was regarded as an artifact of prehistory; Fletcher carefully preserved it and sent it to the Smithsonian Institution. See Fletcher, "Nez Perce Country," 17, Fletcher Papers, Idaho State Historical Society.

50. Gay, *Choup-nit-ki*, 276.

51. Ibid., 98.

52. Ibid., 337 (emphasis in original).

53. Ibid., 226–28.

54. Ibid., 277–79, 242.

55. Ibid., 84, 270.

56. Ibid., 286–88.

57. Camas root is an onionlike bulb that was a staple of the Nez Perce diet. It was harvested by women, and the first root digging was a female ritual. See James, *Nez Perce Women in Transition*, 12–17.

58. Gay, *Choup-nit-ki*, 372–73.

59. Slickpoo and Walker, *Noon-Nee-Me-Poo*, 48, 71–75; Walker, *Conflict and Schism in Nez Perce Acculturation*, 48, 54.

60. McBeth, *Nez Perces since Lewis and Clark*, 144.

61. Gay, *Choup-nit-ki*, 430 (emphasis in original).

62. Ibid., 96.

63. Ibid., 281.

64. Ibid., 379.

65. Ibid., 248–49.

66. Davidov, *Women's Camera Work*, 60.

67. Gay, *Choup-nit-ki*, 175. For more on Native Americans' self-representation in nineteenth-century art, see Lippard, *Partial Recall*, and Berlo, *Plains Indian Drawings*.

68. Gay, *Choup-nit-ki*, 231–32.

69. Ibid., 231.

70. Ibid., 230, 259. For more on this battle, see Mark, *Stranger in Her Native Land*, 186–87, and Morrill, *Out of the Blanket*, 207–8, 233.

71. Morrill, "Old Church Made New," 16.

72. Gay, *Choup-nit-ki*, 267–68, 279.

73. Ibid., 262.

74. Ibid., 352.

75. Slickpoo and Walker, *Noon-Nee-Me-Poo*, 226; "Our Happy Day Named!"; "Cannon Boomed at Noon."

76. Gay, *Choup-nit-ki*, 353–54.

77. Quoted in Mark, *Stranger in Her Native Land*, 294–95.

78. Ibid., 10, 326.

Chapter Five

1. Schneider, "Three Affiliated Tribes," 391–93.

2. Lindsey, *Indians at Hampton Institute*, 30–36.

3. Folsom, "Careers of Three Indian Women," 374.

4. Lindsey, *Indians at Hampton Institute*, 153 n. 88.

5. LMC, *Proceedings* (1898), 54.

6. Quoted in Lindsey, *Indians at Hampton Institute*, 143.

7. "Our New Arrivals."

8. On photography at eastern Indian schools, see Banta and Hinsley, *From Site to Sight*, and Malmsheimer, "Imitation White Man."

9. Banta and Hinsley, *From Site to Sight*, 104–5.

10. Wexler, *Tender Violence*, 113.

11. Ibid., 112.

12. Merish notes that in both the language of economics and the more literary language of sympathy, material goods represent the complexity of a culture's economic and psychological development; see *Sentimental Materialism*, 51.

13. Wexler, *Tender Violence*, 111–12.

14. "Fair for Indian Home Building."

15. "Incidents of Indian Life at Hampton."

16. On general traits of professionalism, see Larson, *Rise of Professionalism*; Lasch, *True and Only Heaven*; Sullivan, *Work and Integrity*; Muncy, *Creating a Female Dominion*; Sawaya, *Modern Women, Modern Work*.

17. *Proceedings* (1898), 54.

18. Folsom, "Careers of Three Indian Women," 374.

19. Emmerich, "'Right in the Midst of My Own People,'" 201.

20. Emmerich, "'To respect and love,'" 101.

21. LMC, *Proceedings* (1898), 54–56.

22. Addams, *Twenty Years at Hull-House*, 242. On the Hull-House Labor Museum and revival of women's crafts, see Boris, *Art and Labor*, 132–33, and Sawaya, *Modern Women, Modern Work*, 24–27. Sawaya describes Addams's encounter with the old woman as part of her "call to vocation" (*Modern Women, Modern Work*, 26).

23. Addams, *Twenty Years at Hull-House*, 243.

24. On modern alienation and the premodern aesthetic, see Lears, *No Place of Grace*, 59–96.

25. For a similar reading of the Hull-House Labor Museum, see Sawaya, *Modern Women, Modern Work*, 19–35.

26. On the Hampton museum, see Lindsey, *Indians at Hampton Institute*, 177–78.

27. Ibid., 178, 192.

28. See Gilman, *Women and Economics*; Matthews, *"Just a Housewife,"* 116–44; Newman, *White Women's Rights*, 132–57.

29. Spector, "Male/Female Task Differentiation among the Hidatsa," 82–90.

30. Schneider, "Women's Work," 109–18.

31. Stewart, "Hidatsa," 338.

32. LMC, *Proceedings* (1898), 56.

33. LMC, *Proceedings* (1900), 110.

34. LMC, *Proceedings* (1897), 100.

35. Lindsey, *Indians at Hampton Institute*, 182.

36. LMC, *Proceedings* (1897), 100–101.

37. Georgi-Findlay, *Frontiers of Women's Writing*, 165–66.

38. Merish, *Sentimental Materialism*, 140–44.

39. Quoted in Lindsey, *Indians at Hampton Institute*, 248.

40. Folsom, "Careers of Three Indian Women," 374.

41. Ibid.

42. Ibid., 374–75.

43. For a definition of professionalism as detachment, see Sullivan, *Work and Integrity*, 6.

44. Emmerich, "'To respect and love,'" 46.

45. Ibid., 56.

46. Report of Anna Dawson, Nov. 1899, LR 58372, BIA.

47. Anna Dawson to CIA, Nov. 1901, LR 74958, BIA.

48. Anna Dawson to CIA, 20 Apr. 1900, LR 18168, BIA.

49. Report of Anna Dawson, July 1901, LR 141682–83, BIA.

50. Report of Anna Dawson, Jan. – Mar. 1907, LR 30856, and Report of Anna Dawson, Aug. 1910, LR 69746, BIA.

51. Report of Anna Dawson, Aug. 1910, LR 69746, BIA.

52. For ways Native American women integrated work into new patterns, see Albers and Medicine, "Role of Sioux Women in the Production of Ceremonial Objects"; Albers, "Sioux Women in Transition"; Rand, "Primary Sources"; and Shoemaker, *Negotiators of Change*. Nancy Shoemaker points out in her introduction to *Negotiators of Change* that most scholars of Native American women's history have conceded that even women who resisted change eventually gave in, but that historians have less of a sense of how and in what ways acceptance changed women's status or maintained societies.

53. Report of Anna Dawson, Aug. 1910, LR 69746, BIA.

54. Report of Anna Dawson, Aug. 1901, LR 43401, BIA.

55. Report of Anna Dawson, Aug. 1910, LR 69746, BIA.

56. For a discussion of Dawson Wilde's field matron activities, see Emmerich, " 'Right in the Midst of My Own People,' " 206 – 10.

57. Ibid., 206 – 8.

58. Ella Ripley to CIA, 26 Oct. 1905 (encl. 1), LR 87626, BIA.

59. The reports of the activities of alumni in Carlisle's journal *Red Man* for February 1914 contain this entry: "Ella Rickert, now Mrs. Ripley, living at Elbowoods, N. Dak., writes that she is keeping house and that her husband is a Government farmer, and that they are doing nicely" ("Concerning Ex-Students and Graduates"). Ripley notes in her letter, "When I was Mrs. Wild's [*sic*] hired girl we used to have good time, she was Miss Dawson then" (Ella Ripley to CIA, 28 Aug. 1905 [encl. 2], LR 87626, BIA).

60. Engs, *Educating the Disfranchised and Disinherited*, 132.

61. See Mary Sylwester's discussion of the Whitman Mission in "Between Memory and the Dream of Home."

62. Ella Ripley to CIA, 28 Aug. 1905 (encl. 3), LR 87626, BIA.

63. Ibid.

64. Ibid.

65. Jacobs, *Engendered Encounters*, 29.

66. Ella Ripley to CIA, 28 Aug. 1905 (encl. 3), LR 87626, BIA.

67. Ibid.

68. Ella Ripley to CIA, 21 Oct. 1905 (encl. 2), LR 87626, BIA.

69. Ella Ripley to CIA, 28 Aug. 1905 (encl. 3), LR 87626, BIA.

70. Amzi Thomas to CIA, 26 Oct. 1905, LR 87626, BIA.

71. Emmerich, " 'To respect and love,' " 250 – 51.

72. Elsie Newton, Inspection Report, 9 Oct. 1911, LR 109158, BIA.

73. Acting Secretary to CIA, 21 Dec. 1911, LR 10915, BIA. According to records at Hampton, Anna Dawson Wilde died in 1968 at the age of 101. See Engs, *Educating the Disfranchised and Disinherited*, 132.

74. Emmerich notes that Native American field matrons often found themselves involved in intertribal politics and that this may have contributed to the decline of their numbers after 1905. See " 'Right in the Midst of My Own People,' " 201.

75. Albers, "Marxism and Historical Materialism in American Indian History," 111.

Chapter Six

1. For more on antimodernism and beliefs in Native American primitivism, see Lears, *No Place of Grace*; Dilworth, *Imagining Indians*, 125 – 72; and Deloria, *Playing Indian*, 95 – 127.

2. Dilworth, *Imagining Indians*, 161 – 63.

3. Brody, *Indian Painters and White Patrons*, 73; Graburn, "Introduction."

4. Berlo, *Early Years of Native American Art History*, 3.

5. See Phillips, *Trading Identities*.

6. Maddox's *Citizen Indians* is a study of the cultural contributions made by members of the Society of American Indians. For a history of the society and of Pan-Indian movements in the United States, see also Hertzberg, *Search for an American Indian Identity*.

7. See, for example, Wexler, *Tender Violence*, 94 – 126; Susag, "Zitkala-Sa"; Bernardin, "Lessons of a Sentimental Education"; Diana, "'Hanging in the Heart of Chaos'"; and Meisenheimer, "Regionalist Bodies/Embodied Regions."

8. McAnulty, "Angel DeCora," 152.

9. On middle-class culture as "therapeutic," see Lears, *No Place of Grace*, 94.

10. DeCora, "Autobiography," 279.

11. Ibid. According to McAnulty's useful biography, DeCora's enrollment at Hampton was facilitated by Julia St. Cyr, an older cousin who had attended Hampton. See McAnulty, "Angel DeCora," 145.

12. DeCora, "Autobiography," 280; Folsom quoted in McAnulty, "Angel DeCora," 147.

13. "Fancy-Work Class"; "Progress of the Fancy-Work Class."

14. DeCora, "Autobiography," 279 – 85; Folsom, "Careers of Three Indian Women," 375; McAnulty, "Angel DeCora," 148; Burns, *Inventing the Modern Artist*, 148 – 49.

15. Agosta, *Howard Pyle*, 1 – 3, 16; Burns, *Inventing the Modern Artist*, 319.

16. DeCora, "Autobiography," 280.

17. Burns, *Inventing the Modern Artist*, 14.

18. See Burns's discussion of gender and civilization rhetoric in perceptions of modern artists in *Inventing the Modern Artist*, 70 – 80.

19. On Pyle's progressivism, see Lears, *No Place of Grace*, 164 – 65.

20. Folsom, "Careers of Three Indian Women," 375.

21. McAnulty, "Angel DeCora," 151.

22. Folsom, "Careers of Three Indian Women," 375.

23. Austin, *Land of Little Rain*, 63.

24. For a discussion of ideas of white women's work and Indian craft, see Dilworth, *Imagining Indians*, 162.

25. DeCora [Henook-Makhewe-Kelenaka], "Sick Child."

26. DeCora [Hinook-Mahiwi-Kilinaka], "Gray Wolf's Daughter."

27. Brodhead, *Cultures of Letters*, 124 – 34.

28. Meisenheimer, "Regionalist Bodies/Embodied Regions," 113, 121.

29. I am grateful to Dawn Makes Strong Move for helping me to verify that the writing on the illustration is Angel DeCora's Ho-Chunk name.

30. Burns, *Inventing the Modern Artist*, 118–19.

31. McAnulty, "Angel DeCora," 155.

32. DeCora, "Autobiography," 285.

33. Angel DeCora to A. C. Tonner, 29 Aug. 1899, LR 40148; Angel DeCora to W. A. Jones, 19 Oct. 1900, LR 52237; Angel DeCora to W. A. Jones, 26 Nov. 1900, LR 58629; Angel DeCora to W. A. Jones, 28 Mar. 1901, LR 24375; Angel DeCora to W. A. Jones, 8 Aug. 1903, LR 51873, BIA.

34. Angel DeCora to W. A. Jones, 19 Oct. 1900, LR 52237, BIA.

35. McAnulty, "Angel DeCora," 161.

36. On craft exchange between Native Americans and whites in North America, see Phillips, *Trading Identities*.

37. "Miss Curtis and Her Work."

38. For a discussion of the significance of *The Indian's Book*, see Carr, *Inventing the American Primitive*, 216.

39. On Boas's work and Native American art, see Berlo, "Introduction," 7.

40. Hegeman discusses this shift in *Patterns for America*, 32–65.

41. Curtis, "American Indian Artist," 65.

42. Ibid. (emphasis in original).

43. Ibid., 63.

44. On the change wrought by cottage industries, see Phillips and Steiner introduction.

45. For discussions of Native American artists and the marketplace, see esp. Cohodas, "Elizabeth Hickox and Karuk Basketry" and "Louisa Keyser and the Cohns," and Steiner, "Authenticity, Repetition, and the Aesthetics of Seriality."

46. Phillips and Steiner, *Unpacking Culture*, 9.

47. Curtis, "American Indian Artist," 64.

48. DeCora, "Native Indian Art" (1907).

49. "Leupp Indian Art Studio."

50. Ibid.

51. Ibid.

52. Angel DeCora to CIA, 16 Dec. 1905, LR 101556, BIA.

53. Fear-Segal, "Carlisle Indian Industrial School."

54. "Leupp Indian Art Studio."

55. See Sarah Burns's discussion of published images of artists' garrets in *Inventing the Modern Artist*, esp. chap. 2, "The Artist in the Age of Surfaces: The Culture of Display and the Taint of Trade," 49–57.

56. "Leupp Indian Art Studio."

57. "Improvements at the Carlisle Indian School," 15.

58. Advertisement, *Indian Craftsman*, Feb. 1909.

59. "Navajo Blankets."

60. Ibid.

61. "Football and Art."

62. On football at Carlisle, see Bloom, *To Show What an Indian Can Do*, and Adams, *Education for Extinction*, 181–90. DeCora later married and divorced Carlisle teacher, artist, and football coach William "Lone Star" Dietz.

63. DeCora, "Effort to Encourage Indian Art," 206.

64. Angel DeCora to CIA, 9 Feb.1906, LR 13647, BIA.

65. Angel DeCora, "Native Indian Art" (1909).

66. DeCora, "Effort to Encourage Indian Art," 206 – 8.

67. Ibid.

68. Ibid., 205.

69. DeCora, "Native Indian Art" (1909).

70. Ibid.

71. Curtis, "American Indian Artist," 65.

72. Boris, *Art and Labor*, 83.

73. DeCora, "Effort to Encourage Indian Art," 207 (emphasis in original).

74. "Leupp Indian Art Studio"; "Effort to Encourage Indian Art," 208.

75. Advertisement, *Indian Craftsman*, Feb. 1909.

76. DeCora, "Effort to Encourage Indian Art," 206.

77. For a discussion of the ways Native Americans incorporated Euro-American designs — particularly the floral — into their craftwork, see Phillips, *Trading Identities*, 155 – 96.

78. DeCora, "Effort to Encourage Indian Art," 207 – 8.

79. Ibid., 207.

80. Ibid.

81. "In Memoriam," *Smith Alumnae Quarterly*, July 1919, Dietz Papers.

82. Curtis, "American Indian Artist," 64.

Postscript

1. Albers, "Marxism and Historical Materialism in American Indian History," 116.

2. Ibid., 116 – 17.

BIBLIOGRAPHY

Primary Sources

Archival Collections

Boise, Idaho
　Idaho State Historical Society
　　Alice Fletcher Papers
　　E. Jane Gay Collection
Cambridge, Massachusetts
　Schlesinger Library on the History of Women in America, Radcliffe Institute,
　　Harvard University
　Jane Gay Dodge Papers
　　Schlesinger A-20, M-69. Folder: Choup-nit-ki, With the Nez Perce. Hand-
　　written manuscript, London, 1909.
Northampton, Massachusetts
　Smith College Archives
　　Angel DeCora Dietz Papers
Washington, D.C.
　National Anthropological Archives
　　Papers of Alice Cunningham Fletcher and Francis La Flesche
　　　Alice Cunningham Fletcher Papers
　National Archives
　　Bureau of Indian Affairs, Record Group 75, Letters Received to the Commis-
　　sioner of Indian Affairs, 1885 – 1910

Published Sources

"Against Indian Women." *Woman's Standard* 1, no. 4 (December 1886): 8.

Beecher, Catharine. *A Treatise on Domestic Economy, for the Use of Young Ladies at Home and at School.* Boston: Marsh, Capen, Lyon, and Webb, 1841.

Beecher, Catharine, and Harriet Beecher Stowe. *The American Woman's Home, or, Principles of Domestic Science.* New York: J. B. Ford and Co., 1869.

"Bits." *Woman's Standard* 1, no. 1 (September 1886): 7.

Black Hawk. *Life of Black Hawk (Ma-Ka-Tai-Me-She-Kia-Kiak).* Edited by Milton Quaife. Chicago: R. R. Donnelly and Sons, 1916.

Brown, Geo. Leroy. "Report on Returned Indian Students." *Southern Workman* 12, no. 12 (November 1883): 113.

Burgess, Marianna [Embe]. *Stiya: A Carlisle Indian Girl at Home*. Cambridge: River-side Press, 1891.

C. T. C. "Women's Wages." *Woman's Standard* 1, no. 3 (November 1886): 2.

Campbell, Margaret W. "An Appeal to the Intelligent Men of Iowa." *Woman's Standard* 1, no. 1 (September 1886): 2.

"Cannon Boomed at Noon." *Lewiston Teller*, 14 November 1895.

Catlin, George. *Letters and Notes on the Manners, Customs, and Condition of the North American Indians*. 2 vols. London: G. Catlin, 1841.

Chapman, Carrie. "The Prayers towards Woman's Enfranchisement an Evolution." *Woman's Standard* 10, no. 12 (February 1898): 1.

Child, Lydia Maria. "An Appeal for the Indians." In *Hobomok and Other Writings on Indians*, edited by Carolyn L. Karcher, 216–32. 1868. Reprint, New Brunswick: Rutgers University Press, 1986.

Code of Iowa, Containing all the Statutes of the State of Iowa of General Nature Passed at the Adjourned Session of the 19th General Assembly. Des Moines: G. W. Edwards, 1873.

"Concerning Ex-Students and Graduates." *Red Man* 6, no. 6 (February 1914): 241.

Curtis, Natalie. "An American Indian Artist." *Outlook*, 14 January 1920, 64–66.

——. *The Indian's Book*. 1907. Reprint, New York: Dover, 1968.

DeCora, Angel. "Angel DeCora — An Autobiography." *Red Man* 3, no. 7 (March 1911): 279–81.

——. "An Effort to Encourage Indian Art." In *Congrés Internationale des américanistes*. Fifteenth session, 1906, pp. 204–9. Liechtenstein: Nendeln, Kraus Reprint, 1968.

——. "Native Indian Art." *Arrow*, 23 August 1907.

——. "Native Indian Art." *Weekly Review*, 30 January 1909.

—— [Henook-Makhewe-Kelenaka]. "The Sick Child." *Harper's New Monthly Magazine*, February 1899, 446–48.

—— [Hinook-Mahiwi-Kilinaka]. "Gray Wolf's Daughter." *Harper's New Monthly Magazine*, November 1899, 860–62.

Dewey, Mary E. "Field Matrons for Indians." *Indian's Friend* 6, no. 9 (May 1894): 6.

Dodge, Dora B. "Woman's Work in Indian Homes." *Indian's Friend* 6, no. 12 (August 1894): 9–10.

"Domestic Training vs. Book Learning." *Indian's Friend* 9, no. 10 (June 1897): 9.

Donley, Mary E. "God Made Woman for Man to Take Care of." *Woman's Standard* 1, no. 4 (December 1886): 5.

Dysart, Esther. "White Slaves." *Woman's Standard* 2, no. 1 (September 1887): 3.

Editorial. *Indian's Friend* 1, no. 2 (October 1888): 1–2.

Editorial. *Indian's Friend* 1, no. 6 (February 1889): 1.

"An Eight-Hour Wife." *Woman's Standard* 1, no. 1 (September 1886): 8.

Eina. "The Mission Indians." *Indian's Friend* 1, no. 7 (March 1889): 1.

"A Fair for Indian Home Building." *Southern Workman* 18, no. 2 (February 1889): 21.

"A Fancy-Work Class." *Southern Workman* 13, no. 11 (November 1884): 115.

"Farm Economies." *Woman's Standard* 3, no. 12 (August 1889): 2.

"Field Matrons." *Indian's Friend* 6, no. 11 (July 1894): 9–10.

Fletcher, Alice C. "Allotting Lands." *Indian's Friend* 2, no. 1 (September 1890): 4.

———. *Historical Sketch of the Omaha Tribe of Indians in Nebraska*. Washington, D.C.: Judd and Detweiler, 1885.

———. "The Winnebagos." *Indian's Friend* 1, no. 12 (August 1889): 2.

Folsom, Cora M. "The Careers of Three Indian Women." *Congregationalist and Christian World*, 12 March 1904, 374–75.

"Football and Art." *Arrow*, 19 April 1907, 3.

French, Julia. "The Institute Paper of Miss French." *Indian's Friend* 9, no. 2 (October 1896): 10.

"From the Letter of a Worker." *Indian's Friend* 8, no. 2 (October 1895): 8.

Garrett, Philip C. "An Observer on the Reservation." *Indian's Friend* 4, no. 12 (February 1892): 48.

Gay, E. Jane. "A Brave Woman Allotting Lands to Indians in Idaho." *Red Man* 10, no. 3 (April 1890): 2, 7.

———. "Brave Women in the Field." *Red Man* 10, no. 9 (December 1890–January 1891): 1–2.

———. "Camp Life Experiences." *Red Man* 10, no. 11 (April–May 1891): 6–7.

———. "Camp Life Experiences." *Red Man* 11, no. 1 (July–August 1891): 7–8.

———. "Camp Life Experiences." *Red Man* 11, no. 2 (September 1891): 6–8.

———. "Camp Life Experiences." *Red Man* 11, no. 3 (October–November 1891): 6–7.

———. *Choup-nit-ki: With the Nez Percés*. Washington, D.C., and North Chelmsford, Mass.: Gay and Gay, n.d.

———. "Miss Fletcher and Miss Gay: Incidental Experiences in Allotting Indian Lands." *Red Man* 10, no. 6 (July–August 1890): 3.

———. "A Woman Allotting Lands to Indians: A Rich and Racy View of a Trying Situation." *Red Man* 9, no. 11 (November 1889): 5, 8.

Gould, Mrs. E. P. "Report of the Home Building and Loan Committee." *Indian's Friend* 5, no. 6 (February 1893): 3.

H. F. C. "Habits, etc." *Woman's Standard* 2, no. 7 (March 1888): 5.

———. "Man's 'Rights' in Women's Property." *Woman's Standard* 1, no. 9 (May 1887): 2–3.

———. "Property Rights of Married Women." *Woman's Standard* 1, no. 9 (May 1887): 3.

———. "Shall Our Country Remain Free?" *Woman's Standard* 1, no. 6 (February 1887): 6.

"Harry Brown's Lesson." *Woman's Standard* 1, no. 7 (March 1887): 6.

"Home Building." *Southern Workman* 16, no. 3 (March 1887): 32–33.

"Homestead Law and Women." *Woman's Standard* 11, no. 11 (January 1899): 1.

Howard, Grace. "Grace Mission." *Indian's Friend* 2, no. 6 (February 1890): 3.

———. "Indian Civilization Work." *Indian's Friend* 3, no. 5 (January 1891): 1, 3.

"The Improvements at the Carlisle Indian School." *Indian Craftsman*, February 1909, 3–17.

"Incidents of Indian Life at Hampton." *Southern Workman*, 19, no. 4 (April 1890): 46.

"Indian Emancipation Day." *Southern Workman* 18, no. 3 (March 1889): 31–33.

"Indian Mothers and Indian Girls." *Indian's Friend* 2, no. 10 (June 1890): 1, 3.

"The Indian Problem Solved." *Woman's Standard* 7, no. 6 (February 1892): 3.

"The Indians Can Vote." *Woman's Standard* 2, no. 1 (September 1887): 8.

"Indian School." *Southern Workman* 13, no. 6 (June 1884): 68.

"An Interesting Letter." *Indian's Friend* 7, no. 3 (November 1894): 5.

"Is Woman a Unit or a Fraction?" *Woman's Standard* 2, no. 7 (March 1888): 8.

J. E. J. "All the Rights She Wants." *Woman's Standard* 1, no. 2 (November 1886): 6.

J. R. "Our Indian House Warming." *Southern Workman* 3, no. 4 (April 1884): 43.

Kinney, Sara T. "Helping Indians to Help Themselves." *Indian's Friend* 2, no. 6 (February 1890): 1.

———. "Indian Home-Building." *Indian's Friend* 1, no. 8 (April 1889): 3.

La Flesche, Susan. "The Home-Life of the Indian." *Indian's Friend* 4, no. 10 (June 1892): 1, 39 – 40.

Lake Mohonk Conference of Friends of the Indian. *Proceedings of the Annual Meeting of the Lake Mohonk Conference of Friends of the Indian.* 26 vols. Philadelphia: Indian Rights Association, 1885 – 1910.

"Leupp Indian Art Studio." *Arrow,* 8 February 1907, 1.

Mallory, Lucy. "The Home of Injustice." *Woman's Standard* 8, no. 12 (August 1894): 6.

Manchester, Grace. "Why some Thoughtful Women are Disinclined to Marry." *Woman's Standard* 7, no. 6 (February 1892): 1, 5.

Martin, E. L. "The Story of Two Real Indian Artists." *Red Man* 5, no. 6 (February 1913): 233 – 240.

"A Miserable Wife." *Woman's Standard* 2, no. 5 (January 1888): 8.

"Miss Burgess Resigns." *Arrow,* 8 December 1904, 2.

"Miss Curtis and Her Work." *Arrow,* 8 December 1905, 3.

"Navajo Blankets." *Arrow,* 5 April 1907, 3.

"News and Notes." *Indian's Friend* 9, no. 12 (August 1897): 4.

"Nez Perce Reservation to be Allotted at Once." *Lewiston Teller,* 30 May 1889.

"Opening of the Nez Perce Reservation in the Near Future." *Lewiston Teller,* 20 June 1889.

"Other Peeps into the Work." *Indian's Friend* 8, no. 9 (May 1896): 9.

"Our Happy Day Named!" *Lewiston Teller,* 14 November 1895.

"Our New Arrivals." *Southern Workman* 12, no. 12 (December 1884): 128.

"The Pagan Origin of Women's Subjection." *Woman's Standard* 7, no. 10 (June 1892): 7.

"Progress of the Fancy-Work Class." *Southern Workman* 14, no. 11 (November 1885): 118.

Quinton, Amelia Stone. "Address." *Indian's Friend* 1, no. 5 (January 1889): 3.

———. "In Care of the Indian." In *Women's Work for Women,* edited by Annie Nathan Meyer, 386 – 88. New York: Henry Holt, 1891.

Read, Lizzie Bunnell. "Equal Rights in Property." *Woman's Standard* 1, no. 1 (September 1886): 6.

———. "Equal Rights in Property." *Woman's Standard* 1, no. 3 (November 1886): 3.

———. "The Married Woman's Bank." *Woman's Standard* 4, no. 7 (April 1890): 3.

Revision of 1860, Containing all the Statutes of a General Nature of the State of Iowa. Des Moines: John Teesdale, 1860.

Revision of 1873, Containing all the Statutes of a General Nature of the State of Iowa. Des Moines: G. W. Edwards, 1873.

Soule, Caroline. *Home Life, or, A Peep Across the Threshold*. Boston: A. Tompkins and B. B. Mussey, 1855. *Wright American Fiction 1851 – 1875*. Digital Library Program, Indiana University, 2002. < http://www.letrs.indiana.edu/cgi/t/text/text-idx?c= wright2;idno=wright2-2284 >. 15 July 2005.

———. *The Pet of the Settlement: A Story of Prairie-Land*. Boston: A. Tompkins, 1860.

———. *Wine or Water: A Tale of New England*. Boston: A. Tompkins, 1862. *Wright American Fiction 1851 – 1875*. The Trustees of Indiana University, 2002. < http:// www.letrs.indiana.edu/cgi/t/text/text-idx?c=wright2;idno=wright2-2286 >. 15 July 2005.

Southern Workman 10, no. 2 (February 1881): 15.

Stabler, Minnie. "Scholarship Letters." *Southern Workman* 14, no. 3 (March 1885): 32.

"Sufferings of Alaska Women." *Indian's Friend* 1, no. 3 (November 1888): 2.

"They Never Strike." *Woman's Standard* 1, no. 4 (December 1886): 3.

Tompkin, Helen. "Another Letter." *Indian's Friend* 7, no. 4 (December 1894): 9.

"Unjust Laws." *Woman's Standard* 12, no. 3 (May 1899): 4.

"The Unpaid Laborer." *Woman's Standard* 4, no. 1 (September 1889): 1.

"Value of Woman's Work." *Woman's Standard* 1, no. 9 (May 1887): 3.

Weeks, Anna. "A Partnership." *Woman's Standard* 1, no. 7 (March 1887): 6.

Wheelock, Jemima. "A Woman's Work in the World." *Red Man* 10, no. 4 (May 1890): 7.

"The Wife Is a Chattel." *Woman's Standard* 8, no. 12 (August 1894): 6.

"Woman and Her Political Peers." *Woman's Standard* 7, no. 6 (February 1892): 8.

Woman's Standard 1, no. 1 (September 1886): 7.

Woman's Standard 1, no. 4 (December 1886): 1.

Woman's Standard 1, no. 5 (January 1887): 1.

"Women of Alaska." *Woman's Standard* 1, no. 7 (March 1887): 5.

Women's National Indian Association. *Annual Report of the Women's National Indian Association*. 23 vols. Philadelphia, 1883 – 1905.

Zitkala-Sa. *Old Indian Legends*. Boston: Ginn 1901, 1902.

Secondary Sources

Adams, David Wallace. *Education for Extinction: American Indians and the Boarding School Experience, 1875 – 1928*. Lawrence: University Press of Kansas, 1995.

Addams, Jane. *Twenty Years at Hull-House, with Autobiographical Notes*. New York: Macmillan, 1930.

Agosta, Lucien L. *Howard Pyle*. Boston: Twayne, 1987.

Albers, Patricia C. "From Legend to Land to Labor: Changing Perspectives on Native American Work." In *Native Americans and Wage Labor: Ethnohistorical Perspectives*, edited by Alice Littlefield and Martha C. Knack, 245 – 73. Norman: University of Oklahoma Press, 1996.

———. "Marxism and Historical Materialism in American Indian History." In *Clearing a Path: Theorizing the Past in Native American Studies*, edited by Nancy Shoemaker, 107 – 36. New York: Routledge, 2002.

———. "Sioux Women in Transition: A Study of Their Changing Status in a Domestic and Capitalistic Sector of Production." In *The Hidden Half: Studies of Plains In-*

dian Women, edited by Patricia Albers and Beatrice Medicine, 175 – 234. Lanham, Md.: University Press of America, 1983.

Albers, Patricia, and Beatrice Medicine, eds. *The Hidden Half: Studies of Plains Indian Women*. Lanham, Md.: University Press of America, 1983.

——. "The Role of Sioux Women in the Production of Ceremonial Objects: The Case of the Star Quilt." In *The Hidden Half: Studies of Plains Indian Women*, edited by Patricia Albers and Beatrice Medicine, 123 – 40. Lanham, Md.: University Press of America, 1983.

Allen, Ann Taylor. "Feminism, Social Science, and the Meanings of Modernity: The Debate on the Origin of the Family in Europe and the United States, 1860 – 1914." *American Historical Review* 104, no. 4 (October 1999): 1085 – 1113.

Allen, Polly Wynn. *Building Domestic Liberty: Charlotte Perkins Gilman's Architectural Feminism*. Amherst: University of Massachusetts Press, 1988.

Ardener, Shirley, ed. *Women and Space: Ground Rules and Social Maps*. Oxford: Berg, 1993.

Arendt, Hannah. *The Human Condition*. 2nd ed. Chicago: University of Chicago Press, 1998.

Austin, Mary. *The Land of Little Rain*. 1903. Reprint, New York: Penguin, 1997.

Bannan, Helen M. "The Idea of Civilization and American Indian Policy Reformers of the 1880s." *Journal of American Culture* 1, no. 4 (Winter 1978): 787 – 99.

——. "'True Womanhood' on the Reservation: Field Matrons in the United States Indian Service." Working Paper no. 18. Tucson: Southwest Institute for Research on Women, 1984.

Banta, Melissa, and Curtis M. Hinsley. *From Site to Sight: Anthropology, Photography, and the Power of Imagery*. Cambridge: Peabody Museum Press, 1986.

Basch, Norma. *In the Eyes of the Law: Women, Marriage, and Property in Nineteenth-Century New York*. Ithaca: Cornell University Press, 1982.

Bataille, Gretchen, ed. *Native American Representations: First Encounters, Distorted Images, and Literary Appropriations*. Lincoln: University of Nebraska Press, 2001.

Baym, Nina. *Woman's Fiction: A Guide to Novels by and about Women in America, 1820 – 1870*. Chicago: University of Illinois Press, 1993.

Bederman, Gail. *Manliness and Civilization: A Cultural History of Gender and Race in the United States, 1880 – 1917*. Chicago: University of Chicago Press, 1995.

Bennett, Tony. *The Birth of the Museum: History, Theory, Politics*. London: Routledge, 1995.

Berlo, Janet Catherine, ed. *The Early Years of Native American Art History: The Politics of Scholarship and Collecting*. Seattle: University of Washington Press, 1992.

——. "Introduction: The Formative Years of Native American Art History." In *The Early Years of Native American Art History: The Politics of Scholarship and Collecting*, edited by Janet Catherine Berlo, 1 – 21. Seattle: University of Washington Press, 1992.

——, ed. *Plains Indian Drawings, 1865 – 1935: Pages from a Visual History*. New York: Harry N. Abrams, 1996.

Bernardin, Susan. "The Lessons of a Sentimental Education: Zitkala-Sa's Autobiographical Narratives." *Western American Literature* 32, no. 3 (Fall 1997): 212–39.

Bernardin, Susan, Melody Graulich, Lisa MacFarlane, and Nicole Tonkovich. *Trading Gazes: Euro-American Women Photographers and Native North Americans, 1880–1940*. New Brunswick: Rutgers University Press, 2003.

Bhabha, Homi. *The Location of Culture*. New York: Routledge, 1994.

Bloom, John. *To Show What an Indian Can Do: Sports and Native American Boarding Schools*. Minneapolis: University of Minnesota Press, 2000.

Boris, Eileen. *Art and Labor: Ruskin, Morris, and the Craftsman Ideal in America*. Philadelphia: Temple University Press, 1986.

Boughter, Judith A. *Betraying the Omaha Nation, 1790–1916*. Norman: University of Oklahoma Press, 1998.

Bowler, Peter J. *The Invention of Progress: The Victorians and the Past*. Oxford: Basil Blackwell, 1989.

Boydston, Jeanne. *Home and Work: Housework, Wages, and the Ideology of Labor in the Early Republic*. New York: Oxford University Press, 1990.

Boydston, Jeanne, Mary Kelley, and Anne Margolis. *The Limits of Sisterhood: The Beecher Sisters on Women's Rights and Woman's Sphere*. Chapel Hill: University of North Carolina Press, 1988.

Brodhead, Richard H. *Cultures of Letters: Scenes of Reading and Writing in Nineteenth-Century America*. Chicago: University of Chicago Press, 1993.

Brody, J. J. *Indian Painters and White Patrons*. Albuquerque: University of New Mexico Press, 1971.

Bromell, Nicholas, *By the Sweat of the Brow: Literature and Labor in Antebellum America*. Chicago: University of Chicago Press, 1993.

Brown, Gillian. *Domestic Individualism: Imagining Self in Nineteenth-Century America*. Berkeley: University of California Press, 1990.

———. "Hawthorne, Inheritance, and Women's Property." *Studies in the Novel* 23, no. 1 (Spring 1991): 107–18.

Brumberg, Joan Jacobs. "Zenanas and Girlless Villages: The Ethnology of American Evangelical Women, 1870–1900." *Journal of American History* 69, no. 2 (September 1992): 347–71.

Buffalohead, W. Roger, and Paulette Fairbanks Molin. "'A Nucleus of Civilization': American Indian Families at Hampton Institute in the Late Nineteenth Century." *Journal of American Indian Education* 35, no. 3 (Spring 1996): 59–94.

Burns, Sarah. *Inventing the Modern Artist: Art and Culture in Gilded Age America*. New Haven: Yale University Press, 1996.

Carby, Hazel. *Reconstructing Womanhood: The Emergence of the Afro-American Woman Novelist*. New York: Oxford University Press, 1987.

Carr, Helen. *Inventing the American Primitive: Politics, Gender, and the Representation of Native American Literary Traditions, 1789–1936*. New York: New York University Press, 1996.

Child, Lydia Maria. *Hobomok and Other Writings on Indians*. Edited by Carolyn L. Karcher. New Brunswick: Rutgers University Press, 1986.

Cohodas, Marvin. "Elizabeth Hickox and Karuk Basketry: A Case Study in Debates on Innovation and Paradigms of Authenticity." In *Unpacking Culture: Art and Commodity in Colonial and Postcolonial Worlds*, edited by Ruth B. Phillips and Christopher B. Steiner, 143–61. Berkeley: University of California Press, 1999.

———. "Louisa Keyser and the Cohns: Mythmaking and Basket Making in the American West." In *The Early Years of Native American Art History: The Politics of Scholarship and Collecting*, edited by Janet Catherine Berlo, 88–133. Seattle: University of Washington Press, 1992.

Coleman, Michael C. *American Indian Children at School, 1850–1930*. Jackson: University Press of Mississippi, 1993.

———. *Presbyterian Missionary Attitudes towards American Indians, 1837–1893*. Jackson: University Press of Mississippi, 1985.

Davidoff, Leonore. *Worlds Between: Historical Perspectives on Gender and Class*. New York: Routledge, 1995.

Davidov, Judith Fryer. *Women's Camera Work: Self/Body/Other in American Visual Culture*. Durham: Duke University Press, 1998.

Dawson, Lillian W. *Jane Gay Photograph Collection Catalog*. Boise: Idaho State Historical Society, 1980.

Deloria, Philip J. *Indians in Unexpected Places*. Lawrence: University Press of Kansas, 2004.

———. *Playing Indian: Otherness and Authenticity in the Assumption of American Indian Identity*. New Haven: Yale University Press, 1999.

Deloria, Vine, Jr., and Clifford Lytle. *The Nations Within: The Past and Future of American Indian Sovereignty*. New York: Pantheon, 1984.

Deutsch, Sarah. *No Separate Refuge: Culture, Class and Gender on an Anglo-Hispanic Frontier in the American Southwest, 1880–1940*. New York: Oxford University Press, 1987.

Diana, Vanessa Holford. " 'Hanging in the Heart of Chaos': Bi-Cultural Limbo, Self-(Re)presentation, and the White Audience in Zitkala-Sa's *American Indian Stories*." *Cimarron Review* 121 (October 1997): 154–72.

Diaz, Abby M. *A Domestic Problem: Work and Culture in the Household*. New York: Arno Press, 1975.

Diggs, Marylynne. "Romantic Friends or a 'Different Race of Creatures'? The Representation of Lesbian Pathology in Nineteenth-Century America." *Feminist Studies* 21, no. 1 (Summer 1995): 317–41.

Dilworth, Leah. *Imagining Indians in the Southwest: Persistent Visions of a Primitive Past*. Washington, D.C.: Smithsonian Institution Press, 1996.

Dippie, Brian W. *The Vanishing American: White Attitudes and U.S. Indian Policy*, Lawrence: University Press of Kansas, 1982.

Douglas, Ann. *The Feminization of American Culture*. New York: Knopf, 1977.

Dowd, Gregory Evans. *A Spirited Resistance: The North American Indian Struggle for Unity, 1745–1815*. Baltimore: Johns Hopkins University Press, 1992.

Downing, Andrew Jackson. *The Architecture of Country Houses*. New York: Dover, 1969.

Drinnon, Richard. *Facing West: The Metaphysics of Indian-hating and Empire-building*. Minneapolis: University of Minnesota Press, 1980.

Dudden, Faye. *Serving Women: Household Service in Nineteenth-Century America*. Middletown, Conn.: Wesleyan University Press, 1983.

Elliot, Maud Howe, ed. *Art and Handicraft in the Woman's Building of the World's Columbian Exposition*. New York: Goupil and Co., 1893.

Emmerich, Lisa E. "'Right in the Midst of My Own People': Native American Women and the Field Matron Program." *American Indian Quarterly* 15, no. 2 (Spring 1991): 201–16.

———. "'To respect and love and seek the ways of white women': Field Matrons, the Office of Indian Affairs, and Civilization Policy, 1890–1938." Ph.D. diss, University of Maryland, College Park, 1987.

Engs, Robert Francis. *Educating the Disfranchised and Disinherited: Samuel Armstrong and Hampton Institute, 1839–1893*. Knoxville: University of Tennessee Press, 1999.

Epstein, Barbara. *The Politics of Domesticity: Women, Evangelism, and Temperance in Nineteenth-Century America*. Lebanon, N.H.: University Press of New England, 1986.

Fear-Segal, Jacqueline. "Carlisle Indian Industrial School: Landscape of Race and Erasure." Paper presented at the American Studies Association Conference, Detroit, October 2000.

Fiedler, Leslie A. *Love and Death in the American Novel*. New York: Dell, 1966.

Fisher, Philip. *Hard Facts: Setting and Form in the American Novel*. New York: Oxford University Press, 1985.

Fitzpatrick, Ellen. *Endless Crusade: Women Social Scientists and Progressive Reform*. New York: Oxford University Press, 1990.

Flexner, Eleanor. *Century of Struggle: The Woman's Rights Movement in the United States*. New York: Atheneum, 1972.

Folbre, Nancy. "The Unproductive Housewife: Her Evolution in Nineteenth-Century Economic Thought." *Signs* 16, no. 3 (Spring 1991): 463–84.

Gay, E. Jane. *With the Nez Perces: Alice Fletcher in the Field, 1889–1892*. Edited by Joan Mark and Frederick Hoxie. Lincoln: University of Nebraska Press, 1981.

Georgi-Findlay, Brigitte. *The Frontiers of Women's Writing: Women's Narratives and the Rhetoric of Westward Expansion*. Tucson: University of Arizona Press, 1996.

Gilman, Charlotte Perkins. *Women and Economics: A Study of the Economic Relation between Men and Women as a Factor in Social Evolution*. New York: Harper and Row, 1966.

Goodburn, Amy. "Literary Practices at the Genoa Industrial School." *Great Plains Quarterly* 19, no. 1 (Winter 1999): 35–52.

Graburn, Nelson H. H. "Introduction: Arts of the Fourth World." In *Ethnic and Tourist Arts: Cultural Expressions from the Fourth World*, edited by Nelson H. H. Graburn, 1–32. Berkeley: University of California Press, 1976.

Grier, Katherine. *Culture and Comfort: Parlor Making and Middle-Class Identity, 1850–1930*. Washington, D.C.: Smithsonian Institution Press, 1997.

Hagan, William T. *The Sac and Fox Indians*. Norman: University of Oklahoma Press, 1958.

Haines, Francis M. *The Nez Percés: Tribesmen of the Columbia Plateau*. Norman: University of Oklahoma Press, 1955.

Halberstam, Judith. *Female Masculinity*. Durham: Duke University Press, 1998.

Hanson, Susan, and Geraldine Pratt. *Gender, Work, and Space*. New York: Routledge, 1995.

Hayden, Dolores. *The Grand Domestic Revolution: A History of Feminist Designs for American Homes, Neighborhoods, and Cities*. Cambridge: MIT Press, 1981.

Hegeman, Susan. *Patterns for America: Modernism and the Concept of Culture*. Princeton: Princeton University Press, 1999.

Herrmann, Anne. "Imitations of Marriage: Crossdressed Couples in Contemporary Lesbian Fiction." *Feminist Studies* 18, no. 3 (Fall 1992): 609–24.

Hertzberg, Hazel W. *The Search for an American Indian Identity: Modern Pan-Indian Movements*. Syracuse: Syracuse University Press, 1971.

Hill, Patricia R. *The World Their Household: The American Woman's Foreign Mission Movement and Cultural Transformation, 1870–1920*. Ann Arbor: University of Michigan Press, 1985.

Hinsley, Curtis M. *The Smithsonian and the American Indian: Making a Moral Anthropology in Victorian America*. Washington, D.C.: Smithsonian Institution Press, 1981.

Hoxie, Frederick. *A Final Promise: The Campaign to Assimilate the Indians, 1880–1920*. Lincoln: University of Nebraska Press, 1984.

Hurtado, Albert L. *Intimate Frontiers: Sex, Gender, and Culture in Old California*. Albuquerque: University of New Mexico Press, 1999.

Improper Bostonians. Compiled by the History Project. Boston: Beacon Press, 1998.

Jackson, Helen Hunt. *A Century of Dishonor: The Early Crusade for Indian Reform*. New York: Harper and Row, 1965.

Jacobs, Margaret D. *Engendered Encounters: Feminism and Pueblo Cultures, 1879–1934*. Lincoln: University of Nebraska Press, 1999.

Jacobson, Matthew Frye. *Barbarian Virtues: The United States Encounters Foreign Peoples at Home and Abroad, 1876–1917*. New York: Hill and Wang, 2000.

James, Caroline. *Nez Perce Women in Transition, 1877–1990*. Moscow: University of Idaho Press, 1996.

Janiewski, Dolores. "Learning to Live 'Just Like White Folks': Gender, Ethnicity, and the State in the Inland Northwest." In *Gendered Domains: Rethinking Public and Private in Women's History*, edited by Dorothy O. Helly and Susan M. Reverby, 167–80. Ithaca: Cornell University Press, 1992.

Jensen, Joan M. *Loosening the Bonds: Mid-Atlantic Farm Women, 1750–1850*. New Haven: Yale University Press, 1986.

Jones, Jacqueline. *Labor of Love, Labor of Sorrow: Black Women, Work, and the Family from Slavery to the Present*. New York: Vintage, 1986.

Kaplan, Amy. *The Anarchy of Empire in the Making of U.S. Culture*. Cambridge: Harvard University Press, 2002.

Kelley, Mary. *Private Woman, Public Stage: Literary Domesticity in Nineteenth-Century America*. New York: Oxford University Press, 1984.

Kerber, Linda K. "The Abolitionist Perception of the Indian." *Journal of American History* 62, no. 2 (September 1975): 271–95.

Kessler-Harris, Alice. *Out to Work: A History of Wage-Earning Women in the United States.* New York: Oxford University Press, 1982.

——. *A Woman's Wage: Historical Meanings and Social Consequences.* Lexington: University Press of Kentucky, 1990.

Kidd Green, Norma. *Iron Eye's Family: The Children of Joseph La Flesche.* Lincoln, Neb.: Johnsen Pub. Co., 1969.

Kolodny, Annette. *The Land before Her: Fantasy and Experience of the American Frontiers, 1630 – 1860.* Chapel Hill: University of North Carolina Press, 1984.

Landis, Barb. "Carlisle Indian School References to the Publication, Stiya." *Carlisle Industrial School Research Pages.* < http://home.epix.net/~landis/stiya.html >. 15 October 2005.

——. "The Serialization of What Became the Book, Stiya." *Carlisle Industrial School Research Pages.* < http://home.epix.net/~landis/stiya.html >. 15 October 2005.

Larson, Magali Sarfatti. *The Rise of Professionalism: A Sociological Analysis.* Berkeley: University of California Press, 1977.

Lasch, Christopher. *The True and Only Heaven: Progress and Its Critics.* New York: Norton, 1991.

Lears, T. J. Jackson. *No Place of Grace: Antimodernism and the Transformation of American Culture, 1880 – 1920.* New York: Pantheon, 1981.

Leavitt, Sarah A. *From Catharine Beecher to Martha Stewart: A Cultural History of Domestic Advice.* Chapel Hill: University of North Carolina Press, 2002.

Limerick, Patricia Nelson. *The Legacy of Conquest: The Unbroken Past of the American West.* New York: Norton, 1987.

Lindsey, Donal F. *Indians at Hampton Institute, 1877 – 1923.* Chicago: University of Illinois Press, 1995.

Lippard, Lucy R., ed. *Partial Recall.* New York: New Press, 1992.

Littlefield, Alice. "Indian Education and the World of Work in Michigan, 1893 – 1933." In *Native Americans and Wage Labor: Ethnohistorical Perspectives*, edited by Alice Littlefield and Martha C. Knack, 100 – 121. Norman: University of Oklahoma Press, 1996.

Littlefield, Alice, and Martha C. Knack. "Native American Labor." In *Native Americans and Wage Labor: Ethnohistorical Perspectives*, edited by Alice Littlefield and Martha C. Knack, 3 – 44. Norman: University of Oklahoma Press, 1996.

——, eds. *Native Americans and Wage Labor: Ethnohistorical Perspectives.* Norman: University of Oklahoma Press, 1996.

Lomawaima, K. Tsianina. *They Called It Prairie Light: The Story of Chilocco Indian School.* Lincoln: University of Nebraska Press, 1994.

Lutz, Alma. *Emma Willard: Pioneer Educator of American Women.* Boston: Beacon Press, 1964.

Maddox, Lucy. *Citizen Indians: Native American Intellectuals, Race, and Reform.* Ithaca: Cornell University Press, 2005.

——. *Removals: Nineteenth-Century American Literature and the Politics of American Indian Affairs.* New York: Oxford University Press, 1991.

Malmsheimer, Lonna M. "Imitation White Man: Images of Transformation at the Carlisle Indian School." *Studies of Visual Communication* 11, no. 4 (Fall 1985): 54–75.

Mark, Joan. *A Stranger in Her Native Land: Alice Fletcher and the American Indians.* Lincoln: University of Nebraska Press, 1988.

Matthews, Glenna. *"Just a Housewife": The Rise and Fall of Domesticity in America.* New York: Oxford University Press, 1987.

McAnulty, Sarah. "Angel DeCora: American Indian Artist and Educator." *Nebraska History* 57, no. 2 (Summer 1976): 143–99.

McBeth, Kate C. *The Nez Perces since Lewis and Clark.* New York: Fleming H. Revell, 1908.

McClintock, Anne. *Imperial Leather: Race, Gender, and Sexuality in the Colonial Contest.* New York: Routledge, 1995.

Meisenheimer, D. K. "Regionalist Bodies/Embodied Regions: Sarah Orne Jewett and Zitkala-Sa." In *Breaking Boundaries: New Perspectives on Women's Regional Writing*, edited by Sherrie A. Inness and Diana Royer, 109–23. Iowa City: University of Iowa Press, 1997.

Merish, Lori. *Sentimental Materialism: Gender, Commodity Culture, and Nineteenth-Century American Literature.* Durham: Duke University Press, 2000.

Mihesuah, Devon A. *Cultivating the Rosebuds: The Education of Women at the Cherokee Female Seminary, 1851–1909.* Urbana: University of Illinois Press, 1993.

Moore, David. "Return of the Buffalo: Cultural Representation as Cultural Property." In *Native American Representations: First Encounters, Distorted Images, and Literary Appropriations*, edited by Gretchen M. Bataille, 52–78. Lincoln: University of Nebraska Press, 2001.

Moore, John H. "The Significance of Cheyenne Work in the History of U.S. Capitalism." In *Native Americans and Wage Labor: Ethnohistorical Perspectives*, edited by Alice Littlefield and Martha C. Knack, 122–43. Norman: University of Oklahoma Press, 1996.

Moore, Lisa. "'Something More Tender Still Than Friendship': Romantic Friendship in Early-Nineteenth-Century England." *Feminist Studies* 18, no. 3 (Fall 1992): 499–520.

Morgan, Lewis Henry. *Ancient Society, or, Researches in the Lines of Human Progress from Savagery Through Barbarism to Civilization.* 1877. Reprint, Cleveland: World Pub. Co., 1963.

———. *Houses and House-Life of the American Aborigines.* Chicago: University of Chicago Press, 1965.

Morrill, Allen C., and Eleanor Dunlap Morrill. "Old Church Made New." *Idaho Yesterdays* 16, no. 2 (Summer 1972): 16–25.

———. *Out of the Blanket: The Story of Sue and Kate McBeth, Missionaries to the Nez Perces.* Moscow: Idaho Research Foundation, 1977.

Muncy, Robyn. *Creating a Female Dominion in American Reform, 1890–1930.* New York: Oxford University Press, 1990.

Murphy, Lucy Eldersveld. "Autonomy and the Economic Roles of Indian Women of the Fox-Wisconsin Riverway Region, 1763–1832." In *Negotiators of Change: Histor-*

ical Perspectives on Native American Women, edited by Nancy Shoemaker, 72 – 89. New York: Routledge, 1995.

Namias, June. *White Captives: Gender and Ethnicity on the American Frontier.* Chapel Hill: University of North Carolina Press, 1993.

Nelson, Julie A. "One Sphere or Two?" *American Behavioral Scientist* 41, no. 10 (August 1998): 1467 – 71.

Newman, Louise Michele. *White Women's Rights: The Racial Origins of Feminism in the United States.* New York: Oxford University Press, 1999.

Nichols, Roger L. *Black Hawk and the Warrior's Path.* Arlington Heights, Ill.: Harlan Davidson, 1992.

Noun, Louise. *Strong-Minded Women: The Emergence of the Woman-Suffrage Movement in Iowa.* Ames: Iowa State University Press, 1969.

Parkman, Francis. *The Conspiracy of Pontiac and the Indian War after the Conquest of Canada.* 1851. Reprint, New York: Dutton, 1908.

Pascoe, Peggy. *Relations of Rescue: The Search for Female Moral Authority in the American West, 1874 – 1939.* New York: Oxford University Press, 1990.

Pearce, Roy Harvey. *Savagism and Civilization: A Study of the Indian and the American Mind.* Berkeley: University of California Press, 1988.

Phillips, Ruth B. *Trading Identities: The Souvenir in Native North American Art from the Northeast, 1700 – 1900.* Seattle: University of Washington Press, 1998.

Phillips, Ruth B., and Christopher Steiner. Introduction to *Unpacking Culture: Art and Commodity in Colonial and Postcolonial Worlds*, edited by Ruth B. Phillips and Christopher B. Steiner, 3 – 19. Berkeley: University of California Press, 1999.

Pratt, Mary. *Imperial Eyes: Travel Writing and Transculturation.* New York, Routledge, 1992.

Prins, Harald E. L. "Tribal Network and Migrant Labor: Mi'maq Indians as Seasonal Workers in Aroostook's Potato Fields, 1870 – 1980." In *Native Americans and Wage Labor: Ethnohistorical Perspectives*, edited by Alice Littlefield and Martha C. Knack, 45 – 65. Norman: University of Oklahoma Press, 1996.

Prucha, Francis Paul. *The Great Father: The United States Government and the American Indians.* 2 vols. Lincoln: University of Nebraska Press, 1984.

Rabkin, Peggy A. *Fathers to Daughters: The Legal Foundations of Female Emancipation.* Westport, Conn.: Greenwood Press, 1980.

Rand, Jacki Thompson. "Primary Sources: Indian Goods and the History of American Colonialism and the 19th-Century Reservation." In *Negotiators of Change: Historical Perspectives on Native American Women*, edited by Nancy Shoemaker, 137 – 57. New York: Routledge, 1995.

Reynolds, Larry J., and Gordon Hutner, eds. *National Imaginaries, American Identities: The Cultural Work of American Iconography.* Princeton: Princeton University Press, 2000.

Rigal, Laura. *The American Manufactory: Art, Labor, and the World of Things in the Early Republic.* Princeton: Princeton University Press, 1998.

Riley, Glenda. *Frontierswomen: The Iowa Experience.* Ames: Iowa State University Press, 1981.

———. *Women and Indians on the Frontier, 1825–1915*. Albuquerque: University of New Mexico Press, 1984.

Roediger, David. *The Wages of Whiteness: Race and the Making of the American Working Class*. London: Verso, 1991.

Romero, Lora. *Home Fronts: Domesticity and Its Critics in the Antebellum United States*. Durham: Duke University Press, 1997.

Rupp, Leila J. *A Desired Past: A Short History of Same-Sex Love in America*. Chicago: University of Chicago Press, 1999.

Ryan, Mary P. *Empire of the Mother: American Writing about Domesticity, 1830–1860*. New York: Haworth Press, 1982.

Said, Edward. *Culture and Imperialism*. New York: Vintage, 1993.

Salmon, Marylynn. *Women and the Law of Property in Early America*. Chapel Hill: University of North Carolina Press, 1986.

Samuels, Shirley, ed. *The Culture of Sentiment: Race, Gender, and Sentimentality in Nineteenth-Century America*. New York: Oxford University Press, 1992.

Sánchez-Eppler, Karen. "Raising Empires Like Children: Race, Nation, and Religious Education." *American Literary History* 8, no. 3 (Fall 1996): 399–425.

Sawaya, Francesca. *Modern Women, Modern Work: Domesticity, Professionalism, and American Writing, 1890–1950*. Philadelphia: University of Pennsylvania Press, 2004.

Schneider, Mary Jane. "Three Affiliated Tribes." In *Plains*. Pt. 1, vol. 13 of *Handbook of North American Indians*, edited by Raymond J. De Mallie, 391–98. Washington, D.C.: Smithsonian Institution Press, 2001.

———. "Women's Work: An Examination of Women's Roles in Plains Indians Arts and Crafts." In *The Hidden Half: Studies of Plains Indian Women*, edited by Patricia Albers and Beatrice Medicine, 101–21. Lanham, Md.: University Press of America, 1983.

Seaburg, Alan. "Caroline Soule." *Dictionary of Unitarian and Universalist Biography*. Unitarian Universalist Historical Society, 1999–2004. < http://www.uua.org/uuhs/duub/articles/carolinesoule.html >. 21 July 2005.

Sedgwick, Catharine Maria. *Hope Leslie, or, Early Times in the Massachusetts*. Edited by Mary Kelley. 1827. Reprint, New Brunswick: Rutgers University Press, 1987.

Shammas, Carole. "Re-Assessing the Married Women's Property Acts." *Journal of Women's History* 6, no. 1 (Spring 1994): 9–30.

Shepard, Paul. *Man in the Landscape: A Historic View of the Esthetics of Nature*. New York: Knopf, 1967.

Sherer Mathes, Valerie. *Helen Hunt Jackson and Her Indian Reform Legacy*. Norman: University of Oklahoma Press, 1990.

———. "Nineteenth Century Women and Reform: The Women's National Indian Association." *American Indian Quarterly* 14, no. 1 (Winter 1990): 1–18.

Shoemaker, Nancy, ed. *Negotiators of Change: Historical Perspectives on Native American Women*. New York: Routledge, 1995.

Siegel, Reva. "Home as Work: The First Woman's Rights Claims Concerning Wives' Household Labor, 1850–1880." *Yale Law Journal* 103, no. 5 (1994): 1073–1218.

———. "Valuing Housework: Nineteenth-Century Anxieties about the Commodification of Domestic Labor." *American Behavioral Scientist* 41, no. 10 (August 1998): 1437–51.

Silbaugh, Katherine. "Turning Labor into Love: Housework and the Law." *Northwestern University Law Review* 91, no. 1 (1996): 3–86.

Silko, Leslie Marmon. Introduction to *Native American Literature: A Catalog*. Ken Lopez Bookseller, 1994. < http://www.lopezbooks.com/articles.silko.html >. 15 July 2004.

Sklar, Katherine Kish. *Catharine Beecher: A Study in American Domesticity*. New York: Norton, 1976.

Slickpoo, Allen P., Sr. and Deward E. Walker Jr. *Noon-Nee-Me-Poo (We, the Nez Perces): Culture and History of the Nez Perces*. Vol. 1. N.p.: Nez Perce Tribe of Idaho, 1973.

Smith, Henry Nash. *Virgin Land: The American West as Symbol and Myth*. New York: Vintage, 1950.

Smith, Shawn Michelle. *American Archives: Gender, Race, and Class in Visual Culture*. Princeton: Princeton University Press, 1999.

Smith-Rosenberg, Carroll. *Disorderly Conduct: Visions of Gender in Victorian America*. New York: Oxford University Press, 1985.

Somerville, Siobhan. "Scientific Racism and the Invention of the Homosexual Body." In *Queer Studies: A Lesbian, Gay, Bisexual, and Transgender Anthology*, edited by Brett Beemyn and Mickey Eliason, 241–61. New York: New York University Press, 1996.

Spector, Janet. "Male/Female Task Differentiation among the Hidatsa: Towards the Development of an Archaeological Approach to the Study of Gender." In *The Hidden Half: Studies of Plains Indian Women*, edited by Patricia Albers and Beatrice Medicine, 77–99. Lanham, Md.: University Press of America, 1983.

Stanley, Amy Dru. *From Bondage to Contract: Wage Labor, Marriage, and the Market in the Age of Slave Emancipation*. New York: Cambridge University Press, 1998.

Stansell, Christine. *City of Women: Sex and Class in New York, 1789–1860*. New York: Knopf, 1986.

Stanton, Elizabeth Cady, Susan B. Anthony, and Matilda Joslyn Gage, eds. *History of Woman Suffrage*. Vol. 3. New York: Arno Press, 1969.

Steiner, Christopher. "Authenticity, Repetition, and the Aesthetics of Seriality: The Work of Tourist Art in the Age of Mechanical Reproduction." In *Unpacking Culture: Art and Commodity in Colonial and Postcolonial Worlds*, edited by Ruth B. Phillips and Christopher B. Steiner, 87–103. Berkeley: University of California Press, 1999.

Sterling, Dorothy, ed. *We Are Your Sisters: Black Women in the Nineteenth Century*. New York: Norton, 1984.

Stewart, Frank Henderson. "Hidatsa." In *Plains*. Pt. 1, vol. 13 of *Handbook of North American Indians*, edited by Raymond J. De Mallie, 329–48. Washington, D.C.: Smithsonian Institution Press, 2001.

Stocking, George W., Jr. *Victorian Anthropology*. Madison: University of Wisconsin Press, 1984.

Stoler, Ann Laura. *Race and the Education of Desire: Foucault's History of Sexuality and the Colonial Order of Things*. Durham: Duke University Press, 1995.

Strasser, Susan. *Never Done: A History of American Housework*. New York: Pantheon, 1982.

Sullivan, William M. *Work and Integrity: The Crisis and Promise of Professionalism in America*. New York: Harper's Business, 1995.

Susag, Dorothea M. "Zitkala-Sa (Gertrude Simmons Bonnin): A Power(full) Literary Voice." *Studies in American Indian Literatures* 5, no. 4 (Winter 1993): 3–24.

Sweet, Timothy. "American Pastoralism and the Marketplace: Eighteenth-Century Ideologies of Farming." *Early American Literature* 29, no. 1 (Spring 1994): 59–80.

Sylwester, Mary. "Between Memory and the Dream of Home: Culture and Geography in Women's Westering Narratives, 1805–1905." Ph.D. diss, University of Iowa, 1998.

Szasz, Margaret Connell. *Indian Education in the American Colonies, 1607–1783*. Albuquerque: University of New Mexico Press, 1988.

Tompkins, Jane. *Sensational Designs: The Cultural Work of American Fiction, 1790–1860*. New York: Oxford University Press, 1985.

Tong, Benson. *Susan LaFlesche Picotte, M.D.: Omaha Leader and Reformer*. Norman: University of Oklahoma Press, 1999.

Tonkovich, Nicole. *Domesticity with a Difference: The Nonfiction of Catharine Beecher, Sarah J. Hale, Fanny Fern, and Margaret Fuller*. Jackson: University Press of Mississippi, 1997.

———. "'Lost in the General Wreckage of the Far West': The Photographs and Writings of Jane Gay." In *Trading Gazes: Euro-American Women Photographers and Native North Americans, 1880–1940*, by Susan Bernardin, Melody Graulich, Lisa MacFarlane, and Nicole Tonkovich, 33–70. New Brunswick: Rutgers University Press, 2003.

Trachtenberg, Alan. *The Incorporation of America: Culture and Society in the Gilded Age*. New York: Hill and Wang, 1982.

Trennert, Robert. "Educating Indian Girls at Nonreservation Boarding Schools, 1878–1920." *Western Historical Quarterly* 13, no. 3 (July 1982): 271–90.

———. *The Phoenix Indian School: Forced Assimilation in Arizona, 1891–1935*. Norman: University of Oklahoma Press, 1988.

Tucker, Cynthia Grant. *Prophetic Sisterhood: Liberal Women Ministers of the Frontier, 1880–1930*. Bloomington: Indiana University Press, 1990.

Vicinus, Martha. "'They Wonder to Which Sex I Belong': The Historical Roots of the Modern Lesbian Identity." *Feminist Studies* 18, no. 3 (Fall 1992): 467–97.

Walker, Deward E., Jr. *Conflict and Schism in Nez Perce Acculturation: A Study of Religion and Politics*. Pullman: Washington State University Press, 1968.

Wanken, Helen M. "'Woman's Sphere' and Indian Reform: The Women's National Indian Association, 1879–1901." Ph.D. diss., Marquette University, 1981.

Warbasse, Elizabeth Bowles. *The Changing Legal Rights of Married Women, 1800–1861*. New York: Garland, 1987.

Weinstein, Cindy. *The Literature of Labor and the Labors of Literature: Allegory in Nineteenth-Century American Fiction*. New York: Cambridge University Press, 1995.

Wexler, Laura. *Tender Violence: Domestic Visions in an Age of U.S. Imperialism.* Chapel Hill: University of North Carolina Press, 2000.

Wiebe, Robert H. *The Search for Order, 1877–1920.* New York, Hill and Wang, 1967.

Wright, Gwendolyn. *Building the Dream: A Social History of Housing in America.* Cambridge: MIT Press, 1983.

———. *Moralism and the Model Home.* Chicago: University of Chicago Press, 1980.

Yohn, Susan M. *A Contest of Faiths: Missionary Women and Pluralism in the American Southwest.* Ithaca: Cornell University Press, 1995.

Young, Mary E. "Women, Civilization, and the Indian Question." In *Clio Was a Woman: Studies in the History of American Women*, edited by Mabel E. Deutrich and Virginia C. Purdue, 98–110. Washington, D.C.: Howard University Press, 1980.

Carter, Sybil, 99, 105–6, 107
Catlin, George, 17–18, 27–28, 30, 189, 207
Chapman Catt, Carrie, 64, 65
Chicago World's Fair. *See* World's Columbian Exposition
Child, Lydia Maria, 23–24, 38, 40
Citizenship: Native American, 1, 11, 141, 214
Civilization policy, 18, 75, 112
Coggeshall, Mary Jane, 45
Collier, John, 213
Contact zone, 4, 5, 14, 146, 215, 221
Cottage industry, 103, 104, 106–7, 109, 198, 199
Crafts. *See* Arts and crafts
Cultural relativism, 195–96
Cultural work, 6, 7, 14, 15, 40, 44, 207
Curtis Burlin, Natalie, 185, 194, 195, 196, 208–9, 214

Darwin, Charles, 59–60
Dawes Severalty Act, 1, 11, 20, 38, 39, 41, 69, 72, 78, 86, 87, 89, 112. *See also* Allotment
Dawson Wilde, Anna, 15, 152–81 passim, 183, 188, 219–20; as professional, 152, 160–61, 168, 169, 171, 172–74, 175–76, 180, 218; home of, 153, 166–67, 168–69, 170, 171, 176, 177, 178–79, 180, 181, 216; education of, 153–54, 165, 168
DeCora, Angel (Hinook-Mahiwi-Kilinaka), 15, 184–214 passim, 216, 218, 219, 220; education of, 185–87; fiction by, 189–91; illustrations by, 191–93, 194–95; design work of, 194, 196–98, 206; educational theories of, 199–200, 205–6, 209–10
Design: Native American, 191–92, 193, 194, 198, 208, 210
Division of labor: and gender, 9, 36, 64, 65, 136–37
Domestic industry, 73, 89. *See also* Domestic production

Domesticity, 2, 4, 5, 7, 8, 15, 216–17, 218, 219, 220; and Native American assimilation, 2, 6, 36, 37, 38, 78, 84–85, 89; Native Americans and, 2, 33, 44, 62–63, 66–67, 151–52, 155, 156, 161, 164, 167, 169, 170, 173–74, 180, 208; and imperialism, 3, 5–6, 14, 20, 135; and professionalism, 10, 89, 152–53, 158, 169, 171, 173–74, 176, 177, 179, 181, 183; and spiritual influence, 28, 29, 31, 35; and Beecher and Stowe, 35–36; and differences between white and Native American women, 39, 67, 181; Native American women's capacity for, 40; civilizing power of, 71–72, 81, 152, 156, 215, 217; and field matrons, 100, 102; as problematic, 112, 137, 149, 210–12; and primitivism, 152, 160, 162, 163, 181, 183, 185, 189. *See also* Domestic work; Housekeeping; Imperial domesticity; Women's work
Domestic labor. *See* Domestic work
Domestic literature, 7–8, 12, 14, 18, 24, 28
Domestic production, 7, 185, 198, 207, 212, 213
Domestic science, 5, 10, 35, 73, 98, 151, 152, 160, 168, 176
Domestic work, 3, 5, 7, 44, 58, 64; cultural meaning of, 6, 7–8, 10, 109, 151; and Native American women, 6, 12, 15, 67, 89, 96, 108; and civilization, 6, 13, 66, 69, 72, 86; and assimilation, 7, 10, 12, 73, 89, 97; and economic value, 7–8, 35–36, 44, 47, 49, 53, 102, 103–4, 107, 108, 109; as moral, 8, 35, 72; as drudgery, 8, 107; and science, 10; and industrialized labor, 55–56; and self-ownership, 56; women's liberation from, 58, 61, 69; and racial comparisons, 61, 66–67, 69, 128, 152; and display, 76; and civic identity, 89; and home economics, 98; and household hierarchies, 134–37; as preindustrial, 162, 163, 168, 170. *See also* Domesticity; Housekeeping; Women's work

Gender and American Culture

Making Home Work: Domesticity and Native American Assimilation in the American West, 1860 – 1919, by Jane E. Simonsen (2006).

Feminism, Sexuality, and Politics: Essays by Estelle B. Freedman, by Estelle B. Freedman (2006).

Republican Women: Feminism and Conservatism from Suffrage through the Rise of the New Right, by Catherine E. Rymph (2005).

Women and Patriotism in Jim Crow America, by Francesca Morgan (2005).

Relative Intimacy: Fathers, Adolescent Daughters, and Postwar American Culture, by Rachel Devlin (2005).

The Freedom of the Streets: Work, Citizenship, and Sexuality in a Gilded Age City, by Sharon E. Wood (2005).

Home on the Rails: Women, the Railroad, and the Rise of Public Domesticity, by Amy G. Richter (2005).

Worrying the Line: Black Women Writers, Lineage, and Literary Tradition, by Cheryl A. Wall (2005).

From Welfare to Workfare: The Unintended Consequences of Liberal Reform, 1945 – 1965, by Jennifer Mittelstadt (2005).

Choice and Coercion: Birth Control, Sterilization, and Abortion in Public Health and Welfare, by Johanna Schoen (2005).

Closer to Freedom: Enslaved Women and Everyday Resistance in the Plantation South, by Stephanie M. H. Camp (2004).

Masterful Women: Slaveholding Widows from the American Revolution through the Civil War, by Kirsten E. Wood (2004).

Manliness and Its Discontents: The Black Middle Class and the Transformation of Masculinity, 1900 – 1930, by Martin Summers (2004).

Citizen, Mother, Worker: Debating Public Responsibility for Child Care after the Second World War, by Emilie Stoltzfus (2003).

Women and the Historical Enterprise in America: Gender, Race, and the Politics of Memory, 1880 – 1945, by Julie Des Jardins (2003).

Free Hearts and Free Homes: Gender and American Antislavery Politics, by Michael D. Pierson (2003).

Ella Baker and the Black Freedom Movement: A Radical Democratic Vision, by Barbara Ransby (2003).

Signatures of Citizenship: Petitioning, Antislavery, and Women's Political Identity, by Susan Zaeske (2003).

Love on the Rocks: Men, Women, and Alcohol in Post – World War II America, by Lori Rotskoff (2002).

The Veiled Garvey: The Life and Times of Amy Jacques Garvey, by Ula Yvette Taylor (2002).

Working Cures: Health, Healing, and Power on Southern Slave Plantations, by Sharla Fett (2002).

Southern History across the Color Line, by Nell Irvin Painter (2002).

The Artistry of Anger: Black and White Women's Literature in America, 1820–1860, by Linda M. Grasso (2002).

Too Much to Ask: Black Women in the Era of Integration, by Elizabeth Higginbotham (2001).

Imagining Medea: Rhodessa Jones and Theater for Incarcerated Women, by Rena Fraden (2001).

Painting Professionals: Women Artists and the Development of Modern American Art, 1870–1920, by Kirsten Swinth (2001).

Remaking Respectability: African American Women in Interwar Detroit, by Victoria W. Wolcott (2001).

Ida B. Wells-Barnett and American Reform, 1880–1930, by Patricia A. Schechter (2001).

Taking Haiti: Military Occupation and the Culture of U.S. Imperialism, 1915–1940, by Mary A. Renda (2001).

Before Jim Crow: The Politics of Race in Postemancipation Virginia, by Jane Dailey (2000).

Captain Ahab Had a Wife: New England Women and the Whalefishery, 1720–1870, by Lisa Norling (2000).

Civilizing Capitalism: The National Consumers' League, Women's Activism, and Labor Standards in the New Deal Era, by Landon R. Y. Storrs (2000).

Rank Ladies: Gender and Cultural Hierarchy in American Vaudeville, by M. Alison Kibler (1999).

Strangers and Pilgrims: Female Preaching in America, 1740–1845, by Catherine A. Brekus (1998).

Sex and Citizenship in Antebellum America, by Nancy Isenberg (1998).

Yours in Sisterhood: Ms. Magazine and the Promise of Popular Feminism, by Amy Erdman Farrell (1998).

We Mean to Be Counted: White Women and Politics in Antebellum Virginia, by Elizabeth R. Varon (1998).

Women Against the Good War: Conscientious Objection and Gender on the American Home Front, 1941–1947, by Rachel Waltner Goossen (1997).

Toward an Intellectual History of Women: Essays by Linda K. Kerber (1997).

Gender and Jim Crow: Women and the Politics of White Supremacy in North Carolina, 1896–1920, by Glenda Elizabeth Gilmore (1996).

Delinquent Daughters: Protecting and Policing Adolescent Female Sexuality in the United States, 1885–1920, by Mary E. Odem (1995).

U.S. History as Women's History: New Feminist Essays, edited by Linda K. Kerber, Alice Kessler-Harris, and Kathryn Kish Sklar (1995).

Common Sense and a Little Fire: Women and Working-Class Politics in the United States, 1900–1965, by Annelise Orleck (1995).

How Am I to Be Heard?: Letters of Lillian Smith, edited by Margaret Rose Gladney (1993).

Entitled to Power: Farm Women and Technology, 1913 – 1963, by Katherine Jellison (1993).

Revising Life: Sylvia Plath's Ariel Poems, by Susan R. Van Dyne (1993).

Made from This Earth: American Women and Nature, by Vera Norwood (1993).

Unruly Women: The Politics of Social and Sexual Control in the Old South, by Victoria E. Bynum (1992).

The Work of Self-Representation: Lyric Poetry in Colonial New England, by Ivy Schweitzer (1991).

Labor and Desire: Women's Revolutionary Fiction in Depression America, by Paula Rabinowitz (1991).

Community of Suffering and Struggle: Women, Men, and the Labor Movement in Minneapolis, 1915 – 1945, by Elizabeth Faue (1991).

All That Hollywood Allows: Re-reading Gender in 1950s Melodrama, by Jackie Byars (1991).

Doing Literary Business: American Women Writers in the Nineteenth Century, by Susan Coultrap-McQuin (1990).

Ladies, Women, and Wenches: Choice and Constraint in Antebellum Charleston and Boston, by Jane H. Pease and William H. Pease (1990).

The Secret Eye: The Journal of Ella Gertrude Clanton Thomas, 1848 – 1889, edited by Virginia Ingraham Burr, with an introduction by Nell Irvin Painter (1990).

Second Stories: The Politics of Language, Form, and Gender in Early American Fictions, by Cynthia S. Jordan (1989).

Within the Plantation Household: Black and White Women of the Old South, by Elizabeth Fox-Genovese (1988).

The Limits of Sisterhood: The Beecher Sisters on Women's Rights and Woman's Sphere, by Jeanne Boydston, Mary Kelley, and Anne Margolis (1988).